Not for SALE

**Manchester United, Murdoch
and the Defeat of BSkyB**

ADAM BROWN and ANDY WALSH

MAINSTREAM
PUBLISHING

EDINBURGH AND LONDON

First published in Great Britain in 1999 by
MAINSTREAM PUBLISHING COMPANY (EDINBURGH) LTD
7 Albany Street
Edinburgh EH1 3UG

ISBN 1 84018 261 X

A catalogue record for this book is available from the British Library

Typeset in Berkeley Book and Gill Sans
Printed and bound in Great Britain by Creative Print Design Ltd

*This book is dedicated to everyone who contributed
anything, however large or small, to the defeat of
BSkyB's take-over of Manchester United*

CONTENTS

ACKNOWLEDGEMENTS

Andy would first of all like to extend his gratitude to his wife Sarah and his sons Patrick and Dominic, who saw so little of him during the seven-month campaign to stop BSkyB that they only knew he still existed because of his regular appearances in the media. To then ask for more understanding whilst this book was being written really was pushing it, and we are grateful for their perseverance and patience.

We are also very grateful to Adam's parents, Richard and Jane Brown, and his brother Matthew, who gave assistance in reading drafts, and especially to Richard for his additional proof-reading at short notice. We would also like to thank Liz Powell and Katherine Beer for being there when needed. Thanks too from Adam to Sam for the Talisker, which helped finish the book off!

Not for Sale itself would not have been possible without the assistance of Bill Campbell at Mainstream Publishing, in accepting the idea and agreeing to turn it around, and we must thank him and his staff for their faith in us.

We would also like to acknowledge Jim White, David Conn, Richard Kurt, Phil Frampton and Chris Robinson for their advice, and Manchester Institute for Popular Culture, Manchester Metropolitan University and Cadre CSM for agreeing to allow us time off at short notice to write the book and for loan of computer equipment.

A special mention needs to be given to the ever-helpful Philip French at the Football Trust, Lucy Ward at *The Guardian* and Liam Hallaghan at Channel Four, who ensured that details on the murky and mysterious world of Westminster were accurate.

We would also like to thank Paul Herrmann, Joel Fildes and Peter Walsh for their photographic assistance, and a big thanks to Elke Szulek for the smokin' cover design.

Last but by no means least, the following all supplied invaluable material for the book, assisted in the recollection of events and/or worked hard for the results recorded here: Paul Windridge, Nick Clay, Mark Longden, Monica Brady, Linda Harvey, Michael Shepherd, Lee Hodgkiss, Jon Paul O'Neil, Mick Meade, Michael Crick, Duncan Drasdo, Mark Southee, Roy Williamson, John Wroe, Jonathan Michie, Roger Brierley, Andy Mitten, Jon Leigh, Steve Donohue, Nigel Krohn, Steve Briscoe, Dave

Kirkwood, Ray Eckersly, Mike Adams, Tom Cusack, Sarah Hatton, Gillian Howarth, Dave Pye, Paul Sneyd, Eddie Taylor, Rob Wilson, Dave Grey, Sue Holland, Howard Jones, Sue Bowers, Mark Kreissl, Alison Pilling, Andy Burnham.

INTRODUCTION

The events of the 1998–99 season were truly ones which will be remembered for many years. Although for many Manchester United fans, the completion of the unique Premier League, FA Cup and European Cup treble may remain the highlight of their lives as fans, for many others, events off the pitch played as important a role. It is those events with which this book is concerned.

The season started much like any other – complaints about the price of tickets, about all-seater stadia, and rumours of a European Super League. We'd heard it before. The revelation on 6 September 1998 that British Sky Broadcasting intended to buy England's richest and most successful club of the decade, Manchester United, shook the football world to its foundations. That the take-over bid was accepted by the United board two days later made many observers decide that this was a *fait accompli*, a logical progression of what had happened to football in the last decade of the millennium, something which nobody would prevent.

Although led by Chief Executive Mark Booth, BSkyB's bid clearly represented the next step in the global ambitions of Rupert Murdoch, whose News International owned 40 per cent of the TV company. That immediately made many Manchester United fans sit up and take notice. Martin Edwards may have been, and may still be, disliked by many at the club, but Murdoch was another kettle of rotten fish altogether. However, no sooner had the story broken than many fans, ex-players and commentators were reflecting on what such a deal would mean for Manchester United and the rest of football. Most did not like what they saw: an increased level of domination of football by television, the end of the independence of a great football institution, the threat to the fabric of British football life, the further exclusion of fans, and further damage to the relationship between sport and the media.

Very, very quickly, a coalition of forces centred around, and led by, the Independent Manchester United Supporters' Association (IMUSA) and brothers-in-arms Shareholders United Against Murdoch (SUAM) were co-ordinating opposition to the deal. That, after seven months of hard campaigning, they got the British government to block the bid and save Manchester United from being another of Murdoch's many conquests, is one of the most remarkable stories of recent times. This book is the story of how a group of football fans stopped the world's biggest media mogul from buying the world's biggest football club.

Nobody believed it could be done. 'You're tilting at windmills,' they claimed. A waste of time. After all, no one stops Murdoch. What could be expected of a government whose leaders had spent the previous five years cosying up to him? What could be expected of an industry which had spent the previous ten years selling anything from tickets to TV rights, shirts to shares, and bed linen to boardrooms to the highest bidder? And who the hell did this bunch of 'raggy-arsed football fans' think they were in the face of such opposition?

This book charts the campaign from the announcement of BSkyB's intention to take over Manchester United, and the plc board's decision to accept the bid on the dark night of 9 September 1998, to its eventual downfall at the hands of the Monopolies and Mergers Commission (MMC) and the Department of Trade and Industry (DTI) on 9 April 1999. It is a story which involves some curious bedfellows for football fans: competition lawyers, parliamentary lobbyists, academics, Sky, City financiers and not least the Office of Fair Trading (OFT) and the MMC.

Whilst we attempt to describe how and why the take-over was defeated and the massive mobilisation of forces involved, we realised very early in writing this volume that we could not cover everything. In a campaign which involved contributions literally from across the globe and from every corner of these isles; which lasted for seven months in which days where nothing happened were far rarer than those where something did; and in a writing process which had to see the completion of the work within three months after the bid was defeated, that simply was not possible. The process of writing a book means editing, and editing means some detail is omitted. Many, many people who will have played a part in the defeat of BSkyB will not be mentioned here, or will only be referred to collectively, and in that this is consciously not a comprehensive account.

It is also true to say that this book should not be seen as an 'IMUSA commemorative brochure' of the take-over defeat, nor a diary of the campaign. It is not intended to be a memento, aimed only at those involved, but an account of what happened and why, which we hope will be of interest to a wide variety of readers. It is, however, clearly written with some bias for which we make no apologies – we were both heavily involved in the campaign from the first day onwards and are both members of the main organisation involved, IMUSA. That is not to say that we haven't attempted to create some critical distance, to reflect and to try to understand why events happened – we have tried at least to be honest and frank – but to say that our perspective may be different from that of other characters in the story (very different in some cases!). Where we have been directly involved in events (and in Andy's case that was most of them!), we have either referred to ourselves in the third person or our accounts are presented as quoted recollections, so that the reader is clear who is talking.

Some angles in the tale are not covered in as much depth as others – there simply is not space. In particular, the daily activities of SUAM, although referred to frequently, are not given the same attention as those of IMUSA. This is not to belittle their role in the story in any way, but is a product of time, perspective and the fact that Michael Crick is currently on the other side of the globe researching a biography of one Rupert Murdoch! Having said that, we hope that what we have described, particularly in chapter three, is accurate and fair. Details of what was happening within Old Trafford, Sky and their parent News Corporation are given when known, but the inside story from that perspective is a tale for another day.

We have also contextualised the events, otherwise a proper under-standing would not be possible. In particular, chapters two and four attempt to establish the commercial and political terrains in which the bid took place and its relation to them: the changes in the football world of the 1990s, the complex relationship of broadcast companies (particularly Murdoch's) with sport, and the balance of forces and political sympathies which the bid exposed in Westminster and New Labour. Chapters one and three by contrast are much more concerned with the day-to-day activities of campaigners, reacting in the heat of events. Chapter five presents an account of some of the contributions (of which there were hundreds) of non-Manchester United supporters. A feature of the campaign was that it touched nerves which stretched across club loyalties and even national divides. Chapter six attempts two things: an outline of the main arguments made to the MMC as to why the deal should be blocked; and personal recollections of a few of those who went before that panel. Chapter seven details the tense build-up to the final rejection of the bid, including the changing role in English football of politics; and chapter eight offers some concluding thoughts and tentative questions regarding the future.

It has been an extraordinary year for football, for Manchester United and for football fans. We hope that this will make a worthwhile contribution to understanding and recording some of the events.

ONE

THE 'BID WEEK' ROLLER-COASTER

The First Call: 6 September 1998

When the news broke, it was like being hit with a cudgel. That was mostly to do with it being early on a Sunday morning. 'It's the PA here, would you like to comment on a *Sunday Telegraph* report that Rupert Murdoch is going to buy Manchester United?' In that bleary state, the first question everyone asked each other was 'What the hell do we do about *this*?'.

The machinations of markets, high level finance and corporate take-overs are not what concern most fans, but they do when it's your football club that's involved. How you respond to it is another matter, though, especially if you've never even owned a share in your life. The executives at BSkyB and Manchester United must have imagined that after the initial shock reaction to the bid announcement, things would quieten down and they could get on with the business of making their own personal fortunes and Murdoch with his global media domination strategy. What they didn't bank on was that at Manchester United there was a well-established and well-organised independent supporters' association, subconsciously created, it seemed, for this very moment.

IMUSA had learnt from experience that when a big United story is breaking, the press will start to call just after six in the morning and this time was no different, with the phones ringing at 6.15 a.m. on Sunday, 6 September 1998. However, nobody had the remotest idea how big this story was. Initially IMUSA refused to comment: it could easily have been pure speculation, although even then IMUSA said that there was no need for the board to sell out to anyone. By eight o'clock and a couple of dozen phone calls later, it was clear that this was for real; the offer was to buy the club for £575m. The immediate response from the officers of IMUSA was that it must be fought at all costs, especially because it was Murdoch. It was not a total surprise – rumours had been circulating for over twelve months that he was buying shares and he had been linked to Spurs in the summer. IMUSA and the United fanzines had a network of snouts and contacts across the globe that MI5 would be proud of and there was rarely a rumour or a story with a United connection that escaped attention. However, this one was still a shock.

With leading figures rapidly at battle stations, Andy Walsh, Chris

Robinson, Lee Hodgkiss and Steve Briscoe arranged to meet up at Old Trafford to deal with the press. The next three hours were an endless round of interviews on the forecourt. Nearly every United fan at the ground that day was against the deal. At this stage it was nothing more than a gut reaction against Murdoch and the uncertainty of what any new owner might mean. On any day of the week the forecourt is busy with fans visiting the ticket office or the shops. But on days of portentous announcements, Reds will wander down just to see what is going on. One punter declared his support for Martin Edwards but it was a lone voice that day and not many had a good word to say for the prime mover behind the sell-off. An attempt was made to find Martin Edwards and to ask him his reasons for the sale, so Steve Briscoe was despatched to Edwards' last known residence only to be told by the occupants that he had moved out some time before. Andy Walsh's son Patrick was drafted to pose with an estate agent's 'For Sale' sign in front of the ground for the attendant press before the officers retired to plan what to do about the deal.

The following few hours were spent considering options and consulting with Reds far and wide to gather as much opinion as possible. This straw poll confirmed the initial thoughts that the deal was unwelcome, and that strengthened resolve. The officers were inundated with calls from the media for the rest of the day, and immediately the pressure began to tell and tempers frayed. IMUSA had to respond because the media was at that stage the only means of getting information across to fans. David Maples, a close friend of Andy Walsh's, was staying at his house for the weekend. David was a veteran of the anti-poll tax campaign and had some experience of organising high-profile public protests so he suggested staging a press conference before everybody was driven insane. A Portsmouth fan, he also felt as threatened by the take-over as the United fans we had spoken to.

Nobody knew at this stage what Murdoch's motives were, what changes were planned for the club and what the background to the deal was. Gathering this information became target number one. Steve Curry and Neil Bennett had written the *Telegraph* story but neither of them was very helpful in providing any more information than had already been in the paper. Resources were split with some of the officers telephoning IMUSA's committee and others charged with calling IMUSA's network of contacts to gauge the mood elsewhere. Journalists were scrambling around gathering information for their own stories and had been badgering IMUSA all day: now it was their turn to give the fans something back as they were called for new information. By piecing together the patchwork of rumour, speculation and fact, fans soon had a fairly accurate picture of where the negotiations for the take-over were up to. The bid had not been accepted by the board but it was known that Martin Edwards and Roland Smith, the plc's chair, were in the thick of negotiations and it looked likely that the offer would be accepted. Reactions from different quarters were also beginning to emerge and the overwhelming prevailing attitude was that there was little that could be done to stop the deal – a fact that nobody at IMUSA was prepared to accept.

In political terms the take-over would be a severe test of the Labour government's resolve. Having established close links with the government, Rupert Murdoch was now making a move which would prove to be intensely unpopular with a large section of the electorate. Some Labour MPs immediately came out against the deal: Central Manchester MP Tony Lloyd, a Junior Foreign Office Minister and United devotee, jumping in before the Millbank thought police told him otherwise; and Worsley MP and IMUSA member Terry Lewis, rallying support within the Parliamentary Labour Party while on holiday.

Locally, a number of councillors did their best to raise a campaign at local authority level, although Paul Dolan's attempts at getting Trafford to examine a potential counter-bid fronted by a consortium of the Manchester metropolitan authorities got short shrift. Within Manchester City Council and Stockport Council, attempts were also made to drum up a civic campaign but these too bore no fruit. Many of the leaders of the local authorities appeared scared of taking on United, not thinking it part of their civic duty to try to save a Manchester institution from Murdoch's clutches. With a few honourable exceptions, backbone and vision are not qualities found in abundance in the town halls.

The response from the press was mostly against the deal, but although most of the football columnists had a few twinges of regret, they largely accepted the 'inevitability' of it all – the next step along the road in the commercialisation of the game. Some members of the press have spent so long as commentators, mixing with the great and the good, that they have forgotten what is like to be a football fan, if they ever were in the first place. Fans opposing the take-over were given no chance.

Andy Spinoza, Manchester City fan, former *Manchester Evening News* journalist and now owner of Spin Media, who cater for Mick Hucknall among others, was typical of those who were sympathetic but told IMUSA that things had already gone too far: 'I fully agree with what you are saying but the game has already changed beyond recognition, you are too late.'

IMUSA's resolve, in contrast, was hardening. There was a common sense of purpose and a belief that this was the last stand. The game may have been heading down this road for some time, but this next disastrous step was not going to have the fans' acquiescence. A United take-over would open the floodgates with other clubs being targeted by media companies and commercial concerns. Football would become a battleground for TV and sponsorship rights and the interests of supporters would be further trampled in the rush. The fact that it was Murdoch did harden opinion, but the belief that a TV company owning Manchester United was wrong would have been there regardless. Above all, there was a recognition that once again fundamental decisions were being made without any input from supporters.

Even those like Spinoza, who sympathised, were not sure that there was anything left worth fighting for, with constant messages that 'the time to have done something was in 1991 when the club was floated'. Too many people were willing to hide behind historical indifference to justify their present inactivity, IMUSA believed. If football fans understood the power they have in the game and spent just 10 per cent of the energy they use talking about it on actually doing something about changing football, life would be very different. IMUSA's job was to lift the sights of United fans and inspire them to take the destiny of the club into their own hands, to secure its independence. Once Murdoch had the club in his grip there would be no way back and Martin Edwards' plea to see if the experiment would work was fanciful. Once sold, there was no return; there were no safeguards for the club built into the agreement, and the only written guarantees were those to protect the interests of Edwards and the board.

These included guarantees about the future roles of Edwards, finance director David Gill and club solicitor Maurice Watkins on United's board. Such undertakings were unusual in that it meant they were being treated differently to other shareholders (a complaint was made to the Stock Exchange Take-Over Panel, without success) and it illustrated the concern they had for their own futures, if not those of the fans. Perhaps the most sickening of these guarantees was that which one insider close to the board revealed: the bid would not go through unless directors' complimentary ticket allocation was protected after Sky took over. All this effort was put in to protect their own self-interest yet there were no guarantees secured for transfer monies, about ticket prices or the role of supporters and the future of the club.

As the first day drew to a close, IMUSA and their allies knew that they had a fight on their hands, but that it was a fight they had to take on.

IMUSA: A Voice in the Wilderness

IMUSA was formed in 1995 because of the creeping change of priorities at Manchester United that had resulted in the fans and the team becoming secondary to the pursuit of commercial success. There was an overt attempt to re-engineer the social makeup of the game following the publication of the FA's *Blueprint for Football* in 1991 and Manchester United's board had gone about the task with a single-minded zeal. Redevelopments, firstly at the Stretford End and then at the United Road stand, had seen traditional areas of support uprooted and replaced with corporate hospitality and executive seats. The displaced were scattered around the ground, which had a devastating effect on the atmosphere. This was exacerbated in 1994–95 when United's security firm, the heavy-handed Special Projects Security, tried to intimidate those few who were attempting to create a better atmosphere into a silent and passive role at matches.

Football fans don't readily turn out on the streets to campaign against such changes. Football is an escape from logic and reason for a couple of hours and few want that 'free time' invaded by peripheral thoughts. The match and the team's performance are all that matters. What was witnessed that year devalued the match-going experience to such an extent that something had to be done. The final straw was a tannoy announcement at the home game against Arsenal in April 1995 telling everyone to sit down after some in the crowd were standing to sing and try and lift the team. Ferguson had asked for more encouragement from the crowd, yet the club's hierarchy seemed determined to stop that happening. The anger the announcement generated led to an act of civil disobedience, with a spirited rendition of 'Ferguson's Red and White Army' with three-quarters of the ground on their feet in defiance.

Immediately after the game the fanzine editors convened a meeting at The Gorse Hill pub in Stretford to explore the idea of establishing a supporters' group, independent of the club. For the majority of United fans living in Manchester there are no official supporters' clubs to join and the official branches tend to restrict their activities to travel arrangements for matches and ticket distribution. The hierarchy within Old Trafford frowns upon any activity beyond the odd social event and complaints, let alone campaigns, have resulted in ticket allocations being mysteriously reduced. United have steadfastly refused to establish any more branches because of the demand for tickets and there are none in Manchester itself. The club makes no effort to engender a 'club spirit' and attachment with the fans other than encouraging them to buy merchandise from the Megastore.

Following a couple of open meetings to test the mood for the new group, the Independent Manchester United Supporters' Association was established with an elected committee of twenty. Founding members were balloted on what they saw as their chief concerns and the following agenda was adopted: a more lenient approach to those standing in seated areas; the use of further ground development to improve the atmosphere; an end to price increases way above the rate of inflation; regular dialogue between the board and IMUSA; a fair distribution of away match tickets, based on loyalty; and encouraging more young, local people to attend, by way of pricing structures and pay-on-the-day admissions.

This overall view of the game coupled with a desire to see sport triumph over commercialism is at the very core of IMUSA's philosophy. The fans' voice is rarely heard; though various fan groups have tried hard over the years, the authorities and clubs only pay lip service to supporters' concerns. Most protest groups lack durability, it is very difficult to keep them going on a voluntary basis, so authorities tend to let them burn themselves out. The prevailing attitude is that fans don't matter, taking for granted that fans will be there emptying out their pockets come what may because they have no choice. A football fan cannot change 'brands' if the one they are used to is no longer attractive or becomes too pricey. A fan is born into a club and doesn't leave; failure or exclusion will not result in supporters going elsewhere.

Representation of fans is notoriously difficult and it was an early decision of IMUSA not to claim that it spoke for *all* Manchester United fans. However, it is clear that the organisation does represent a sizeable portion of the match-going support, with every fanzine at Old Trafford backing IMUSA and regular editorial space given in each edition. The siege mentality at United has meant that a sense of unity has developed, against both the club hierarchy and the outside world, and this has meant that the disunity among fans experienced at some clubs has not happened. Although some fans will say IMUSA is too critical of the club, the organisation has steadfastly avoided commenting on issues to do with the playing side.

There was an early lesson in this respect, a handful of months after IMUSA was formed. When Paul Ince was in dispute with Manchester United and on the point of leaving, some IMUSA officers visited him to persuade him to stay. Although the intention was to get a resolution of differences, the visit was viciously misrepresented and attacked by some in the press (especially the *Manchester Evening News*) and compounded by an injudicious statement by the then Press Officer of IMUSA. A lesson was learnt to avoid team affairs and although some mud stuck, Alex Ferguson has since expressed his support for IMUSA by attending meetings.

Some of the organisation's biggest success has come in relation to travel to European matches, with the lifting of restrictions on independent travel and better ticket distribution. The organisation was also centrally involved in the response to attacks on United fans by police in Porto in 1997. Acting alongside the Football Supporters' Association (FSA) and the club, IMUSA helped to secure an exoneration of United fans by UEFA and action was taken against the Portuguese club. This tentative thread of co-operation was strained the following season when over forty fans were ejected from Old Trafford and had season tickets removed for standing in seated areas. However, through discussion and negotiation, IMUSA was successful in having the season tickets returned and a potentially explosive confrontation was eventually avoided. The key to such successes has been IMUSA's willingness to be receptive to the views of fans, with monthly committee meetings open to all members and no one individual allowed to dominate proceedings. IMUSA's committee is elected every year and a tremendous amount of work is put in by many people out of a dedication to the club and a burning belief that the fans must be given a voice in the game.

When the BSkyB take-over shattered the Sunday morning peace in September 1998, there was a robust organisation, with a high press profile and deep and genuine links with the core support of Manchester United, ready to fight for the integrity of the club.

Face to Face: The Secret Meeting With Sky

Given the comments against the deal which had been made on the Sunday, it was a shock when out of the blue, on Monday, 7 September, Chris Haynes, Sky's Head of Press and Publicity, contacted IMUSA's vice chair and *Red Issue* editor Chris Robinson and invited him to a meeting with Vic Wakeling at the Midland Hotel in Manchester the next day.

This meeting was kept secret both in line with Sky's wishes and because, however confident IMUSA were that it was right to meet, the organisation could not be confident how it would be construed. With the bid story confirmed, Chris Robinson and Andy Walsh decamped to the Midland Hotel. Chris describes it thus:

> Andy and I decided that the best tactic to adopt at the meeting was to listen. In the car on the way into town we speculated about what Sky might have to say and our curiosity intensified as we explored the possibilities. We concluded that their motivation must be to reassure us of their intentions and try to understand our open hostility towards them. We arrived in the cavernous lobby of the Midland Crowne Plaza and Chris Haynes felt that it would be preferable to move to a less public location, so we adjourned to Joop, one of Manchester's trendier bars.
>
> Our thoughts in the car had been correct – Vic Wakeling was curious as to why we were so vehemently opposed to the bid and Sky. He asked whether we would have had the same reaction if someone else were to make an offer or was it Sky in particular? We explained that it did not matter who it was, that we wanted the club to remain independent, but that Sky was a particularly unwelcome predator.
>
> Wakeling was amiable and listened very attentively but was keen to dissuade us from the view that Sky were some kind of ogre with no feeling for the game. Indeed, he even suggested at one point that

he would like to see a return of terraced areas at Old Trafford to improve the atmosphere. He assured us that everyone working for him was a football fan who understood the fans' concerns and he could not understand the antipathy towards them. As far as he was concerned Sky had pumped millions of pounds into football and through its marketing had lifted the game's profile. We tried to explain how the rearrangement of fixtures and kick-off times was often a great inconvenience to match-going supporters, resulting in major disruption to people's lives and how they had played a key part in the commercial changes in football, which we vehemently disapproved of.

Before the meeting we had taken the opportunity to speak to a few people who had met Wakeling and he was described as a genuine person and football fan. We left feeling that it was certainly far easier to feel animosity towards Rupert Murdoch and later Mark Booth [Sky's Chief Executive] than it was towards Vic Wakeling.

The assessment of the meeting was that it had been worthwhile because up to that point IMUSA had only been able to make its views known to Sky through the media. To have the opportunity to explain the position in a calm atmosphere could only be to IMUSA's benefit. Chris and Andy had shown Sky that 'we're not just a rabble but have a clear vision of what a football club should be'. More importantly IMUSA had let Sky know that it wasn't going to be a two-minute protest movement and that any deal would be fought to the end. At that point in time, of course, it was not clear which way the bid was going to go as United's board had yet to formally accept Sky's offer. Ironically, unbeknown to the two officers sat in Joop chewing the fat late that Tuesday afternoon, the deal was finally being settled two hundred miles away in London. In contrast to the Manchester meeting, United's Chief Executive Martin Edwards looked far from calm, portrayed in the papers in a fist fight with photographers at Euston station!

On Monday *The Telegraph*'s story had been confirmed beyond question. Michael Crick got the scoop of the day as he located the secret negotiations between Sky and United's directors. The film he did for *Newsnight* was brilliant, complete with shots through the window of the key players involved – real cloak-and-dagger stuff. Despite the anger fans felt about the deal, for those involved it was also very exciting. With one of IMUSA's own tracking the rats to their lair, it was the first time IMUSA had been slap bang in the middle of such a press frenzy. Michael had already penned a sharply critical opinion piece in the *Evening Standard* and this caused some debate about objectivity at *Newsnight* about whether he should be fronting a film on the same issue. *Newsnight* decided the way around the problem was to trail the film as an opinion piece but then failed to do so, causing all manner of problems in the weeks to come, including the wrath of Sky's Tim Allen.

Having met Sky, the next stop for Andy and Chris was the eerily quiet Red Café at Old Trafford. Chris Robinson was due to be taking former IMUSA Press Officer and *Red Issue* contributor Richard Kurt for a farewell meal and he had chosen the Café to pen a review piece for the next fanzine. However, more pressing matters were now on the menu. The Red Café epitomises the rampant commercialism of Manchester United, the logic of which had now driven the board to consider selling the whole club to someone who was undoubtedly a commercial expert but knew nothing of the traditions on which the club had been built. Wall-to-wall video screens reran great games of the past bringing memories flooding back. The meeting with Wakeling had rounded off a hectic couple of days and although there was some reflection on the achievements so far, confidence was high among the three would-be rebels as they plotted what to do next. It was so high in fact, that Richard began planning the dust cover of the book he was going to write about the defeat of Sky!

What Do We Do About This? The First Meeting

Having mulled things over, Richard, Chris and Andy headed up to the Stretford Trades and Labour Club where IMUSA's officers and close allies were gathering for a hastily arranged eight o'clock meeting. On their way the phone rang: the deal had been done. Sky had increased their offer to £623m – £2.40 per share. There had been objections from Greg Dyke, board member and Pearson TV executive (and now BBC Director General), who was there to advise on TV-related matters, and David Gill, finance director. Dyke had held out but was told by his legal advisers that he had no choice but to go along with the rest of the board. On the way to the labour club as many media contacts as possible were called – IMUSA were going to need to build credibility with some of the bigger hitters on the broadsheets if a momentum was to be maintained in the campaign, and what better way than being the ones to tell them the big news? So hot was the news that when, on arrival, Chris Robinson spoke again to Chris Haynes and Vic Wakeling, IMUSA were now informing the head of Sky Sports that a deal had been agreed between his board and United's! Even those waiting at the labour club had heard and the mobiles were in a frenzy.

IMUSA's local media contacts – the ones who had been amongst their most valuable contacts for years rather than the national journalists who had befriended the organisation in the previous forty-eight hours – got the drop on the story. The organisation's usual haunt, O'Briens at Stretford Arndale, had been forsaken to avoid media intrusion. It was discovered later that this had been a wise move, as two tabloid journalists and a Sky camera crew had turned up at the pub. Jean and the staff at O'Brien's may have been none too pleased that somebody else was getting the custom – she and landlord Terry O'Brien had always allowed IMUSA the use of the pub whenever it was needed – but these were times of necessity. There was a job to do, a campaign to plan and the media were not going to be allowed to determine the pace or direction of events. Having spent much of the previous forty-eight hours talking to the press, now was the time to get on to a campaign footing.

The Tuesday officer's meeting was the first time everyone actually sat down to discuss a considered response to the bid. Up to that point everything had been a knee-jerk reaction. The issues had been discussed over the phone but such discussions are never complete and not all the officers had spoken to each other. Now there was an actual bid on the table – the club had been sold for £623.4m. In attendance were: Andy Walsh, Chris Robinson, Mike Shepherd, Mike Adams, Steve Briscoe, Lee Hodgkiss, Dave Kirkwood and Gillian Howarth from the committee, along with Adam Brown and Richard Kurt. Mike Shepherd recalls the meeting:

> Lee Hodgkiss gave a brief resumé of how the news had broken and what had been happening since. This was the first time I'd met up with anyone since it had broken. Lee reported that the phones had not stopped ringing and those people doing press and media work just hadn't had a moment's break. I was immediately conscious that the press was being very demanding and that as an organisation we needed time and space to think, get our ideas together and make them public. I made the point that we shouldn't run around at their behest giving them copy to broadcast and sell newspapers simply because we were the big story right now. I also made the point that we shouldn't get giddy or be intoxicated by journalistic attention. We needed to get our message right and then use the press to talk through them to our members and the public.

As if to illustrate Michael's point, one national journalist rang Andy Walsh on his mobile for a quote and was politely told that a press statement would be made at quarter past ten. Unlike others who appreciated this, it was not good enough for this individual and he attempted to bully his way to a quote. Obviously not satisfied with the response from Andy, the journalist then rang Lee Hodgkiss, unaware that he was on the opposite side of the room. By the time Steve Briscoe's and Chris Robinson's mobiles had subsequently rung with the same call, it was decided to switch them all off. This became a rule for all future meetings.

Two things needed to be arranged, and fast. One was a press conference, which was to be held at 11 a.m. the next day, Wednesday, 9 September. This would outline IMUSA's opposition to the bid and its plan of action, and it would provide a sharp contrast to Sky and United's joint jamboree. Secondly, primary among IMUSA's activities was to be a public meeting to demonstrate the strength of feeling. The question was raised as to whether this should be a rally, a call to arms, or a debate. At that early stage there were still doubts about the strength of feeling, and whether a rallying cry would fall on deaf ears. However, it was soon concluded that with Murdoch's press machine behind them the proposers of the bid needed no assistance from IMUSA in getting their propaganda across. There would be a rally, with a neutral chair. Who would do this, what its format would be and where on earth it would be held were matters to be decided within the next twelve hours.

It was a long, tense meeting, but before going to bed that night the press release was finalised and dispatched. Sometime after midnight Dave Lavery, the club secretary, threw everybody out – they were a very helpful lot, but IMUSA had outstayed their welcome this time!

Meet the Press

Nobody really knew what to expect. Sky and United would lay on the vol-au-vents and velvet seats at their announcement of the agreement. IMUSA had the upstairs room at Stretford Trades and Labour Club, complete with what looked like left-over Christmas tinsel as a backdrop. The press conference was due to start at 11 a.m. and it had already been a hectic morning.

Some people had met up at Andy Walsh's house and put the finishing touches to the statements that were to be made before setting off for the short walk to the labour club. Adam Brown had been on a wild goose chase to secure a venue for a public meeting the following week, which had to be announced that morning. The committee had decided that Manchester Town Hall might be too small, as they were expecting up to a thousand people. Through a work contact Brown had tried to contact the manager of the Apollo, a concert venue in Ardwick, on the edge of the city centre, and just as famous for the ease of jibbing in for free as it was for the classic punk concerts staged in the '70s and '80s. Although that time in the morning was obviously too early for the music business, Ian Cockburn, a City fan, deserves credit for calling the next day to offer the venue for free, albeit too late for IMUSA. The idea of the Bridgewater Hall was mooted the previous evening and that prestigious new venue was secured with minutes to spare, but at a cost.

On turning the corner into Sydney Street, all fears that the press would find the Sky/United press conference more attractive were dismissed, as the street was crammed full of satellite vans and outside broadcast units. The labour club's concert room was packed with about seventy members of the press. Mark Longden and Michael Shepherd had set up the PA system and the whole event went out live on a number of radio stations.

It was an enormous success. With questions flying in from all sides, the panel members – Walsh, Briscoe, Hodgkiss, Robinson and Ray Eckersley representing the fledgling Shareholders United Against Murdoch – handled the pressure superbly. There was to be no equivocation, IMUSA would fight the proposed take-over tooth and nail. Emphasis was placed on the tradition of Manchester United and that it was not for Martin Edwards or anybody else to sell the club off like some second-hand Jag. IMUSA would call a rally for the Bridgewater Hall the following week to which the public would be invited. The deal was bad for fans and shareholders. At the officer's meeting the night before, Michael Shepherd had made a defiant speech. One of his best lines was used to encapsulate the mood:

> Rupert Murdoch may have walked all over the United States of America and the rest of the world but he is not going to walk all over Manchester.

Mark Longden collected business cards from the assembled journalists for future use. That night all the evening news programmes had IMUSA's press conference as the lead item, knocking Tony Blair and the Clinton–Lewinsky affair off the top spot.

That evening there was also the small matter of a football match to go to. The fans arriving at Old Trafford for the home game against Charlton had not had much time to take in the news of the take-over and all around the ground people were discussing the implications for the club. There was confusion: whilst most were against the idea of the club being sold off, some believed the hype that Murdoch would provide the money for transfers, previously denied by the plc. This was to be a fallacy which Sky stuck to, even after their eventual defeat. There were some fans with hastily produced placards and T-shirts decrying Murdoch and two young females became the darlings of the media with their 'Stop Murdoch' painted faces. Melissa Moore took matters into her own hands and daubed a protest across one of the Red Café billboards. However, there was no mass demonstration and some – even within IMUSA – could not see how the defiance displayed in the press over the previous few days would ever carry the campaign through to a successful conclusion. The press was derisory, with Jeff Powell, who had already belittled the fans' chances of victory, almost ecstatic:

Beaten Italian World Cup managers go home to worse than this, a thousand times worse. Not one rotten tomato, let alone a crate load, was thrown in anger as Martin Edwards took his seat last night . . . As public demos go this was more querying the council planning application than bringing down the government . . . Hardly a pamphlet in sight, never mind a barricade . . . Who's going to stop him? . . . What chance the simple fans?

How he would eat his words. However, the committee meeting the following night was a chance to air anxieties. It was agreed that Alex Ferguson would be reassured that campaign activities would not disrupt the performance on the pitch and any event at the ground would be in support of the team. There were sufficient numbers of fans rallying to IMUSA's banner to lift the mood and it was agreed that the real test of strength would be the Bridgewater Hall meeting the following Tuesday. It was vital that this meeting was a success and a dozen or more people volunteered to work night and day over the next few days to ensure it was. IMUSA needed hard evidence of Murdoch's previous business ventures. Peter Harwood and David Conn agreed to trawl through the various books that profiled Murdoch and News International and Nick Clay agreed to swing some time off work to co-ordinate things. It was going to be tight, but that meeting would be the time to put some meat on the bones of contention.

Rallying the Troops: The Bridgewater Hall

That opposition was solidifying became clearer as the days went on. The messages IMUSA were receiving piled in during the week and are described in chapter five. Even local luminaries were beginning to turn. One time Edwards stalwart, journalist David Meek, equivocated on a 'debate' with Adam Brown on Granada Television and officials from that station made their opinions crystal clear by leaving their seats empty at Saturday's match against Coventry. Nerves were still jangling, though, as the Tuesday meeting approached.

Aiming for a thousand people was ambitious. IMUSA's largest previous attendance was around the five hundred mark, and although this was a much bigger issue, fans tend to content themselves with a gripe over a pint. It was a balancing act, though: a half-empty hall would not send out the right message and locking people out would alienate potential supporters. A lockout may have created a better news story, but it was more important that as many Reds as possible were given the opportunity to have their say than worrying about what the critics might think. The silky-tongued patter of the Bridgewater personnel reassured IMUSA that the upper tiers could be closed off, reducing the capacity to a thousand and that it could be lit in such a way that it wouldn't appear too cavernous. However, unlike the generosity of Ian at the Apollo, the Bridgewater Hall wanted payment. The initial figure was a whopping four and a half grand, but once they'd added on extra security staff (they were a bit nervous about the quality of the clientele in their prejudiced way), radio microphones and the rest, it rose to £6,115.80. And that was the charity rate!

The Bridgewater Hall is a product of the times, a 'public' facility, built with public money but run as a private enterprise. Here was a section of Manchester's public who needed somewhere to meet for a couple of hours, to discuss the sale of one of Manchester's most enduring institutions. Fans' taxes had probably paid for the building in the first place but the proprietors wanted an exorbitant fee. The Apollo, a private concern, were happy to take the publicity alone; the publicly supported Bridgewater however, one of Manchester's flagship new buildings, were charging IMUSA through the nose. A starker comparison you could not find: black tie and cocktail dresses or bondage pants.

Dave Kirkwood, IMUSA's treasurer, would never have sanctioned the booking at the price being asked, but a decision had to be made on the hoof in time for the press conference the week before. Dave, as treasurers do, had kittens when he eventually found out. 'How are we going to find six thousand pounds when we don't have six hundred quid in the bank?' he asked. It was a good question. An attempt was made to reassure him but nobody knew where the money was going to come from. The best that anyone came up with was a collection on the night but that was scuppered when the Bridgewater said they wanted half of the money up front. Then the prospect of getting a sponsor was raised. 'Surely the *Daily Mirror* would pay for the meeting?' somebody asked, but this idea was rejected, as the last thing IMUSA needed was the *Daily Mirror* or anybody else being in a position to hijack the campaign. If IMUSA had co-operated in this and other demands that leaders pose for photographs with *The Mirror's* campaign posters, it would also have made IMUSA a ready target for all those who had an axe to grind with *The Mirror*. They had demonised both Eric Cantona and David Beckham and IMUSA had to guard against being used by the media, reflecting the very arguments being used against Sky's take-over of the club. Mutual benefit was acceptable, control was not. It had to remain a fans' campaign, independent of outside influence. Many fans still had to be won over and that task would be made much harder if it involved somebody else's baggage, such as the latest banality from the likes of Harry Harris.

A public appeal for funds would be made alongside private approaches to celebrity United fans. Adam Brown contacted Spinoza to try and get a commitment from Mick Hucknall, although he, along with about every other United celebrity, well and truly proved their credentials by turning IMUSA down. Andy Walsh did a *Newsnight* interview immediately after the Charlton match and put the call out. The next day there was a phone call from a Phil Symes. Phil relayed that a client of his in the music industry wished to make a donation of £6,000 to cover the costs of hiring the hall. By that time it was clear that much more than £6,000 was going to be needed and he was asked whether the mystery benefactor would be willing to increase his offer to £10,000. On the Friday came a second call confirming that the benefactor was the former Queen drummer Roger Taylor and that he would give us the £10,000. Phil was keen that Roger's identity was kept quiet until the Monday as there would be a press launch in London, but the news was manna from heaven, not least for poor Dave K.

The secrecy sparked off a competition on local radio where listeners were asked to phone in with suggestions as to who the mystery benefactor was and there was huge interest from the media. On Monday morning Andy Walsh was getting a taxi to the airport to go down to London for a meeting with IMUSA's *pro bono* lawyers when the taxi driver informed him that their drivers were running a sweepstake on who it might be. Most people were convinced it was Mick Hucknall so when Roger 'came out' there was another round of stories about why he would be so generous to IMUSA, not being a United fan. Ironically, and to Roger's credit, none of the celebrities that regularly appear in the media to declare their allegiance to the Red cause even bothered to answer IMUSA's letters. Roger's son Rufus was a United fan and there was rumoured to have been a poisonous story in a Murdoch rag about Freddy Mercury some years before, but Roger said that his prime motivation was to support the ordinary man in the street against the big corporation. Whatever the reason, IMUSA were grateful, and later in the year Roger even released a special edition single to publicise the campaign.

The key aim of the Bridgewater Hall meeting was to give maximum opportunity for fans to have their say. Fans needed to air their views; everyone had heard IMUSA's time and again over the previous week; and IMUSA themselves needed reassuring that they were reflecting the trend of opinion. Lee Hodgkiss made the opening remarks, with SUAM's Michael Crick and *Guardian* columnist, author and United fan Jim White also on the platform, and Andy Walsh finishing off. Then it was over to the floor. To give the meeting some semblance of impartiality, not to mention professional handling, Man City fan Jimmy Wagg, presenter on local BBC radio station GMR and a staunch defender of ordinary fans, took the chair.

A monumental amount of planning was needed. A leaflet had been produced at cost price by Kendal press in Trafford Park and distributed by thirty volunteers at the Coventry game on the previous Saturday. A banner for the stage was needed, as was a more substantial document outlining

IMUSA's opposition and detailing facts about Murdoch and the sale of the club.

Nick Clay virtually moved into Andy Walsh's house to co-ordinate efforts. Here he explains his recollections of organising the meeting:

If Monday 14th was hectic, Tuesday was madness. Roger Taylor's name had been revealed. There was controversy about how much the event had cost. There were all the last-minute problems associated with organising an event such as this – 'What do you mean the banner has to be fireproof?' Meanwhile I was so pumped up about the event, I was telling all the journos that the hall 'would be packed to the rafters' – a fine example of the kind of giddiness that would hit each and every one of the campaign team at various times that week. On several occasions the team would meet, discuss whom we had spoken to and a way forward – it may have been senior politicians, football administrators, football 'dignitaries' or City types. At times the enormity of what we were doing would hit us and we would all collapse in fits of laughter! Moments like that were priceless and showed how at one we all were, strangers but sharing the cause of United.

So to Tuesday. Volunteers and the IMUSA committee were out in force in the afternoon, and tasks were delegated accordingly. The nerve centre for operations by this time was Andy and Sarah's bedroom. Around a dozen lads were camped in there, at one point just sitting around and waiting. It must have been quite a shock for her when she returned from work to find all those (very) strange men hanging out in her room.

On the back of the experience I had picked up over the last couple of days, I was to stay on the front desk and organise the press interviews. Even by mid-afternoon, the Bridgewater Hall seemed like the centre of the media world – the Superbowl and the Cup final rolled into one. The media circus we had whipped up was in danger of going out of control. Channel 4 wanted to do a big piece on the campaign, featuring Andy as some kind of heroic David against Murdoch's Goliath. They even wanted to film Andy at work on the campaign in his house! Only if you've ever been for a pint in Terry O'Brien's pub, in the Stretford Arndale Centre (IMUSA's meeting place), would you fully appreciate the surprise of the regulars when a TV camera crew turned up, mistakenly believing we were camped in there.

Given my role on Tuesday evening, I saw very little of the meeting. I know many, despite the fact that the meeting was sandwiched between two home games, were disappointed with the attendance. The Murdoch press was quick to make capital out of the block of empty seats, irrespective of the fact that almost a thousand United fans turned up, all opposed to the bid. There were also a couple of Murdoch weasels present, skulking around backstage, no doubt hoping to catch us smoking dope or organising 'hoolie' fights. Instead they saw only what appeared to be (at least on the surface!) a polished performance. Smooth on the surface, panic stations underneath. Yes, the evening truly set the tone for the next six months!

Despite not being able to see the event unfold, it was an unforgettable evening. On the front desk, it was chaos: fans were keyed up by the speakers and were desperate to help and contribute. My role was with the press, however, and making sure journalists who wanted an interview had their request fulfilled. The logistics meant nipping into the auditorium from time to time to pull various committee members out. Once it had gone past nine o'clock I noticed several of the journalists had come out of the hall to write their reports and articles. In a flash of inspiration, I went into 'spin doctor' mode, working the corridors, drumming home our message. 'This is what I want you to put – Murdoch needs United; United don't need Murdoch.' I sat alongside a radio journalist and helped him to edit his recording of the meeting to fit our message.

I can't deny it was a real buzz as I went around. *How could we lose?* I can recall talking to Joe Lovejoy about what I wanted him to write. How disappointing it was therefore to find the actual meeting receive so little press attention after the event! When the meeting broke up, it was euphoria as we decamped to the bar, joined by some trusted journalists.

Accounts like this are typical of that first week, the roller-coaster ride as ordinary fans were thrust into the maelstrom of the campaign, developing new skills as they went, growing in confidence, growing in stature. However, IMUSA needed as many fans on board as possible and it was a handful that had come this far.

IMUSA decided that those who attended needed something to take away with them, something that they could use to illustrate the arguments that would be put against the bid. In any campaign people are won over by what they hear or see written down; as it was not going to be possible to speak to everybody, campaigners needed to put together a brochure explaining some of the worst fears. This brochure had to be professional and substantial to last the duration of the campaign if necessary.

IMUSA was extremely lucky to have two dedicated designers ready to turn out work at the drop of a hat. Phil Shaw runs his own graphic design company, called Portfolio, in Bolton's bandit country and Paul Windridge is an award-winning designer based in Leamington Spa. Both are dedicated Reds and have been totally committed to what IMUSA was fighting for. They probably both felt like volunteering to be sectioned after what they were put through that first week as leaflets were demanded from them and a banner had to be turned round in double-quick time. Paul Windridge recalls how he discovered what he was letting himself in for at the match against Coventry.

Andy and I had already discussed the possibility of producing a separate leaflet for the actual Bridgewater meeting on the Friday and we had arranged to meet at half-time in the Coventry game. Little did I know what was in store for me! At the sound of the half-time whistle I wandered below K Stand to meet with Andy. As I already knew he wanted me to produce a leaflet I had written down a list of questions I needed answering. In time the answers to my questions became obvious. Problem was we didn't have the time! That afternoon under K Stand, I remember Andy's words well:

'Are you sure you can do me a leaflet for Tuesday?'

'Sure. What format do you want it to take?'

'I need you to dish up some dirt on Murdoch's dirty dealings – Times newspapers, LA Dodgers, Oz Rugby League, etc.'

Then we got down to the nitty gritty and the realisation set in that I had now dedicated myself to producing not what I envisaged would be another single-colour A5 leaflet, but a four-page A4, two-colour leaflet containing four and a half thousand words.

'Ten thousand printed by when?'

'Tuesday afternoon at the latest. Are you sure you can do it? I don't want you to take this on if you haven't got the time.'

Time – it's nearly 4 p.m. on Saturday and I have just agreed to research, write, edit, design and print 10,000 four-page, two-colour leaflets in two days. Maybe I'd better miss the second half and go straight home – but I couldn't even do that. I'd been driven up by Mick Meade in his car and he'd got the keys.

The research for the brochure was an example of what can be achieved when people are motivated and illustrates the power of the Internet. Paul Windridge again:

I was travelling back to the Midlands with two willing helpers in Mick Meade and Alan Dobson – at least, I assumed they would be willing! But I'd reckoned on needing at least two or possibly three more and then a few other researchers. I knew that Linda Harvey would be one of them and was fairly sure that Jon Leigh would be another. I then phoned Sean Hennessy on Mick's mobile on the way down the M6, as the last piece of the jigsaw. Sean was more than a little surprised to be asked as he lives in Boston – not Lincolnshire, but New England, USA! At first he was reluctant to join in with our happy band of writers – understandably, because he lived away from the bosom of the club – but I assured him that he would surely be the right choice for the article on the LA Dodgers. He was originally from New York and I later found out his grandmother was an avid follower of the original Brooklyn Dodgers and had been heartbroken when they were franchised off to LA.

Without the Internet and e-mail, the success of our campaign would have been in serious jeopardy. The production of the Bridgewater leaflet would definitely not have been possible in such a short time-scale, that's for sure. It was imperative that everyone who was going to be working together on the leaflet was contactable by e-mail and preferably also had access to the Internet.

The brochure very nearly never saw the light of day at all because Nick Clay became locked out of Andy Walsh's house whilst Andy was on his way to Blackpool to lobby the TUC. Articles continued to be gathered from newspapers around the world and Mick Meade recalls one incident in particular:

> Everything had to be factual and copyright laws could not be infringed. At one stage I found a report in the archives of the *Sydney Morning Herald* that was gold dust to the campaign, but lunchtime on a Sunday is the dead of night in Sydney and getting authorisation to use the article was not easy. I did eventually get hold of the night chief of staff who duly sent an e-mail giving such authorisation (with best wishes for success and a few other unrepeatable comments about Murdoch).

Eventually the brochure was produced, outlining IMUSA's opposition to the club being sold, the loss of its independence and the particular threat which a Murdoch-owned company would pose. It was a fantastic achievement and served up a powerful message for those coming into the Bridgewater Hall.

To broaden the appeal of the campaign IMUSA solicited messages of support from all quarters and at the meeting messages from fans of other clubs (see chapter five) as well as local politicians and councillors were read out. Ex-players such as Willie Morgan, Brian McClair and Sammy McIlroy lent their support and a letter was even delivered to the former home of Sandy Busby, son of Sir Matt. Unknown to IMUSA, Sandy had moved sometime before and the house was now a nursing home. In one of the more bizarre episodes of the whole campaign, Lee Hodgkiss got a phone call from the matron apologising for the fact that one of the residents had *eaten* the letter and the only bit that had survived contained Lee's phone number on it!

In another twist, the Irish Prime Minister Bertie Ahern, renowned for his allegiance to United, had been reported making a comment opposing the bid. Time was short, so what better to do than phone him, Prime Minister or not. Lee dialled directory enquiries and asked for the Taoiseach's office. To his surprise he got straight through to his private secretary, who told him that Bertie was off to China on an official visit but assured Lee that as the Taoiseach felt so strongly about the deal IMUSA would definitely get a message of support, which they did. Buoyed by success with Bertie, Hodgkiss repeated the process with Downing Street, but Alistair Campbell's grip was too strong. The resident of the White House was then considered but it was decided that as President Clinton had the little matter of a black dress on his mind at the time he would be left in peace!

The Bridgewater Hall meeting was nerve-racking for all of those leading the campaign. This was the first true test of support and the event had to be a success. So much time had been put into organising it that no time had been left to plan what was to be said. Two hours before the meeting Lee Hodgkiss and Andy Walsh hid away from the phones and the chaos at Andy's house and camped at Andy's sister-in-law's to write Lee's opening remarks. The first task on arriving at the Bridgewater Hall was to complete all the interviews that had been lined up, and then it was ahead with the meeting. The staff of the Bridgewater didn't quite know what to make of it all and, either through nerves or bureaucracy, declared that the doors could only be opened at the designated time, leaving many people waiting in the pouring rain outside. IMUSA members went outside to apologise but the mood amongst the punters was so upbeat they didn't seem to mind. The speakers for the night were all arriving and needed to be briefed; Mark Longden and Jane Battye were organising the IMUSA stewards; and after some final arrangements at the front of the auditorium it was time to kick off.

Jimmy Wagg opened the meeting by taking a show of hands on who was opposed to the bid and not a single hand stayed down. Lee made his opening remarks and read out the messages of support with those from ex-players receiving the loudest applause. Michael Crick started with a few wisecracks – 'Mark Booth probably believes that Best, Law and Charlton are a firm of Manhattan attorneys and that the Neville brothers are a blues band,' he said, referring to the Sky executive's inability to name United's left-back the week before. Michael went on to soberly set out the task that was facing us, explaining how difficult it would be to defeat a take-over of this kind. He urged everyone to buy shares and carefully explained that 10 per cent would help stop BSkyB getting overall control. Jim White did an impassioned and humorous knock-about and Andy Walsh summed up the proceedings, IMUSA's position and the determination that was to be characteristic of the campaign. The punters were so inspired at the end that over two thousand pounds was raised in the collection and one collector, Roy Williamson, remembers a particular incident:

> One guy walked past those with the collection buckets outside. We had a little grumble that he had given nothing and then ten minutes later he came back with a hundred quid. He said he had been so inspired that he went straight to the cashpoint and drew out the money and put it straight in the bucket. We were gobsmacked.

This kind of support from ordinary fans was to be repeated throughout the campaign. Phil Bedford, a Brummie Red, whose banner-making skills and vocal support for United at away games are legendary, gave a substantial donation. Mick Meade, Peter Corscadden, Guy Hodgson, Jim White, Jon Leigh and a couple of anonymous Manchester businessmen also gave considerable sums of money. At the other end of the scale IMUSA had old age pensioners and school kids sending what they could afford into the fund, ordinary people whose only desire was to see United safe. In contrast, those pushing the bid forward, the directors of the plc, listed £2m as costs incurred in the bid process in their 1999 half-year accounts – causing the club to pay for a deal which only served to enrich their already bloated bank accounts. Almost every penny the club makes comes, in one way or another, from ordinary fans: even the TV revenues are earned from the subscriptions that fans pay the TV companies. Now, whilst campaigners were devoting their lives to the cause and fans were donating what cash they could, the money they'd given in support of the team was being used to sell the club to Rupert Murdoch! Few contrasts made the campaigners' blood boil more than this.

Despite their expensive advice, according to those closest to the deal the truth was that the directors of Manchester United were hopelessly out of their depth. They had presided over a business that had outgrown their expertise and now they wanted to cash in. Like a bunch of schoolboys, they were more bothered about impressing their mates with how easily they could get tickets for the match than they were about securing guarantees from Murdoch about the future of the club. The history and traditions of Manchester United Football Club were being auctioned off by men who could only see the cash value that their shareholdings could bring. There was no sense of duty as custodians of the club, no acknowledgement of the emotional attachment that millions of fans have with the team. With

Edwards and Smith arrogantly assuming that the success of the club was down to their flotation in 1991, rather than the management team or the loyal support of fans over many years, they believed they owned it and could do with it what they liked.

But the fans knew that the club was more than a line on the share pages of the stock exchange and that first week demonstrated that belief. In fact it was clear within days of the bid announcement that for many of those involved, their lives had been changed irrevocably. Andy Walsh took unpaid leave to co-ordinate matters and his wife Sarah had to put up with her home being the property of a bunch of football fans on an impossible mission. Although she says that, given both her and Andy's previous political involvement, it 'wasn't as much a shock to me as it might have been to someone without that background,' the fact that he didn't even see his kids for two weeks was a heavy toll for any family to bear. Others took time off work; some suddenly developed advanced dental problems which required almost daily treatment; sales meetings were hastily arranged in Manchester; tasks were 'taken home' to 'get peace and quiet from the office'; holidays were taken; and relationships were strained to, and beyond, breaking point on more than one occasion. It was a titanic effort and the human cost should never be underestimated. But, by the end of that second week, everyone involved knew that there was still a very long way to go.

TWO

FROM FLAT CAPS TO FAT CATS

Tragedy, Taylor and Television

Once upon a time, football was a game. The People's Game. Enjoyed by millions of working men, all of whom seemed to wear flat caps. If we are to believe the nostalgia, football was fair and square, sheer endeavour on the field determined success and failure, players played for the good of the game and fans applauded the opposition's fancy footwork. Then something happened. Players got greedy. Fans started fighting. England never looked like winning the World Cup again. Before we knew it, the game was in a mess. Financial instability, internecine fighting within the football authorities, deaths at football grounds. The age of innocence was over.

The World Cup of 1990, the Taylor Report and the formation of the Premier League introduced, in the words of the game's new paymasters, Sky TV, 'a whole new ball game'. Well, not quite, it was still football, Jim, just not as we knew it. Football clubs were suddenly big business. They began to 'realise market potential'. They were bought or sold to holding companies listed on the stock exchange, where institutional shareholders became anxious for share price and dividend increases. The shareholders even started determining transfer policy and that the supporters pay more and more to watch the game.

If football lost its innocence in the 1970s and 1980s, then in the 1990s it grew up, bought a suit and started thinking about how it would finance that luxury retirement home. Whatever the myths of football's bygone years, and they are legion, those in positions of power in the game at the turn of the decade decided that it was time to cash in on football's myth, get a return on its appeal, and sell its soul.

The watershed, of course, was Hillsborough. Football had reached such a nadir that it was possible for ninety-six people to be crushed to death at an FA Cup semi-final because of the dire state of the ground and policing tactics which – like much Continental policing to this date – presumed hooligan intent first and worried about the physical well-being of fans a very poor second. The events of this tragic day are well documented elsewhere (see Rogan Taylor's excellent account), but two things should be highlighted. First is that the speed of development of the English football industry in the 1990s would not have happened as it did without Hillsborough and the 'commercialisation' of football cannot be properly understood without recognising the pivotal importance of 15 April 1989. The second is that football's, and arguably the nation's, response to Hillsborough has been piecemeal and has largely served to further financial above other interests, not least justice for the families concerned.

The main lever for football's development was Lord Justice Taylor's final report, a 109-page indictment of the way football was run in Britain. 'The picture revealed is of a general malaise or blight over the game due to a number of factors,' he wrote. 'Principally these are: old grounds, poor facilities, hooliganism, excessive drinking and poor leadership.' [HMSO: 26] Most people remember the report for its conclusion that the only way to avoid another disaster like Hillsborough was for football stadia to be made all-seater, something which was introduced in the top two divisions in England within five years of the report. However, it said much more than this. For instance, it argued that if stadia were to be made all-seater, 'it should be possible to plan a pricing structure which suits the cheapest seats to the pockets of those presently paying to stand,' citing the £6 and £4 then charged at Ibrox as reasonable.

Further, Taylor highlighted the failure in governance of football:

> As for the clubs, in some instances it is legitimate to wonder whether the directors are genuinely interested in the welfare of their grass-roots supporters. Boardroom struggles for power, wheeler-dealing in the buying and selling of shares and indeed whole clubs sometimes suggest that those involved are more interested in the personal financial benefits or social status of being a director than of directing the club in the interests of its supporters. [HMSO 1990:53]

However, these concerns were sidelined rapidly and the then Tory administration had little sympathy for such restrictions on the free market. Clubs, as clubs do given free rein, used the introduction of all-seater stadia to make as much money as they could; at Manchester United prices have increased 400 to 500 per cent in the nine years since the report. If they had stuck to the price range Taylor recommended, with the cumulative rate of inflation, we'd now be paying something between £9 and £10 per match.

The World Cup of 1990, when England reached the semi-finals and Gazza burst into tears, marked not only a symbolic full-stop to the dark days of the 1980s where hooliganism occupied the front pages and the long-ball game the back pages, but was also a wake-up call to the lucrative possibilities of television. The rights to the tournament were sold for a record fee and huge numbers of viewers tuned in. Club chairmen, Greg

Dyke and analysts such as the then Premier League consultant Alex Fynn began to realise that football wasn't getting its dues.

Hot on Taylor's heels came the Premier League, forged by the legendary white heat of the Football Association who, in their *Blueprint for the Future of Football*, backed the calls of big First Division clubs for a breakaway league. Some form of breakaway had been likely for some time and the self-styled 'Big Five' clubs (Manchester United, Arsenal, Liverpool, Tottenham and Everton!) had been progressively securing a bigger share of football's financial pot for some years. The formation of the Premier League meant that they could not only decide how much TV money they retained for themselves (previously 50 per cent of TV revenue was redistributed), but they could exclude the remaining seventy (now seventy-two) clubs from any decision-making. The Football League's attempts, in 1990's *One Game, One Team, One Voice*, to unify the organisation of football had been deftly side-stepped: instead of one organisation we were to have three. As David Conn writes in *The Football Business*:

> It seems unthinkable that the man [Graham Kelly] with the top job in football really backed a rich man's breakaway . . . allowing the clubs to keep all the money, actually to avoid a constructive suggestion for unity . . . It was the FA's responsibility to safeguard football, to insist that the new television money be spent wisely, to rebuild the whole of English football after its disgrace and disaster . . . [to] ensure that the historic, incomparable love of the English for the game of football which they gave to the world was nurtured, treasured, not exploited, stretched, tested, weakened, cheapened. [Conn 1997, 284–5]

The Premier League was now in a position to negotiate an exclusive TV deal. BSkyB outbid the competition from ITV with the co-operation of the BBC, who gained a revamped *Match of the Day* slot. The Premier League clubs got £305m over five years, with only £3m to be redistributed to the Football League. Given that a legal challenge to the breakaway from the Football League achieved a settlement which said that they should not be 'financially disadvantaged', the Premier League could be rather pleased with themselves. A further deal, worth £743m over the years to 2001 followed.

For BSkyB the deals were a saviour. Sky TV spent so much seeing off the challenge from British Satellite Broadcasting and their natty 'squarial', that it was losing £10m a week in 1990, threatening the very viability of Murdoch's parent company News Corporation. They had to achieve a critical mass of subscribers, and fast. Sport was the answer and in the words of one executive, in Britain that meant getting football 'first, second and third'. [Conn, p16] Exclusive access to live Premier League football was all bait that was needed. Murdoch's 'battering ram' put paid to another ont door. It is important to note that all the key players in the 1998 take-ver plans were active at this early stage: Martin Edwards pushing for a breakaway, Greg Dyke (who opposed Sky's bid for United) and BSkyB to whom Dyke lost out in 1991.

In just three years, from 1989 to 1992, the organisation, governance, finance, and physical shape of English football was changed forever. At each turn, the wishes of a small élite of clubs was granted. They were now to have brand new stadia – subsidised by the public purse to the tune of £200m – all kitted out in plastic seats, neatly patterned to spell the name of the latest sponsor; they would charge what they liked as Taylor's price recommendations were conveniently forgotten; they didn't have the tiresome need to consult with those cheeky mites from the lower divisions; and they had a bundle of new cash which they could stuff in their pockets, only tossing the odd copper into the outstretched hat being proffered by the League clubs. They had their cake and they were scoffing it too. One other factor came into play. Several of the clubs decided that the best way to raise even more money was to form holding companies to be floated on the stock exchange. We will return to this shortly.

At a European level, things were also moving. Silvio Berlusconi, owner of the Mediaset empire, had rescued AC Milan from bankruptcy in 1986, giving Arrigo Sacchi money to forge the legendary team of Gullit, Van Basten and Rykard, who lifted the European Cup in 1989, 1990 and 1994. From a very early stage Il Cavaliere, as he was known, had his sights firmly set on the mountain of cash possible from selling football through tele-vision. In 1988 he set up the first satellite television match, between AC Milan and Manchester United, during the ban on English clubs competing in Europe. With an audience of fifty million across Europe, it was an early signal of the potential (and greed) to resurface ten years later in the months before Sky's bid for United. [*The Times*, 2 August 1998]

However, Berlusconi's dreams of a European Super League were not to be realised at that time. But, in another portentous statement some time later, he argued that for his Milan team to be eliminated from the European Cup competition in the early stages, was 'not modern thinking'. The idea that Europe's major clubs be subject to the whims of a cup competition just didn't fit with the balance sheet. The chance factor in the sport of football just shouldn't get in the way of a healthy profit. In 1994 the European Champions' Cup introduced a league structure in its early stages. The Champions' League guaranteed six matches' worth of television income to each of the qualifiers, more for those that progressed to the quarter-finals, and also diminished the effect of shock defeats at the hands of part-time Scandinavians, with a league structure there to reassert the 'natural' order of things. Somebody, though, should have told Manchester United, who in

1994 followed a 4–0 defeat at the hands of Barcelona with a 3–1 loss to Gothenburg and exited the competition. However, even then they went home with a handy wad in their pockets, considerably more than when they had lost out to Galatasaray a year earlier. If you didn't win on the field, the lesson went, you could at least win in the bank.

Culturally, things were also changing. Football had hit the depths in the 1980s with Bradford (fire), Brussels (Heysel) and Birmingham (fan stabbed to death) preceding Hillsborough. English clubs were banned from Europe. Margaret Thatcher speculated whether the game could (or should be allowed to) survive. To say that you were a football fan was an admission likely to get you chucked out of a pub, rather than earn you points in the Groucho club. If the World Cup of 1990 showed how much could be made from television, it also showed publishers, chat-show producers and pop stars the benefits of claiming your life-long love of the beautiful game.

True, the ground work had been done, with both the Football Supporters' Association and fanzines showing that not everyone who went to the game was a rampaging hooligan. Arthur Smith's *An Evening with Gary Lineker* and then, most importantly, Nick Hornby's *Fever Pitch* gave the game a middle-class, cultural cachet to which middle England flocked. It was hip to be a fan; it was *de rigueur* to wear your old-fashioned football shirt; it must have been written into the contracts of almost every indie band signed from 1992 onwards that football allegiances be stated, or created. A new pricing structure for football, the FA's *Blueprint* and Sky's coverage all led to a new audience being targeted – the A, B and C1 social classes rather than the lumpen proletariat (a better audience for advertisers, you see). By the mid 1990s things were looking, and feeling, very different.

Manchester United plc – Winning off the Pitch

One club above any other symbolises the changes in English football in the last decade because, when it came to balance sheets, Manchester United led the way. For a long time the most popular team in England, the club turned itself from rich to super-rich in a handful of years. In 1991 Manchester United FC became Manchester United plc. Three small letters, but a world of difference.

As Michael Crick highlighted in his book, *The Betrayal of a Legend*, the Edwards family regime at Old Trafford had not been shy in terms of making money before the plc. A share issue, on the advice of Sir Roland Smith (now Chair of the plc), and what amounted to insider dealing in the late '70s had reinforced the family's grip on the club and allowed them to start to realise some dividend payback, which increased from £312 in 1978 to £50,419 a year later. As the FA relaxed its rules on dividends and payment of full-time directors, Martin Edwards became the main beneficiary: by 1987 he had received £233,684 in dividends and was being paid £96,000 a year as United's Chief Executive, by far the highest-paid football club Chief Executive anywhere. However, such money-making by Edwards was nothing to the personal fortune he was to amass in the flotation of Manchester United on the stock exchange.

Spurs had been first out of the blocks in 1983, although the disaster of their Hummel sportswear arm resulted in the club's shares being suspended. However, Irving Scholar's pioneering efforts had been closely watched elsewhere. It might seem a bit strange that clubs raising capital by floating shares on the stock market had not been done before (it was suggested in the Chester Report in 1969): after all, the 1980s was the decade of the mythical share-owning democracy, when flotations seemed an almost weekly occurrence. 'Tell Sid,' the adverts said. Well, nobody seemed to have told football. In fact there was a very good reason for this; the Football Association had a rule, dating back to the early part of the century, which effectively prevented clubs floating on the stock exchange. Rule 34 decreed that not more than 5 per cent of the face value of shares could be paid in dividends and payment of directors was outlawed.

The idea behind this was to stop speculators buying football clubs to be used as a source of profit. It was designed to preserve some essential ideals about football: that it is a sport first and business second and that the introduction of the notion of a club as a source of profit, rather than a club as a mutual pooling of resources, would pervert the game. Rule 34 is still on the FA's statute book as a condition of membership, although modified to allow payment of up to 15 per cent of share value and payment of a director as long as he/she works full time at the club.

Nobody seems quite sure what happened to Rule 34 when Tottenham and Manchester United decided that they would float on the stock exchange. Technically, Manchester United Football Club (along with Manchester United Merchandising and Manchester United Catering) became wholly owned by Manchester United plc, a holding company, and therefore, they argued, they were exempt from the ruling. It was not Manchester United *Football Club* who would pay dividends on shares, but the *plc*. Likewise it would be the plc which paid the directors. But surely the FA realised what was happening, that their rule, which had been in place for most of the century and which is to this day a condition of FA membership, was being ignored?

But why did football clubs want to float anyway? Was it just the avarice of chairmen and directors who had inherited or bought shares at minimal cost who now wanted to realise their potential, as Conn describes in *The Football Business*? There was certainly motivation here for Martin Edwards. Son of former Chairman and Manchester butcher, 'Champagne' Louis

Edwards, Martin inherited control of the club when his father died in 1980. Almost immediately he was involved in controversy, accusing Granada TV of contributing to his father's death through its *World in Action* exposé of dealings in the meat business. A £600,000 investment by Martin in the share issue of 1979 had become a 50.6 per cent stake – half a million shares – which he negotiated to sell for £10m just ten years later.

In 1986 he had tried to sell the club to Robert Maxwell in the face of vocal opposition from the Stretford End, but the deal fell through. In 1989 he tried again to sell his share of the club to Michael Knighton. Although a deal seemed to have been done and Knighton appeared before the Stretford End at the start of the season, kitted out and juggling a football, the deal foundered as Knighton's backers pulled out. The deal meant that control of the club was to have been sold for £10m (it was valued at £20m in total), £500,000 less than United were to pay for Japp Stam a decade later. The failure of the Knighton deal spurred Edwards and the club towards the stock market.

Edwards claims that he 'was the last director to be persuaded it was a good idea . . . [and] fought against flotation but in the end realised it was good for the club'. He continues, 'I *could* now take the credit for that, but I was against it. I accept now that I was wrong.' It's a curious thing to say, especially when he does appear to want credit, saying, 'When I am dead, people might actually look back and think that I didn't do a bad job for this club.' [*Sunday Telegraph*, 13 September 1998] He also ominously admitted, 'If you float, you lose your independence . . . it does not protect you from the sort of offer we have received from Sky.'

With the prospect of the Premier League becoming a reality, the situation suddenly looked very different to Edwards and the board in 1990–91. United had won the FA Cup, they were back in European competition after the five year ban, and the commercial prospects of the football business looked decidedly different than they had in 1989. A flotation was certainly more likely to succeed for Manchester United in 1991 than for Spurs in 1983. However, the board argued that they needed to float the club to raise revenue for the Taylor-required rebuilding of the Stretford End, United's main remaining terraced area. This rebuilding was to cost £12m and £6.7m was to come from the flotation. The shortfall and loss in capacity meant extra strains on the income streams of the club and thus at the same time prices were increased. The club, despite making a £5m profit in 1990 which increased to around £7m in 1991, and being valued at £47m on flotation – twice its value in 1989 – claimed that they had no option given the new government requirement on all-seater stadia. Fans weren't so sure.

The share issue, in June 1991, was criticised by fans for a number of reasons. Firstly, the timing. It came immediately after the end of the season, when Reds had just paid for a trip to Rotterdam for the successful European

Cup-Winners' Cup final, and many had just had to pay for the renewal of their season tickets. The minimum share issue of £194 was considered a prohibitively high price for 'joining our team and being part of our future', as the official programme put it. [*United Review*, 20 May 1991, p21]

Far from being a means of democratising football – letting supporters actually own their club through public share issues – the Manchester United experience left over half the shares with the club's underwriters, large financial institutions with little or no interest in football. Ownership may have been widened, but to whom? The editor of Manchester United's biggest-selling fanzine, *Red Issue*, argued that the share issue had been opposed for a number of reasons:

> I suspect that two factors kept more Reds from investing, when it came down to it. The first is the well publicised fact that most of us had just shelled out a couple of hundred quid on the trip to Rotterdam and renewed our season tickets, another £194 for shares did not exist. Second and less publicised was the realisation amongst many that whilst under the 'reasons for and proceeds of offer', £6.7m was towards the redevelopment of the Stretford End, £6.4m was going to Martin Edwards [United's chairman]. The thought of lining his pockets must have put some people off. [*Red Issue*, Volume 4, Issue 1]

A further share issue was made in 1997, again ostensibly to finance ground improvements, including the North Stand. What the share and price strategy which the club pursued meant was that it avoided getting into debt, or having a 'bond scheme' as Arsenal and West Ham did, to finance rebuilding. Indeed, United retained considerable assets by selling shares and making fans pay higher prices, so perhaps it's not surprising that top of the list of fan complaints since has been those phenomenal price increases.

In 1990 a standing season ticket (then called a League Match Ticket Book) cost £76. In 1992 it was £152 – a 100 per cent increase in two years. At a time of economic recession, in the wake of Taylor's recommendations and when the prime economic strategy of the government was to keep inflation low, this was a particularly steep increase for fans to meet. If a supporter transferred from standing accommodation in the Stretford End to seating accommodation – all fans had to be in seats by 1994 anyway – the increase in the price of a season ticket was huge, from £108 in 1991 to £266 in one year. [*United Review*, Volume 53]

Martin Edwards defended the increase on the grounds that the club would lose revenue from a drop in capacity:

> We knew when the Stretford End was demolished we were losing something like 12,000 or 13,000 spaces. We sat down with a

calculator and a pencil and said, 'What do we need to make up that lost income? What do we need to charge?' And that is exactly how we arrived at the £14, £12 and £8 standing for this [1992–93] season . . . what we needed to replace that income. [*Open Space*, BBC2, March 1993]

All this was despite strong arguments from supporters that the club were not building, or thinking, big enough, with many claiming that a three tier Stretford End should have been built. The subsequent decision in 1998 to add an extra tier on to both the Stretford End and K Stand End, illustrates the shortsighted and costly nature of the board decisions at the time. Money was lost by having to build stands twice and for losing out on the extra seat revenue from a bigger capacity. But why worry when fans would pay? Although required rebuilding was complete by 1994, prices continued to spiral. In 1998 a season ticket in K Stand was £340 and in 1999 this was increased by several times the rate of inflation to £380 in a year when the club made £20m profit.

Significantly, in defending the initial wave of price increases, the club argued that, 'by choosing the only available option, that of a public share flotation we are, of course, committed to a dividend policy'. [BBC2, 1993] And what a commitment that became. The payments of money from the plc to its shareholders – i.e. payments of money going out of both Manchester United and out of football altogether – are: 1992: £2,189,000; 1993: £2,372,000; 1994: £2,554,000; 1995: £2,737,000; 1996: £3,221,000; 1997: £4,026,000; 1998: £4,416,000; 1999: £1,429,000 (interim only so far, likely to be another £3m). In total a projected £27,373,000 has gone out of the club, justified by a need to raise just £6.7m for rebuilding in 1991.

In that time the club has enjoyed record profits – £27.5m in 1997 and £20m in 1998 – making it by far the richest club in Britain and in Europe. Its turnover of around £90m is twice that of Barcelona. Edwards, who now has between 14 and 15 per cent of shares in United, has already received around £33m from share sales. On top of this he was receiving £536,000 a year in salary and bonuses in 1997, plus dividends from his shares, totalling somewhere around the £1m mark. A year. The value of his remaining shares were worth £64m before the Sky take-over raised its ugly head. For an investment of £600,000 in the rights issue of 1979, Edwards' share worth was nearly £100m. [Conn, p179] Not bad, especially when he was being paid a handsome salary every year on top. The Sky deal was to send that scale of return into the stratosphere.

To satisfy the voracious appetite for profit of shareholding institutions, the club began to market its 'brand'. The 'Souvenir Shop' sounds fantastically quaint in these days of the Super Store and Megastore and, with plans for new shops at seemingly every major Far East airport, United hotels, United pizza and United whisky on the go, it is in a different league. In what has been seen as a final symbolic act, the plc removed the words 'Football Club' from the club crest 'to concentrate brand identification'. Where once stood a football team, with a tradition and glory and passionate support, now stood a marketing exercise with a past to resell and a present to be 'spectated' and bought.

But there is a more general sense in which fans feel things have changed since the club became a plc. The famous Old Trafford atmosphere has vanished, except on rarefied European Cup nights; the Stretford End was replaced with a Family Stand and Club Class sections bang in the middle; fans were displaced around the stadium; new executive areas took pride of place in the North Stand; 'day-trippers' and 'glory hunters', complete with bags of merchandise, seemed to become the norm at home games; and, with an ageing crowd, any sense of a community of fans has been reduced to gatherings under the stands at half-time, sipping over-priced lager and talking of how things used to be.

In deflecting criticism, it was fortuitous for Edwards and his new financial buddies that, under manager Alex Ferguson, United suddenly became a team that could do the business. United have won the Premier League five times in seven years; the FA Cup four times; the League Cup; the Cup-Winners' Cup; and now the European Cup. That includes three League and Cup doubles in an era which has only seen seven in all as well as the first treble in history. Although United have been a 'big club' for many years, their acceleration through the '90s would leave Schumacher on the starting grid. And who has been there to pick up the loose change? Edwards, the directors and shareholders.

There has been some opposition, however. The initial round of price increases saw the formation of a fledgling supporters' organisation, HOSTAGE. Holders of Season Tickets Against Gross Exploitation is perhaps the most phenomenally cumbersome moniker a fans' organisation has ever had, and although it was renamed United Supporters' Association soon after, it died on the wing before causing a flutter in the heart of the board. The fanzines – Red Issue, United We Stand and Red News – have been a rich and constant source of criticism during these years, a voice-piece for the disaffected, a constant reminder of the cultural legacy to be defended, for which they should all be immensely proud. Though the fanzines prosper, IMUSA has joined the fray.

Other criticism has focused on a perceived conservatism within the plc evidenced through both a reluctance to raise money from sources other than fans' pockets and for restricting the manager's ability to buy new players. During the summer of 1997 this criticism became particularly forceful as one star player after another seemed to reject a move to the club because of its wage structure. Now, although such a reluctance to pay exorbitant wages can be applauded on grounds of common decency – surely £20,000 a week is enough for anyone? – remunerative morality was hardly Edwards' and the board's motive. Indeed, Edwards himself sold a small portion of his shares in 1998 for a whacking £33m – so it's okay to pay yourself, just not those who actually play football.

One defence of the plc route for football clubs has been that they are subject to the rules of the stock exchange. As such, they are perhaps exempt from the criticism levelled increasingly at non-plc football clubs that they operate in a murky financial world of cash payments and creative tax returns. What they cannot be defended on is grounds of democracy. At every turn in the plc's short history, the ire of supporters and small shareholders has been raised. Yet the board, frequently bombarded by hostile questions and statements at the plc's AGM, has failed even to pay lip service to consulting supporters and/or shareholders.

At the root of this dissatisfaction is a feeling among many fans that by floating on the stock market the club has lost part of its identity, its local connections and history, its obligation to the community and its role as a sporting rather than a money-making institution. Such concerns, though prevalent before September 1998, were to take centre stage when the take-over by BSkyB was announced.

The Train Keeps A-Rolling – European Super League '98

If the early 1990s had set things up nicely for the corporate arm of the game, the latter stages of the decade seemed to offer new opportunities. One was a renewed interest in a European Super League; the other was the possibilities of pay-per-view (PPV) television.

On 19 July 1998 the *Sunday Telegraph* reported that new moves were afoot to create a European Football League of Europe's élite clubs. This new competition was to be run outside the auspices of UEFA and was to restrict access for Europe's rich clubs. It was hardly even newsworthy to see that Manchester United's name was attached to the project. Although earlier attempts at a Super League, such as that proposed by Berlusconi in 1990, did not even envisage United as one of the UK's leading players, times had changed and the idea of the project 'having legs' without United was far-fetched. The club, of course, denied any involvement in a statement on 20 July which said that, 'It is just pure speculation. We are getting a little fed up with the speculation linking us with a European Super League. It is not on our agenda.' [*The Guardian*, 20 July 1998] But it was on their agenda, which they admitted two weeks later at a Premier League meeting on 3 August.

A hitherto unknown consortium called Media Partners, backed by American bank JP Morgan, fronted by Rodolfo Hecht Lucari and financed partly by Formula One's Bernie Ecclestone, had been holding meetings with various chairmen of Europe's biggest clubs. They met in London on 3 August. Their proposal is believed to have included a thirty-two-club competition, with a top division of sixteen who were guaranteed participation for at least three years. This top flight of sixteen would include Continental giants Juventus, Barcelona, Real Madrid and Ajax, and Arsenal and Manchester United from England, with Liverpool a possibility. They were to be offered £3m to join, with promises of a further £20m for taking part and a total of £40m for the winners.

The European Football League (EFL) would have spelt disaster for those clubs on the fringes of the competition or excluded altogether if they played football in one of Europe's poorer countries. It was bad news for UEFA too, who immediately opposed it. It was also bad news for the credibility of national leagues, such as the Premier: after all, if your richest clubs are guaranteed their European gravy train, why slog it out through the bleak English winter and suffer damaging injuries to your best players? Treating the League as minor competition, if not leaving it altogether, seemed a likely prospect. The outlook for the remaining seventeen Premier League clubs was not good and the League took immediate action to get assurances from Arsenal, Manchester United and Liverpool that they weren't intending to compete.

The threat of expulsion from domestic leagues was a real and powerful one, at least in the short term, and a meeting of the Premier League guaranteed that any plans to join the EFL were put on hold. In return, the Premier's Chief Executive, Peter Leaver, promised that they would work within UEFA's Professional Clubs Committee to secure an expansion and better financial return from existing European competitions, including a further watering down of the Champions' League and the combining of Cup-Winners' and UEFA Cups.

Although the EFL was ultimately defeated, at least for the time being, it had been a watershed in asserting the power of the continent's richest clubs over the continent's governing body. Major changes had been wrought in the structure of European competition, in the sole interests of the richest clubs. England were now to have three possible places in the Champions' League and the 'pyramid' of European football was rapidly being decapitated.

An oft-quoted but ill-defined group of clubs was emerging, the 'G14'. That they took their name from the grouping of the world's richest nations is hardly a coincidence: it also signalled that they were more about making money than defending the cultural traditions of European football, or about sporting excellence. Football's supporters, still the life-blood of the game even in the harsh light of clubs' executive offices, had opinions, but they simply weren't being considered. IMUSA opposed the project and, amazingly, there was now sympathy even within UEFA for fans:

> Europe's top clubs yesterday expressed fears at a meeting in Geneva that they are losing contact with the fans as football grows into a multi-million-pound industry. Bombarded daily by talk of super leagues, battles over television rights, bickering over a biennial World Cup, stock flotations and doping scandals, the business of football has recently overshadowed the playing of football, leaving many supporters uninterested and disillusioned. 'Money talks and the . . . changes of clubs into capital companies is difficult for the real fans to digest,' acknowledged Gerhard Aigner, the General Secretary of UEFA. [Reuters, 27 February 1999]

Despite the setback, Media Partners' Rodolfo Hecht Lucari warned in September 1998 that he 'had never been so optimistic about the eventual success of the venture'. [*Sunday Telegraph*, 13 September 1998]

Carving Up the Continent: The European Sports Market

What is interesting in the context of the Sky bid for United is that neither Berlusconi nor Rupert Murdoch initially appeared involved in Media Partners' EFL. That wasn't the whole story, however. In fact Murdoch was busy putting together interventions in Italy, France and Germany and Berlusconi's Mediaset were believed to be part of the Media Partners set-up.

In September 1998 Murdoch teamed up with Telecom Italia to table a £1.4 billion bid for the rights to broadcast Italian Serie A football. An attempt at allying themselves to RAI, the state broadcaster, to form a single digital pay-TV network, would have potentially put them in direct competition with Telepiu, owned by the French Canal Plus network who already had a pay-TV deal with four of the top Italian teams, Juventus, AC Milan, Inter and Napoli (an estimated 70 per cent of the pay-TV market) and possibilities of others yet to come.

Such a conflict threatened the stability of the Italian league and the centre-left government stepped in. Already keen to stop Murdoch gaining influence in Italy and control over the rights to its football, the Italian government issued a decree outlawing any deal involving RAI and Telecom Italia. This was backed by the Italian Parliament, and so Murdoch withdrew his interest in Telecom Italia.

He wasn't finished, however. Seeing as Canal Plus, through Telepiu, had the rights to most of Italian football and also that, to some analysts, 'Europe's pay-TV markets, divided by language, are not, for the moment, big enough to sustain two competing platforms' [*The Economist*, March 1999], Murdoch turned his attention to the French station. He was negotiating a merger with Canal Plus in which BSkyB were to have a 25 per cent stake. There were a number of problems, however. Murdoch had approached Canal Plus a year earlier, but backed off. His interest in Italy, which finally ended in January 1999, had annoyed Canal Plus, with whom he would have been the chief competitor and Murdoch himself was also wary of any deal in which he was the minor partner. Then there were the competition issues, one legal, the other football. Karel Van Miert, the EC's Competition Director General, was already getting sniffy about media conglomerations and both he and DGX (Culture and Sport) were beginning to investigate the sport–TV relationship. The EC's determination to support European production and culture against American competition was another threat.

Secondly, the BSkyB–Canal Plus merger raised concerns within UEFA and the EC, particularly in the light of the Manchester United take-over proposal. Van Miert was already involved in negotiations, which are still ongoing, about the competition issues raised by a UEFA ban on two clubs owned by the same person or group in the same football competition. Canal Plus own Paris St Germain and BSkyB were bidding to own Manchester United. SUAM's Michael Crick was quick to point out the potential problems:

> One can easily see a terrible situation where it's a choice between Manchester United and Paris St Germain – and one shouldn't assume that just because Manchester United are the bigger club that Paris St Germain will be forced to give up their place. In any case what would French supporters think of that? And what if Paris St Germain are the French champions and Manchester United only qualify for the Champions' League as runners-up? It would be a nightmare to sort out . . . But it just shows the kind of problems that will arise if the authorities allow BSkyB to take over Manchester United. [PA]

In the end it was the tussle over who got the top job which put paid to the Canal Plus–BSkyB deal: 'The management is the tough point and it is not negotiable. We will have the leadership or there is no accord,' said Canal Plus chairman Pierre Lescure. But the process had highlighted the increasingly desperate machinations and scrambles to achieve dominance over European football's television rights, a battle which was reaching boiling point in England.

Failure with Canal Plus was beginning to dent Murdoch's 'determination to carve out a leading role in the lucrative business of televising European football, the key vehicle for building subscription-based TV networks'. [*Financial Times*, 18 September 1998] The problem lay not only with competition issues, but with the nature of the European television market.

> For a notoriously single-minded man, Rupert Murdoch's behaviour in Europe has been odd. Every few months there are new talks with a new potential partner; then something goes wrong, he loses interest, and a few months later he pops up in a different boardroom. But the problem is not so much that Mr Murdoch has turned peculiar; it is that Europe's television business is a peculiarly hard one to operate in. [*The Economist*, March 1999]

So, next stop, Germany. Also in September 1998, Murdoch teamed up with Berlusconi's Mediaset (believed to be one of the Media Partners), and Saudi investor Prince Alwaleed bin Talal to buy a 25 per cent stake in German media group Kirch. This eventually not only landed Murdoch with a stake in the rights for the German Bundesliga and German Champions' League games, but also formed a nascent European media network.

This is the real prize. It is a well-recognised Murdoch tactic to buy into partnership deals, dominate them and then expand them. The attempts in Italy, France and Germany to get a toehold is really about guaranteeing as much of the European football pay-TV market as possible. The take-over bid for Manchester United cannot be seen outside this context. The EFL had been blocked, but once a dominant position could be achieved in this market, involving the top clubs from the major footballing nations, the prospects of a European Super League were sure to resurface. Rumenigge's vow that 'we'll be back', after the sidelining of the Media Partners plan, seemed ominous.

Indeed, Murdoch's vision extended way beyond Europe. The newly elected head of FIFA, Sepp Blatter, raised the prospect of a biennial World Cup in a speech in January 1999. It was as much an attempt to reassert the pre-eminence of national team competition over the increasingly powerful clubs, as it was a serious proposal, but the reactions spoke volumes. UEFA's Lennart Johansson merely reiterated the supremacy of the clubs shown in the revamping of the Champions' League – 'The risk is that the representatives from the big clubs in Europe say to me this is too much. We cannot accept yet more demands on our players.' Yet Murdoch seemed to welcome the idea – 'There's no reason why it shouldn't be every second year' – but he added that he 'would like to see a biennial World Cup for clubs instead'. [*The Guardian*, 13 January 1999] The fears of United fans that the club would be turned into a footballing Harlem Globe Trotters, in new, tradition-less and unwanted competitions, seemed well grounded. The news in June 1999 that United were to play in the World Team Championship in Brazil, at the expense of the FA Cup, proved they were right.

Braking the Juggernaut? – Pay-Per-View, the OFT and the RPC

The issue of pay-per-view television also got increased airings in the year before Sky's attempt to buy Manchester United. The introduction of digital channels seems to offer unlimited opportunities for showing more football on television, and, given football's proven ability to secure subscriptions, it is pivotal in the battle between BSkyB and their main rival, OnDigital. PPV would be a central plank in paying for securing those rights. Even without the digital opportunities, Sky had always said that PPV – in which subscribers would have to pay an extra, one-off fee for matches – was still an option. They began to use it extensively in televised boxing and proposed to do the same for the Premier League in the 1998–99 season.

Manchester United were aware of the possibilities of PPV. Indeed, they had gone so far as to establish their own TV station, MUTV, in partnership with Sky and Granada TV long before the take-over deal was an option. However, should PPV be approved by the Premier League, and should BSkyB be allowed to buy Manchester United, the infrastructure was in place to fully exploit the development.

The clubs – particularly those with the highest numbers of viewers and most often on television – stood to make a mint, as did Sky. The 1998 proposal involved an initial four games a weekend being screened on Sundays, three of which would be pay-per-view matches. The second stage would have involved moving the entire Premiership programme to Sundays on PPV. Martin Edwards seemed confident of securing agreement to the deal, and as Chief Executive of the most watched and televised club, stood to gain most: 'My own research shows that the majority of clubs are in favour of the idea,' he said.

However, at a meeting of the Premier League on 29 May 1998, the member clubs refused to back its introduction the following season. It was a surprising turnaround, and the first time BSkyB's proposals had been knocked back since the inaugural deal in 1992. Although Chief Executive Leaver claimed, 'The Premier League is determined to ensure that there is an opportunity to consider all of the issues in detail and to act in the best interests of the game and its supporters,' observers concluded that a majority of clubs felt that they had more to lose given the likely concentration of PPV's benefit with the biggest clubs. Sky may have put a brave face on things – 'The proposals were never going to be agreed today but Sky shares the Premier League's wishes to get it right for all football fans'

– but the failure to secure the deal was not only a blow to future income streams, but also a blow to the corporation's confidence that it could take the Premier League with it, come what may.

Although the story of football in the 1990s is nothing short of a revolution in the game, the traffic has not all been in one direction. For a start, Manchester United may have taken off into the stratosphere commercially, but that 'success' raised significant opposition among fans. It is also, of course, one success story among many failures. We shall look at the number of clubs which teetered on the brink of existence at the end of the 1990s in chapter six, but it ought to be stated here that despite the untold riches pouring into the game at the top level, its redistribution throughout football is diminishing. For where there are winners, there are also losers.

However, even the top clubs were not having things all their own way, and some of these factors played a critical role in the timing of the take-over bid. We have already touched on two of them: the failure of the EFL and the rejection of PPV by the Premier League. However, even the stock market – football's 'new home' – began to be unimpressed. As one report highlighted, by mid-1998 the 'UK football index . . . almost halved from its 1996 peak . . . [and] all Premier League clubs lost ground.' [Salomon Smith Barney 1998: 4] Prices of all football shares from 1998 to January 1999 fell, bar four (Manchester United, Spurs, Sunderland and Newcastle) and the latter of these has since dropped dramatically. The message to Murdoch was that if he wanted to see a return on his investment, he would be better off with United – who had performed consistently well on the stock market since flotation – than almost all others. Indeed, the poor performance of many clubs led some analysts to argue that any future flotations were unlikely.

There was other criticism of the plc process in the 1990s. Douglas Hall and Freddy Shepherd, who own over 60 per cent of Newcastle United, were notoriously caught on camera in a Spanish brothel in a gross display of bravado about the profits they were accruing from the sale of club shirts. Although forced to resign from the board, they were reinstated several months after the incident. Conn has mounted the fiercest critique of the plc process in *The Football Business*, arguing that the FA abdicated its authority and failed to uphold the spirit, if not the letter, of its own rules by letting clubs float in the first place. The future regulation of plcs is something which the Football Task Force is wrestling with at the time of writing, an issue which we will return to. There was more: UEFA had managed to head off the EFL; there was an increased awareness at the European Commission of the threat to both European culture and tradition, and to a successful sporting industry, that over-penetration by television represented; and the British government launched a major investigation of football's commercialisation in the shape of the Football Task Force in 1997. If the tide hadn't turned then at least there were some ripples of discontent.

However, in the UK, by far the biggest threat to the comfy world of money-making in the Premier League has come from the Office of Fair Trading. It was the threat that this organisation of civil servants posed, above all, which made BSkyB sit up and decide that they had to protect their jewel in their crown, their saviour, their golden goose – exclusive rights to live Premier League football.

Television, in particular BSkyB, was heavily integrated into English football. If the Premier League was the juggernaut cab that ditched the wearisome load of the Football League in 1992, then BSkyB were on hand to pump in the fuel. By 1998, 20 per cent of the Premier League's income came from television and nearly all of that was from BSkyB. But not everything was rosy. The OFT decided that seeing as everyone else from David Mellor to Zoë Ball were dipping their fingers in football's pie, it was about time they had a go.

What they found when they looked under the pastry was a strange kind of business where competing firms formed a joint organisation, co-operated with each other to organise competition, and then banded together to sell exclusive rights to a fraction of the matches to one television company. Not only that, but the firms involved then divvied the loot up between them, making sure that as little as possible fell through their fingers to those languishing in the Football League. Now, the OFT could arguably be forgiven for thinking that football in the 1990s was *only* about watching games on TV and that that was what mattered to the consumer – it's what Sky had been telling everyone for years – but then to take the Premier League to court for acting as a cartel, so that each club had to arrange its own television deals, so that the 'consumer choice' of PPV could be ushered in, so that the rich got even richer and the poor poorer, and so that fixture chaos and self-interest ruled, all *in the interests of fans*, seemed to miss the point just a tad.

The process is this. The OFT investigated the Premier League's second exclusive TV deal with BSkyB and the BBC. They decided that by selling TV rights collectively, they were acting as a cartel, against the law. They also decided that, because Sky 'only' showed about sixty games a year – quite enough for most, to be honest – the deal deprived clubs, fans and other TV companies of the right to show the remaining live matches. So they took the Premier League, BSkyB and the BBC to the Restrictive Practices Court to get the deal nullified. The overwhelming defeat of the case was not expected at the time, and the prospect seemed to be that all clubs would have to make individual deals. It put both the Premier League and BSkyB on to a war footing.

The case was an unusual one in football, for it uniquely managed to unite almost every interest in the game in opposition. For the Premier League, the case threatened their very *raison d'être*: if they weren't there to sell TV rights to their competition, what were they for? If clubs were to sell TV rights by themselves, with no obligation to redistribute income amongst the others in the League, then they might as well go back to the old League structure, as the new situation would fulfil the wishes of the big clubs to retain income. Or worse, it might spur on those clubs likely to be involved in European competition to form a new league, without the tiresome mid-week trips to Wimbledon and Southampton to worry about. The Premier League stuck an estimated £20m behind winning the case, it meant that much to them.

For the Football League clubs, the prospect of the OFT winning the case raised the spectre of a further concentration of television income in the hands of the few: they would even lose the pittance which the Premier deemed fit to chuck in the League's direction. The dire financial health of many of their clubs would look decidedly terminal.

Even fans didn't like it. The fixture chaos wrought by Sky's schedules would seem small fry when you had twenty clubs, each with their own deal, trying to maximise the market for their games by not clashing with another. With individual TV deals would almost certainly come PPV deals, increasing the cost to those who wish to watch football on TV. Finally, fans of clubs such as Coventry and Southampton, who at least received a proportion of income every time Manchester United play on TV, main-taining some redistribution, would now get nothing and they would be forced to rely solely on the audience they could generate.

Given that the government, in the shape of its Sports Minister at the DCMS and its recommendatory body, the Football Task Force – which includes every representative organisation in football – came out against the OFT, you began to wonder just whose interests the OFT thought they were defending, except some civil servant who didn't like a technical breach of Fair Trading legislation.

But the process generated some interesting reactions. The Premier League who, like almost every other organisation in football, steadfastly refuse to seriously involve supporters in decision-making (you can almost hear them now, bleating on about Supporter Panels and Surveys) suddenly instructed their solicitors – in particular Tracey Petter at Denton Hall – to get fans on board. The two national fans' organisations, as well as indepen-dents at Newcastle, Southampton and IMUSA, were all contacted and asked to give evidence to the RPC. Rather inadvisedly, some of these agreed without conditions, as if the Premier League *per se* was something to be defended in the fans' interests.

At the end of August 1998 IMUSA met with the Premier League's solicitors Denton Hall, agreeing to give a statement in defence of the current TV rights arrangements. A week later the Sky bid was announced and Peter

Leaver stated on Radio 5 Live that he did not see anything wrong with the deal and that it wasn't a matter for them to be involved in. IMUSA immediately contacted Mike Lee at the Premier League and explained to him why it was crucial for the Premier League to oppose the take-over, not least because of the threat the deal posed to the long-term future of the collective sale of rights. Lee was distinctly unhelpful and extremely patronising so IMUSA decided to withdraw its support. This was a difficult decision as IMUSA fervently believed in collective selling. In the end the IMUSA officers were left with little choice given limited resources, as the priority was to try and save the club. This immediately prompted Peter Leaver to call Andy Walsh to reassure IMUSA that he was taking the issue seriously. IMUSA remained unconvinced. Adam Brown reported that Leaver was being obstructive at the Task Force (Leaver accused him of 'trying to hijack the Task Force' in his attempts to get a Task Force statement against the deal) and this confirmed the suspicion that Leaver was playing a duplicitous game.

Another series of conversations with Denton Hall and Mike Lee followed. The Premier League refused to be 'negotiating with potential witnesses' but IMUSA refused to spend time and money supporting the collective sale of rights when Murdoch was planning something else entirely. The Premier League's short-termism was astounding. IMUSA's decision was not supported by all other supporters' groups, although there was considerable sympathy and Southampton's ISA were not happy about defending the Premier League in the first place. Despite IMUSA making it clear to Denton Hall that they had no intention of turning up, IMUSA were still listed as a witness in the case and Denton Hall acted surprised when IMUSA did not appear!

The great and the good (or powerful and bad) of football certainly were not getting it all their own way. Halfway through the bid process, at the turn of the year, both Graham Kelly, Chief Executive of the FA, and Keith Wiseman, FA Chairman, were forced to resign. They were soon followed by Peter Leaver and Sir John Quinton, their counterparts at the Premier League. Accusations of organisational and financial impropriety put paid to their aspirations and opened up a vacuum at the top of the game, into which a host of competing interests were sucked (see chapter eight). The message it put out was that no one was beyond reproach.

For BSkyB, the OFT and growing uncertainty about the future was a major threat to both their domination of Premiership coverage and their grip on the UK pay-TV market, itself entering a new period of competition as the digital TV battle with OnDigital heated up. The strategic position of BSkyB, which had been supported through the 1990s by possession of Premier League rights, was now under threat and a key money-spinner, PPV, had been rejected by the chairmen. The battle for digital television in many ways echoed the battle with BSB at the start of the decade, although arguably with much bigger stakes: the pay-TV market in 1990 was almost non-existent; by

1998 it was well established and the potentially much bigger digital market was being embraced by everyone, including the BBC and Channel 4.

In November 1998, BSkyB announced that its profits were being hit by the competition with OnDigital – down by £9.6m for the three months to September 1998. However, although 100,000 digital dishes had been sold, only 30,000 of these were to customers who were not already Sky subscribers. Sales of analogue dishes fell dramatically, by 143,000 in the same period, and the total number of Sky subscribers was down by 17,000 on the previous quarter. [*Financial Times*, 1 November 1998] One of the cornerstones of Sky's ability to maintain their position, to see off OnDigital and then to expand their dominance of the European pay-TV sports market was Premier League football. The situation was to be exacerbated by OnDigital's securing of half of 1999–2000's Champions' League games, in a joint £240m four-year deal with ITV. With the various challenges to BSkyB's dominance of football in the UK now materialising, the stage was set for the drama to commence in earnest.

Enter Murdoch, Stage Right

Rupert Murdoch was probably one of the few people in a position to make a bid for Manchester United at the time. His initial bid of £575m, and subsequent agreement of £623.4m, was a colossal sum and the highest economic value ever placed on a football club. To recoup that amount of money meant being able to exploit Manchester United's global appeal within his own global media empire. It was the strategic value of the club as much as the amount of turnover and profit it could generate which really counted. After all, who buys a firm for £623.4m when the most it has ever made in annual profit is £27m: it would take something like twenty-five years to pay back the basic investment.

Murdoch's global empire – News Corporation – operates nearly eight hundred separate businesses in around fifty-two countries. It declared profits of $561m in 1996. Almost all of News Corp's profits are declared in low-tax countries such as the Netherlands and Bermuda, with losses recorded in the countries operating News Corp's main subsidiaries, Australia, Britain and the US. In total News Corp paid an estimated 7.8 per cent tax in 1996–97. The growth in size of News Corp in the last decade or so has been fuelled by enormous borrowing – something which brought it to the edge of disaster in 1990 as Sky TV battled it out with BSB, only to be saved by the Premier League deal. It is believed that the corporation had an estimated $13 billion debt before making the play for Manchester United.

News Corp's subsidiary, News International, owns only 40 per cent of BSkyB because of UK competition law restrictions, due to News International's powerful position in the UK print media. However, recently Murdoch has taken the chair of BSkyB. One reason given for this is that he wants control of the crucial battle with OnDigital. Another is that BSkyB Director Jean-Marie Messier of French media group Vivendi (who own 37 per cent of BSkyB and 34 per cent of Canal Plus), may soon make a play for control. Murdoch may be forced to choose between control of his UK television arm of News Corp and relinquishing control of some of the print media. [*The Guardian*, 16 June 1999] Whatever happens, News Corp was in a unique position to exploit the ownership of Manchester United through its UK and global media empire: 'From the initial spin to delivering United matches, domestic and European, around the planet, it is difficult to imagine any organisation which could match the global infrastructure Murdoch already has in place.' [*The Guardian*, 8 September 1998]

One of the most quoted arguments Murdoch has put forward about the place of sport within his global media empire is this:

> Sport, and football in particular, 'absolutely overpowers' film and all other forms of entertainment in drawing viewers to pay television. 'We have the long-term rights in most countries to major sporting events and we will be doing in Asia what we intend to do elsewhere in the world – that is, use sports as a battering ram and a lead offering in all our pay television operations,' he said. [*The Guardian*, 7 September 1998]

This is the absolute crux of the BSkyB take-over of Manchester United. As IMUSA stated when the take-over was announced, 'Every company he [Rupert Murdoch] owns or buys out is simply a means to an end.' With the various threats to Sky's exclusive position in televising British football, and the complications within the European field, Sky had to secure rights to as much Premiership football as possible to ensure that viewers continue to subscribe to its main sports channels, and take up digital options, to see off the competition. 'The calculations behind the buy-out are relatively straightforward. Sky needs must-buy content, i.e. Premiership football, to convince viewers to subscribe, especially to its new 200-channel digital service.' [*The Guardian*, 8 September 1998]

In the US and Australia he has pursued a similar strategy. To boost take-up of his Fox Sports Channel in the US, Murdoch has purchased a number of sports teams, including the LA Dodgers baseball club, which he got for $320m. In that case a leading player, Mike Piazza, was sold to Florida Marlins over the head of the coach in a deal involving a marketing man, an accountant and two television executives. Sporting decisions didn't come into this equation.

Murdoch wrought havoc in Australian Rugby League in 1994 trying to boost ratings for his Foxtel cable network. The ARL had a five-year deal with a rival company, to which all twenty clubs had firm loyalty agreements. Murdoch, seemingly blocked from influence, secretly established a rival Super League, offered huge cash bonuses and double salaries direct to players, circumventing the clubs, and leaving clubs the option of joining the Super League or facing a mass defection of players and rival Super League clubs being set up on their doorstep. The result was confusion, soaring player costs, recriminations and a collapse in attendances and ratings, leading to negotiations to reverse the process by the end of 1997. [*LA Times*, 25 August 1997] Although a different tactic to the United take-over plan – Murdoch was buying players here to guarantee TV contracts rather than a club – it was a dire warning of the lengths to which he would go to secure his TV sports rights.

Once contracts were guaranteed, the strength of Murdoch's media empire meant he could exploit them globally. 'He is uniquely placed,' a media analyst of Henderson Crosthwaite said. 'He can broadcast into South America, he can broadcast into Asia, he can broadcast into the Far East and he can broadcast into the United States.' Supplementing dish sales and subscriptions to his sports channels was the ability to market secondary goods, and in this Manchester United – already the leading football brand in the world and one of the leading sports brands – were particularly attractive. 'Mr Murdoch does believe that there is a huge related market, not just the football, but related merchandising opportunities in his global conglomerate,' said Bob Nobay, of the London School of Economics. [*The Guardian*, 8 September 1998]

Another reason why Manchester United were so attractive on a global scale was that they had a huge supporter base across the world, but especially in the Far East. True, Premier League football itself was hugely popular – why else do we have the utterly bizarre floodlight failures caused by Malaysian betting syndicates? – but globally, as in the UK, United were the top prize. Murdoch had already had his hands burnt in India, where there are still three outstanding warrants for his arrest for material broadcast on his Star network, and he is desperate to maximise his penetration of the opening Chinese market. The importance of the Far East, the way he would use ownership of Manchester United and the implications for the club were highlighted during the take-over process. On two occasions, the press reported that BSkyB executives had approached the pin-up superstar of Japanese football, Nakarta, with the idea of signing for United. Nakarta's signing for Italian side Perugia had sparked mass sales in Japan of Perugia shirts bearing his name; estimates are in the region of one million. Combine the profit from merchandise sales and subscriptions to see him playing for Manchester United and suddenly Alex Ferguson's management of team affairs appears secondary in the global scheme of things.

This was the chief concern of supporters. With such a huge global strategy in play, how could the interests of one small part in the chain be expected to prevail? At times the interests of a successful Manchester United and the global strategy of the Murdoch empire may coincide, but when push came to shove, there was only going to be one interest that counted and that was the parent company's.

One final issue was raised by Murdoch's purchase and that was that, in addition to News Corp's colossal debt, the securitised loan with which he would buy Manchester United would have to be paid back. Some city analysts estimated that this could be in the region of £50m a year, at least in the short term. For a club which turned over £90m and made a profit of around £20m, it raised serious questions about where that additional revenue would come from. Selling players? Money-spinning, TV-driven tournaments? Excessive marketing of product? Matches scheduled to suit a Far Eastern TV audience rather than a UK one? Whatever the case, United fans were sure whose interests would come first if the deal were allowed to go through.

Murdoch may have known the power of football in selling satellite television subscriptions, if not actually anything about the game itself, and, given the mounting issues – the RPC, PPV, the protracted attempts to get a foothold in Continental Europe, Manchester United's own TV channel, the possible regulation of football and the sale of TV rights – he decided he'd better do something. Premier League football had saved Sky TV at the start of the decade: Murdoch wasn't about to let his own private battering ram to dish sales slip through his hands. In a typically audacious move, Murdoch and his cohorts at BSkyB decided that if it was ruled that he couldn't have the whole cake – exclusive Premiership and European coverage – he'd make damn sure he got the bit with the cherry on it. So he decided to buy the biggest, richest and most successful club, and the one with a massive global following: Manchester United.

THREE

TILTING AT WINDMILLS:
THE CAMPAIGN STRATEGY

Once the dust had settled on the first tumultuous week, it became easier to see how the land lay. Who was with you? Who was against? What were the issues to target? What was the best option for fighting the deal? Even some allies who were prepared to stick their oar in claimed that IMUSA was 'tilting at windmills', fighting a good fight but with little hope of victory. However, a clearer campaign strategy began slowly to emerge and the route for the next few months became set.

Know Your Enemy

'The deal,' said Martin Edwards, 'has strengthened Manchester United, not weakened it. We have secured a safe future and a prosperous future for them.' Sky added that: 'This is good for BSkyB, good for Manchester United and good for football. It is the next logical step in Manchester United's successful story. Together we can create a fantastic business for the twenty-first century.' That a fantastic business was not what United fans really cared about didn't seem to matter.

Beyond the two main protagonists, there was a general acceptance that it would go through, an apathy which has allowed too much to pass in the last decade of football as 'progress'. The tie-up of the biggest football club with the biggest broadcaster of the sport was presented to the world as the 'next logical step along the road of modernisation'. It was as if Adam Smith's free market 'invisible hand' was guiding football's future and choice in the matter was redundant.

> Mr Murdoch's take-over is only the inevitable consequence of the march of the corporate suits on the people's game which began in the early '80s . . . Well, football is being run like a proper business now and there is no going back to the cottage industry which the fans find so charming with hindsight. The supporters sit in greater comfort and safety now and watch exotic footballers from foreign climes with huge excitement. But there is a price to pay and the

national game made Rupert Murdoch its Chancellor of the Exchequer the day it let Sky finance the entire, booming operation. [*Daily Mail*, 9 October 1998]

The great myths were paraded before fans: there was nothing they could do about it; the decision lay with the stock market; there was no turning the clock back. Some even joined in with the mantra that 'Sky would allow the club to outbid any other club in the world for a player's signature' – the central plank of the pro-bid propaganda. The board knew they were on fertile ground here – the debate about the club's inability to attract the world's top stars like Ronaldo, Salas and Zinedine Zidane had been raging for some time amongst United's support. A strict control over wages and an unwillingness to be imaginative in remuneration packages offered to players had made the board an easy target. The main problem for the board is that they are not trusted; they have blotted their copybook so many times over the years that even a New Labour spin-doctor would struggle to get them a good press. This is a board who told those fans who could no longer afford to go to first team games to go to the reserves as 'it is much cheaper and there is lots of room'. A board that plays brinkmanship with their most successful manager since Busby over a new improved contract. The fans' rationale is clear: if United is the richest club in the world, then it should be competing for the signatures of the world's top players. What is the use of all these riches if they are not spent in pursuit of the prizes on offer? The suspicion is that the board is salting money away for itself or some new marketing initiative in Borneo.

Here was their ideal response – 'sell the club to a corporation eight times bigger and we can say we can buy anyone'. The fact that BSkyB's parent company had allegedly almost gone 'bump' a few years before and that no promises were ever made on transfer funds or that United were already twice as rich as Juventus didn't seem to matter. There was a feeling of inevitability about the whole concept of Manchester United being sold.

Some fell for this line. Even Pat Crerand, IMUSA's president, appeared to have swallowed the bait. Pat didn't like Murdoch and felt increasingly uneasy with what the club had become. But he believed that the commercial juggernaut was hurtling along at such a speed that it was impossible to stop it. Besides, the fact that the club was now quoted on the stock market as a plc meant that it had stopped being a 'club' years ago. Like many of United's hard-core supporters, Pat didn't like what he was witnessing, but Alex Ferguson had fashioned a team that was playing a kind of football which more than softened the blow.

To his credit, however, he soon turned around. Pat knows that the price of football is already beyond the reach of those who are on less than average wages and his early view of the Sky bid was based on a belief that there was nothing ordinary people could do about it. After discussing it with fellow Reds he changed his mind, albeit with a somewhat defeatist air: 'Aye I know what you're saying, I know you are right, but nobody listens to the likes of us. I wish you luck in trying to stop it but you've got one hell of a job.' A few weeks later Pat was challenged on a Piccadilly Radio phone-in by a City fan and declared his opposition to the bid. He claimed to have been convinced by those arguing against the deal and he no longer thought it was in the club's best interests. It was a brave thing to do, admitting that you were wrong when you are such a public figure, but a fitting testament to the man's humility and honesty.

To be honest there were few allies to the board. The attitude of journalists tended to be that the take-over was regrettable but inevitable. Others who leant their weight to Edwards' ambitions included Anthony H. Wilson, Granada TV presenter and head of Factory Records. A maverick at the best of times, he railed against those opposing the deal as standing in the way of United's global domination enterprise; that it would make the club 'bigger'; even that it was a reward for all Edwards had done for the club! He claimed those in opposition were the 'Mary Whitehouses of football', a minority of busybodies and stuck in the past. Others argued along similar lines, including Blakley MP Graham Stringer; and celebrity fans like Zoë Ball swallowed the Sky propaganda without even taking the wrapping off. However, throughout the campaign there were far more who thought that it couldn't be stopped than thought it was actually a good idea.

Countering the Propaganda

There was a growing certainty among those opposing the bid that they had right on their side – 'I knew we would win all along,' one claimed much later, 'because we were right in our arguments.' The gut reaction to Murdoch had been important at the beginning, but many fans needed to be convinced that he would be worse for United than the current board. Murdoch's track record had to be exposed and the production of the four-page pamphlet for the Bridgewater Hall meeting had solidified the knowledge that his pursuit of money outstripped his knowledge of, or desire to safeguard, any sport he got involved in. In this Murdoch was an ally: the board, and Edwards in particular, were so unpopular that almost anyone else would have seemed an improvement. Anyone, that is, except Murdoch.

However, IMUSA had to develop beyond that. Another line of attack was that the club was being sold too cheaply and that it had a much better future remaining as an independent entity. Indeed, one board member,

Greg Dyke, was putting these very points. In a rare moment of foresight the plc had invited Dyke on to the Old Trafford board to advise them on TV and broadcasting matters. The challenge from the Office of Fair Trading to the Premier League's collective sale of broadcasting rights is covered elsewhere, but this threat and the advent of digital TV were matters on which the plc needed strategic advice. In addition, United were to launch their own cable channel, MUTV, which came on air during the week of the bid announcement. Dyke told the board that the offer from BSkyB was selling United short but they weren't interested. Perhaps the size of the personal financial bonus was too big a temptation for them; perhaps they were frightened by what Manchester United had become; insiders say they were certainly out of their depth.

Tom Rubython in *Business Age* magazine, argued that 'the board was in a panic'. Faced with the rising costs of players' wages and transfer fees at the same time that merchandising revenues appeared to be reaching a plateau, they argue that the board were worried that 'the club could take a nose-dive financially'. Backed by cautious advice from their bankers HSBC, the board were happy to sell. Some City analysts had valued United at close to one billion pounds, almost double what Murdoch was willing to pay. Advisers tend to be cautious, but during the bid process United's weren't just cautious, they were out-negotiated. Only by insisting that somebody took a second look at the figures did Dyke manage to persuade BSkyB to increase their original offer of £575m to £623.4m, worth a colossal £87m to Martin Edwards personally.

Rubython rather rashly declared that nothing could stop Murdoch's purchase of United but nonetheless believed that 'Edwards had left £400m on the table'. He claimed that if United had looked longer term at the potential TV rights then there was no need to sell the club at all, predicting an increase in TV revenues:

> The deep irony of the sale of Manchester United for £623m is that BSkyB would have paid at least £500m for the TV rights alone and left ownership of the club in the hands of the current share-holders.

Such an argument has been supported by evidence since. In June 1999 FC Barcelona signed an advance deal for the TV rights to the club's games for 2003 to 2008. This one deal alone is worth over £260m. The price graphically illustrates how crazy United's plc were to ignore the advice of Dyke. With much uncertainty about the future sale of rights, there was nothing being offered by BSkyB that Manchester United could not do for itself. Although many fans opposed the individual sale of rights, and PPV *per se*, there would be nothing wrong with United having a contractual tie-in with a company such as BSkyB, but there was absolutely no need to sell the company's independence to get it.

In fact, with the MUTV project, United had already done a tie-in deal, as joint partners with Sky and Granada TV. The fact that Granada found themselves facing the prospect of losing a tripartite agreement and being out-voted two to one at MUTV in the future, before the channel was even launched, caused much consternation. This was no way to do business and the number of empty seats in the directors' box at games in that part of the season showed that it wasn't only Granada that was unhappy.

The board had also let the club become a take-over target. The attractions were clear to any outsider without considering the power and leverage in the market that BSkyB were really interested in – access to football's TV rights. One side-effect of the conservative wage policy and the commercial strategy was that Manchester United plc was a cash-rich company. The board had been warned over twelve months before the Sky bid that the club was a potential take-over target because of its 'flabby balance sheet' but this had not been taken seriously. The phenomenal amount of money generated by season ticket sales alone meant that 'United were a huge cash machine churning out the readies year after year' as one accountant described it. When the fortunes of a football club are in the hands of a plc board of directors, their legal responsibilities are to the shareholders and not the club and its supporters, something Sir Roland Smith has reiterated since the defeat of the deal. [Radio 5 Live, 4 July 1999] Yet fans complained that an individual with £2.40 spare to buy one share has more say in the running of a football club than a supporter who, in the treble-winning season, may have spent thousands of pounds following the team home and away. Plc status itself, then, became something campaigners argued against, making the club susceptible, as it does, to periods of intolerable instability. A privately owned club with shares in the hands of supporters would not be under the same external threats and pressures.

IMUSA also began to look further afield, to the effects of the take-over beyond Manchester United. It was evident that it wasn't in the club's interests. It was clear that the motivation was Murdoch's desire to secure Premier League rights, rather than further the fortunes of Manchester United. It was also clear the club was being under-sold and had a much better future as an independent entity. But what was also evident was that it would damage football as a whole and gradually these issues rose up the agenda – arguments for the outside world rather than the United faithful, perhaps, but increasingly important ones, as illustrated later.

Given that IMUSA had only had limited success in forging a dialogue with the board, there was also a sense that by becoming a small part of a much bigger machine, a subsidiary of BSkyB, the take-over would further remove the club from connections to its community, its fans and its locality. Who would fans be trying to appeal to: the club board, the BSkyB board, News International or News Corporation? And what did any of these know about what mattered to fans, the history of the club or the concerns of match-going supporters? However, dissatisfaction with the status quo never disappeared and new debates about the future organisation of the club and football started to emerge.

Campaign Strategy

From the earliest days there was a steady growth in IMUSA's campaign strategy which reached a crescendo in the presentation to the MMC. The campaign timetable looked like this: IMUSA's best hope of victory was to get the Office of Fair Trading to recommend to the Secretary of State for Trade and Industry, Peter Mandelson, that the bid should be investigated by the Monopolies and Mergers Commission. The OFT had two weeks to consider it and in that time IMUSA and SUAM intended that they be left in no doubt as to the depth and strength of feeling against the deal. This meant organising a massive lobbying campaign that was to include use of the Internet, letter writing, and a lobby of Parliament. Once at the MMC, campaigners would make their arguments on competition grounds, but at this stage that was a very long way off. Alongside this timetable was the development of Internet use; the opening of an office space; a constant PR battle; the development of a shareholders' organisation; and developing links with some important allies.

One key factor was to keep campaigners busy and maintain the different strands involved to guard against the burden being focused on the few. Communication also had to be maintained with the fans who were less involved, to update events and present new arguments. On two occasions, 10,000 four-page leaflets were produced by Nick Clay and the *Red Attitude* fanzine and distributed at matches by volunteers including Roy Williamson and Duncan MacIntyre as well as many others. Attempts to get leaflets into the ground were largely blocked by United's SPS security who confiscated them. SPS, who tend to act more like defenders of a police state than stewards at a football match, even went to the lengths of stopping one fan from entering because he was wearing a 'BSkyB Not Wanted' T-shirt; and two SPS goons were later mandated to 'keep an eye' on Andy Walsh and those he sat with. The campaign was hotting up.

On the Web

The Internet and the World-Wide Web played as important a role in the success of the campaign as any other single factor. As Paul Windridge explains elsewhere, the Bridgewater Hall document would not have been possible without it. Equally, when it came to lobbying MPs and government departments the Internet came into a class of its own.

Linda Harvey and Nick Clay had been trying to convince the committee of the need to use the Internet as a campaigning and recruitment tool without much joy. Most of the committee knew little of the Internet and were doubtful of the benefits that could be gained. Linda persuaded Paul Busby to give IMUSA some space on his website but Paul could not offer enough space to satisfy IMUSA's growing need. However, IMUSA's Internet evangelists found extra help and support when Monica Brady was elected to the committee in 1998. Monica was technically better qualified to set up and maintain the website and was able to dedicate more time to the work during the campaign. Duncan Drasdo also emerged on the scene in September 1998 and immediately started on his crusade to make IMUSA more aware of the technology that was available. His experience demonstrated how easy it was for IMUSA to lose people it had spent valuable resources recruiting.

> I'd been an IMUSA member pretty much from the start although I'd not been actively involved. I felt in the dark and out of touch. After the bid was announced I saw on Teletext that there was to be a meeting at the Bridgewater Hall and eventually got a phone number for Andy Walsh's house where there appeared to be about fifteen lads beavering away on various things.

Duncan had gone to some lengths to find the campaign and when he barnstormed his way into his first committee meeting making dozens of suggestions for the campaign he immediately raised suspicions. Many were convinced that the campaign was open to infiltration from agents provocateurs and spies who could have wrecked the careful work IMUSA had been doing. At a meeting in week two of the campaign, Ray Eckersley, who is one of IMUSA's more cautious members, was extremely colourful in his language when enquiring of Duncan's identity. Ray declared that he had received eighty-four e-mails since the previous meeting from 'this Drasdo character' and explained in graphic detail what he would do should he ever clap eyes on him. Duncan was sitting opposite Ray and introduced himself, prompting an unrepeatable response.

Once Duncan had proved his Red credentials, he began to stir the technophobes out of their collective complacency and persuaded local

Internet company XTML to host IMUSA's website for free and pay for the registration of two domain names (imusa.org and imusa.org.uk). They helped publicise the site and Peter Stewart from XTML went out of his way to help with resources and ideas. XTML's own site, Virtual Manchester, was already running a petition against the take-over and another XTML wizard amended it so that everybody that signed received a reply from IMUSA telling them what to do next. The petition collected over three and a half thousand signatures and was eventually presented to the DTI. The spin-off was a database for use in the lobbying work.

An e-mail list was established where interested parties could register for updates on the campaign and send their own ideas and thoughts. Other related lists were in existence already, but IMUSA's was reserved specifically for the campaign matters and all enquiries for David Beckham's autograph were politely redirected elsewhere by Linda, who had by now become the list moderator. In addition to autograph requests, Linda receives dozens of enquiries from students, most of whom appear to want someone to write their dissertation for them. Although she tries to make sure that everybody gets a reply, as yet IMUSA does not provide a dissertation-writing service.

The website was extensively developed by Monica and became an ideal repository for documents and newspaper articles, furthering the initial evidence-collecting undertaken for the Bridgewater pamphlet. In the early days, all papers were bought to monitor the PR battle and developments. It was costing IMUSA a fortune. One member who had got involved through the Internet, Ronak Joshi, volunteered to trawl the papers and post any relevant material to the mailing list. By the end of the campaign the archive on the site was so extensive that journalists were phoning up, having used it for research, to congratulate IMUSA on the depth of coverage.

The XTML petition, the names on the mailing list, contacts through other websites and campaigners' own e-mail contacts were a massively valuable tool and they were all used to distribute standard letters for onward transmission to MPs and Ministers as well as Manchester United directors and the OFT. Duncan again:

> I got the e-mail and fax numbers for the OFT and distributed them. Many people would never have bothered writing a letter but they would send a fax or e-mail while sitting at their PC. Once they'd done something, they were drawn in like the rest of us. Overseas Reds contacted us wondering whether it was worth them bothering. My answer was yes – although they had no direct political influence, if I were Peter Mandelson I would be astonished if I got loads of such correspondence from around the world. It would make me sit back and think, maybe this isn't quite straightforward; this is bigger than I thought.

With e-mails filling the DTI's files and direct-dial faxes flying across the ether, it certainly had an effect. The OFT received a record number of submissions, numbering over 350, and over one weekend their fax machines were emptied of paper. Over 200 MPs were persuaded to sign the Early Day Motions (see chapter four), and because IMUSA had started distributing the number of the fax located in the Secretary of State's office, even Stephen Byers commented on the volume of correspondence he had received:

> 'I now know that Manchester United even has 8,000 supporters in Kuala Lumpur,' he said with the weary air of someone who had received a letter from many, if not most, of them in recent weeks. [*Sunday Telegraph*, 11 April 1999]

The offices of government and their quasi-judicial bodies had never seen anything like it from football fans.

IMUSA was also able to get its ideas across to the Manchester United diaspora in the four corners of the globe. Many overseas Reds remained suspicious of IMUSA as a 'Manchester Mafia' that looked down on all those who did not have a Manchester post code, although some, like Ole Pederson of the 35,000-strong Scandinavian supporters' branch became a regular contributor to the mailing list. Other more established websites also offered help. Barry Leeming – 'The Mad Dane' – circulated his Manchester United contacts on the World-Wide Web and posted information on to other mailing lists. Mike Slocombe, a Cardiff City fan and one of the country's leading web designers runs an 'underground e-zine' (www.urban75.com) and he created a special 'Slap Murdoch' game on his site which injected a bit of humour into the proceedings. By clicking on a picture of Murdoch his face became contorted as if you had just given the Dirty Digger a punch. Some people would visit the game religiously as each small victory was achieved in the campaign.

Of course, security is a big issue on the Internet and opening up the debate about campaign strategy to the IMUSA list would have created security problems – there was no point planning campaign moves in a forum where Sky could gain access. Indeed, Duncan Drasdo actually uncovered a 'spy' on the list.

> After hearing that Sky had recruited a PR agency in Manchester, we saw Staniforth PR join the mailing list. They used an official Staniforth e-mail address, which was not a very clever piece of undercover work. However, this was a sign that they were taking us seriously and we had to be careful.

Guerrilla tactics became more and more effective. At one time, when news on the campaign was quiet, IMUSA and SUAM decided to highlight the fact that, although the bid document sent to shareholders had no information on how to reject the bid, it was easily done, by throwing the 'Acceptance of Offer' form away. To demonstrate this fact, a ceremonial burning of the acceptance forms was staged outside BSkyB's Manchester offices. Mark Longden bolted some legs to an old satellite dish to act as a crucible and the press were invited to come along. The whole event was devised, discussed and publicised solely through the Internet.

That same day, BSkyB set up a freephone 'Take-over Hotline' to advise shareholders how to fill their forms in. This caused a great deal of anger, because when they were asked how to reject the bid, they would give no information – hardly a share-holding democracy! Jonathan Michie recalls a typical experience:

> A member of SUAM telephoned the BSkyB Helpline to say that they were confused by the bid document. The Helpline adviser replied that 'quite a few people are', adding that 'it's all sort of mumbo-jumbo, isn't it?' When asked about the option of not selling shares to BSkyB, the worker admitted that 'it doesn't make that clear' and even reported that 'lots of people ring up and say "well, what do I do if I don't want to accept it?" because they haven't really made that option clear'. When told by the SUAM member that they thought it should be made clearer the Helpline worker responded, 'I think so too!' The take-over panel [at the stock exchange] were provided with a copy of the tape recording but still failed to act.

Some of the e-mail list members decided that enough was enough and that they would jam the switchboard with faxes on repeat auto-dialling. One anonymous IMUSA guerrilla recalls the incident:

> It was treble satisfaction: it was messing up their propaganda machine, it was costing me nothing, but they were paying for all the calls and all the staff. They had to take on extra staff and open more lines because of all the complaints from people who could not get through – which consisted mainly of complaints to the media from us. Childish pleasures but pleasures all the same!

Contacts with MPs were improved and both list members and website visitors got access to who their MP was and how they were to be contacted. The help of another technical Red wizard, Bill McArthur in Toronto, was drafted in and a programme to query the House of Commons database of MPs was developed. The results were cross-referenced to IMUSA's membership database for mail-shots and Bill's technical expertise was used on more than one occasion to mass-mail the thousands of e-mail addresses that had been collected. The web also proved useful in attracting more non-United fans to the cause. A separate website was created called 'FART' – Fans Against Rupert's Take-over! The website carried the eye-catching slogan 'FART for victory' and arguments for opposing from a non-United fan perspective were posted creating more contacts and support across club divides.

The Internet and e-mail were new campaigning tools for fans and proved absolutely vital. Not least, of course, because it helped sustain regular contact and information sharing among the core members of IMUSA, out of the public eye in a way in which phone conversations could never do. In this, and in targeting fax machines and government departments, e-mail proved to be IMUSA's 'killer app'.

The Office

The campaign activities were still centred on Andy Walsh's house, but had started to spill out to other houses on the street, including his sister-in-law Liz's house across the road which ended up being used as an annexe for meetings to avoid the constantly ringing phones. People would make an appointment and turn up at Andy's house for a coffee before being shown over the road once the previous meeting had finished. A rota had been established with someone assigned to answer the phones on a daily basis. Along with everything else he had to do, Nick Clay became a co-ordinator and campaign supervisor making sure that the relevant people returned phone calls and that messages were passed on. However, it couldn't go on like this forever and space was needed away from the hearth.

Manchester property developer Tom Bloxham had offered to find some space to relieve the situation, but had nothing available for a few weeks. So, when Manchester bike courier Matt Tansy told campaigners that architects Dominic Sagar and Neil Stevenson had space in their central Manchester offices, IMUSA jumped at the chance. Matt had already offered to deliver IMUSA material around town and was keen to use his contacts to get the campaign extra help from the Manchester business community.

Following an appeal by Lee Hodgkiss at the Bridgewater Hall, office equipment and stationery had started to arrive and Ian Hindle came up with a computer. Visitors and journalists could not help but be impressed by what met their eyes as they walked in to IMUSA Central. Staffed entirely by volunteers, the office was a hive of activity. Reporters from all over the world were beating a path to IMUSA's door and the story was big news in dozens of countries. In Germany the campaign IMUSA waged has actually resulted in the Bundesliga devising ways of protecting the interests of supporters in football clubs and these restrictions have effectively killed off the chase to the market that many clubs were contemplating – a far cry from the reception given IMUSA by English football authorities! There was, as expected, keen interest in America and Australia but the global appeal of English football and Manchester United gave rise to headlines on every continent.

Some of those running the office were actually 'on the sick' from their jobs, so many TV interviews saw lots of shots of the backs of people's heads working away on computers to avoid detection! Months after IMUSA left, Dominic and Neil were still getting press enquiries, and although they passed these on, some journalists insisted on a reaction from 'IMUSA's landlords'! Four people who had not previously been involved with IMUSA volunteered to run the office – Andy Marsh, Roland Urey, Val Evans and Pauline Rashid, who had previously been dealing with correspondence from her house. Dozens of others would play a role but these four were the mainstay of the work, updating the database, replying to correspondence and making sure that the progress of the various strings of the campaign were monitored.

The occupation of the offices was not without incident, though. Sean Hennessey, president of the Boston Reds in the States, was over for a visit and took his turn manning the office when a shooting occurred. Originally from New York, he was obviously used to the odd gun going off because when the police turned up appealing for witnesses he said he hadn't heard anything despite being less than thirty yards away from the scene! The office did, however, make the campaign more businesslike: IMUSA now had somewhere central to store leaflets and campaign material, as well as having somewhere for people to meet. The extra space and help made things run much more efficiently as the campaign took on a long-term footing. After writing to MPs about the EDM, a database was set up to monitor the response and target areas of weakness and a similar exercise was carried out for the official supporters' club branches. At last IMUSA had a home to go with their Home Page.

The PR Battle

From day one IMUSA had been clear and confident in its message: the bid would be opposed and IMUSA believed that they could win. However, cynicism, apathy and hostile attempts at undermining the campaign were constant threats.

IMUSA has been careful not to claim that it represents all United fans but that it does represent a significant trend of opinion. As with any protest group, it is a minority of people who become actively involved and, typically, this was presented as being 'unrepresentative'. Sky and Martin Edwards claimed the 'silent majority' backed the bid because IMUSA and SUAM only had a few thousand members. As it was, there was considerable evidence that the two in fact represented the overwhelming majority of opinion. The *Manchester Evening News* ran a couple of phone polls in the first week of the bid. The first recorded a 96 per cent vote against the deal, and the second, probably undertaken at the club's insistence and deliberately vaguely phrased, came out with over 80 per cent voting against Sky. Another poll conducted independently on the Internet showed 85 per cent in opposition; and even research undertaken by John Williams at Leicester University for the Football Task Force showed that about 80 per cent of fans across all clubs opposed media companies owning football clubs.

Over the four years of IMUSA's existence a good deal of information has been gathered on how the media works and great care is taken when dealing with them. This was just as well because the media was a crucial battleground for the campaign. IMUSA tried to restrict itself to the matters directly affecting the match-going fan and, however hard it was not to degenerate into ranting and/or personal abuse, common sense and reason had to prevail. To ensure that the 'message' was not going wrong, with cameras and microphones being shoved into people's faces on an hourly basis, fellow fans were constantly asked for their thoughts of particular media appearances.

One key PR policy was that the campaign was not to be presented as a personal crusade – interviews about personalities were politely refused and the focus was maintained on the issues. IMUSA had to avoid the accusation of 'Swampyism' where one individual is elevated above a campaign. One journalist who sought such an interview was Brough Scott, former jockey and now newspaper reporter. Brough wanted an Andy Walsh profile and argued that it would benefit the campaign. On accepting that he would get nowhere, he didn't slam the phone down like some before him but heaped praise on IMUSA for what had been done so far and offered encouragement. At the time, Brough could not know the impact of his comments; spirits were low and IMUSA were flying by the seat of their pants. Receiving such handsome tribute from an outsider boosted the campaigners.

Another key moment in relation to this was at the end of the first week when Andy Walsh conducted a live interview for Alex Brody's Radio Four slot. The programme was prefaced with a montage of many of the interviews given by Andy that week. 'For the first time I actually realised how far we had come,' he recalls, 'but it was vital to emphasise that this was about more than a few mouthy individuals and by now involved hundreds.'

A PR professional on the show backed this up with fulsome praise for the organisation's campaign, 'combining passion with professionalism'.

IMUSA dropped some clangers. Early comments arguing that Murdoch might move the ground did not have credibility and IMUSA was ridiculed. Comments made that 'the reception Martin Edwards got when he tried to sell the club to Robert Maxwell will look like a tea party compared to what will happen if the deal goes through' was perceived as referring to the Charlton game and as wishful thinking. Predictive pronouncements were out.

A good lesson was learnt from BSkyB in relation to this. At no time did Sky ever say whether any money, or how much, would be made available for buying new players. However, there was a constant assumption that United would be considerably richer. By saying nothing, Sky allowed the myth to be perpetuated, aided and abetted by their cronies at sister media outlets. In fact, under Alex Ferguson, the team was more successful and the club richer than ever. They had the resources to buy anyone they wanted, even without Sky. Yet headlines such as 'Gold Trafford' on the front of *The Sun*, and the use of pictures – Alex Ferguson reclining alongside a headline 'Sit Back and Enjoy the Ride', or a smiling picture of the manager from several years previously alongside news that 'his job is safe' – peddled Sky's message without them saying, or committing themselves, to anything. IMUSA were watching and learning.

The one big problem Edwards and Murdoch actually had was Alex Ferguson's silence. If they could get him to endorse the deal it was as good as done but he steadfastly refused to comment on the bid specifically. They dissected an interview on Sky TV in which Ferguson said many things including that he thought Sky's TV coverage had been good. This quote was splashed everywhere, sympathetic journalists then constructed a story around the quote. There had been painful contract negotiations some time previously, when many of those close to the manager believed that he was so despairing at the antics of Martin Edwards and the board that he was going to leave. Sky's PR team started to push stories of a big money contract for Alex if the deal went through. They missed the point. Patronising him by promising big money if he backed the deal was more likely to push him out of the club than tie him to it. That would be a disaster. Indeed, those close to him say he never wants to leave United and why should he? From the debris left by managers preceding him Alex Ferguson has built a team in his own likeness, one that is strong, determined and hungry for success.

As badly as Sky needed Alex Ferguson's endorsement, IMUSA needed it more. IMUSA needed a leg up but Ferguson was out of reach. Though he may not have spoken in favour of the deal, he was not about to come out and oppose it either. At the end of the day he was an employee and, if they chose to, the board could sack him. Looking back now it is difficult to see that happening, especially after the season just gone, but this was September, early season and the circumstances were very different. Some of those close to Ferguson at the time said he was very down in the first few days of the bid, his relationship with Martin Edwards at its lowest ebb. Ferguson needed to look after his own interests and with the upheaval at the club, anything was possible.

IMUSA decided to take a leaf out of Sky's book, and go for perception over substance. The man who had an opinion on everything to do with Manchester United had not said a word in support of the deal. So this was put on leaflets, in newsletters and repeated in interviews with the media. IMUSA weren't saying 'Alex Ferguson is against the bid', but things were left unsaid, allowing people to draw their own conclusions, prompting journalists to ask him the question. IMUSA were also saying to the plc and BSkyB that they knew what game they were playing and IMUSA were doing it too, backed by enough signs to suggest they were right.

There was also a perception by many that at the very worst the club would carry on as it was, 'Murdoch ain't going to buy the club to run it down' said one. One close colleague of Martin's and a senior Old Trafford insider described him as 'the greediest man I have ever met'. Therefore fans may have been willing to believe the notion that things would get no worse, but a vital element in IMUSA's PR battle was the fact that Martin Edwards was seen as the architect and this sowed enough doubt to put many people off.

This was another of Sky's big mistakes. If they had come in saying Edwards would go, it really would have been a new ball game. No doubt Edwards wanted to stay on at Old Trafford, but it was a fatal error of judgement from Mark Booth to promise to keep everything as it was. Yes, say Alex Ferguson stays; but keeping Martin Edwards was too much! IMUSA were constantly reminded on phone-ins and in the fanzines that having campaigned for years to get rid of Edwards here was an ideal opportunity that was being spurned by refusing to endorse Sky's bid. That was a mistaken hope, but how different things might have been if Sky had promised to jettison Edwards.

A comment Ferguson made, but which was lifted out of context at the time, was that 'Sky has been good for football' and that all the money in the game was all down to them. BSkyB may have paid a lot of money for TV rights, but the fact that the Football Trust was responsible for pumping millions of pounds into stadium development and the fans had seen ticket prices quadruple was left unsaid. That perception had to be challenged but because Sky's own promotion of the game exhorted fans to believe that they had 'the best league in the world', some fans and media commentators alike had started to believe it.

Perhaps the greatest thing, which counted in IMUSA's favour right at the start, was that this was *Murdoch* taking control. If virtually any other company had come in for United, the job of persuading United fans that outside control was a bad idea would have been much harder. Murdoch is such a demonic figure that many joined in opposition to him out of a gut instinct. However, the long-term success was that that perception was used to open minds and further other arguments. This worked to such an extent that many more United fans now believe that success can be achieved independently than ever did before. Any company casting covetous eyes in the direction of M16 now better have a good sales pitch because United fans will have some very searching questions to ask about future intentions, and they will take some convincing that outside help is needed.

It was also clear that the battle was not going to be won by United fans alone; details of how other supporters' groups got involved are elsewhere in this book. IMUSA received an offer of free printing from Geoff Mullarkey, a United fan who had attended the Bridgewater Hall meeting and who owned a large packaging and printing firm. He suggested a red card protest to encompass the widespread opposition to Sky at other clubs as well as sending a message from Old Trafford which did not undermine IMUSA's promise to Alex Ferguson not to disrupt the team. Although there were reservations that such protests had been done to death in earlier football campaigns, IMUSA were in no position to look a gift horse in the mouth and they decided to do 'a card protest which wasn't a red card protest'!

Geoff arranged to print one million white cards urging football fans everywhere to boycott Murdoch products and stop Sky subscriptions. The cards were going to be distributed to all supporters' organisations with a different card being distributed to United fans for the home game against Liverpool. The United card also urged fans to join in a rendition of the popular terrace chant the 'United Calypso' just before half-time. The song was a classic from the '50s and had been resurrected by supporters only to be given an appalling disco reworking by United's merchandising monster and further bastardised by Sky by inserting 'BSkyB' into the lyric! In the end the logistics of distributing the cards to other clubs proved too much but the publicity generated gave IMUSA considerable assistance and worried Sky, who set up a special help desk to intercept customers cancelling their subscriptions. The card did three things: it attempted to shake fans out of their apathy; it asked for consumer action against the deal; and it urged them to get behind the team. It was partly a response to the press attacks after the apathy shown at the Charlton game but, at the same time as wanting protest, IMUSA did not want to lose sight of the fact that they not only wanted to fight Murdoch but also wanted to improve the match-going experience and the atmosphere.

Shareholders United Against Murdoch was born on the morning of Tuesday, 8 September, two days after the *Sunday Telegraph* story. The morning after his *Newsnight* piece, Michael Crick received a phone call from an old school friend, Richard Hytner, chairman of the French-owned advertising agency Publicis, who suggested a shareholders' group to oppose the bid. Between them they gathered together twenty or so interested individuals over the course of the next week and SUAM was launched. Old Manchester Grammar School contacts such as Richard Lander were chased up and other exiled Mancs such as SUAM Treasurer Roger Brierley got in touch. This coalition of predominantly middle-class professional people, largely based in London, complemented IMUSA's strengths. With SUAM's roots firmly grounded back home in Manchester and bound together by a blinding vision of an independent Manchester United, the group set about making as much noise as possible. Though IMUSA and SUAM worked closely together, co-ordinating efforts and ensuring that neither embarrassed the other, they remained two distinct organisations giving the anti-Murdoch camp two bites at the cherry. SUAM's immediate aims were two-fold; firstly to persuade shareholders to hang on to their shares; and secondly to get the bid referred to the MMC.

Michael Crick worked virtually full-time on SUAM matters for the rest of September. Scheduled to fly to the States on the Thursday of bid week to cover the Clinton/Lewinsky affair for the BBC, his bosses were furious when he did an interview outside Old Trafford with *Newsnight* rival *Channel 4 News*. His editor, Sian Kevill, said that he was distracted, that his mind was on other things and he was pulled off the Clinton story. Michael agreed to return to *Newsnight* when things had died down a bit. One other early minor hiccup for SUAM was when one founding member discovered that his company worked for Murdoch and quickly and quietly had to withdraw. Later, many celebrities who claimed to have a soft spot for Manchester United and who were written to by IMUSA, were to cite Murdoch's grip on the world of entertainment as a reason why they themselves would not get involved. SUAM's initial running costs were covered by an anonymous donation of £11,000. Though everybody was happy to receive the monies, Richard was asked to give assurances that if the source ever became public then nobody would be embarrassed by the fact – nobody wanted to be linked to Saddam Hussein or Francis Lee!

Amidst issuing press releases and doing media interviews it was realised that SUAM would have to write to every shareholder and a letter was written and printed up by Scan Plus in Trafford Park. Michael paid a friend, Martin Tomkinson, £200 to obtain a copy of the complete shareholders list from Companies House, which ran to some 1,400 pages and contained over

28,000 names. A printer in Manchester's Cheetham Hill district agreed to run off the sticky labels and Geoff (Red Card) Mullarkey supplied the envelopes. All that was required after that was enough volunteers to stuff the 28,000 envelopes. For two nights up to sixty people folded, stuck and stuffed in the upstairs room of O'Brien's until three in the morning, before the mountain of envelopes and a cheque for over £7,000 for postage was handed in at the Post Office. SUAM's initial start-up money was heavily dented. Through sending out this letter SUAM got a lot of people writing in, pledging support and offering help, and shareholdings of over 700,000 shares were pledged to the campaign. Although a tiny portion of the total 260 million shares, it was a significant block in such a short space of time.

The letter had been timed to coincide with BSkyB and Manchester United's offer document, but beat it to the doormat by about a week. When the offer document did come out, SUAM were furious that it gave the impression that shareholders had no option but to sell their shares. Subsequently every opportunity was used to point out to shareholders that they did have a chance of rejecting the offer.

Sky and United went on the offensive, complaining to the take-over panel about SUAM's letter, asking how assertions contained in it, that Greg Dyke was opposed to the bid and that Murdoch had almost gone bankrupt in 1990, could be justified. SUAM struck back and put in a formal complaint of their own to the panel about the misleading nature of the offer document. The take-over panel said that the document was typically worded. SUAM responded that many thousands of fans owned shares, and many United shareholders weren't normal shareholders and therefore not accustomed to such language – Sky's own Helpline had admitted as much. Although the take-over panel refused to order that the offer document be reissued, valuable publicity had been gained informing shareholders that they need not accept the offer. Sky's complaint against SUAM hardly got a mention.

On the morning of the Charlton game, 10 September 1998, United and Sky held their press conference, which Michael went along to:

> Foolishly I asked Martin Edwards why he hadn't secured any promises from BSkyB of investment into the club – after all, I added, even Michael Knighton had promised £10m to redevelop the Stretford End and another £10m for new players. 'And we all know what happened to Michael Knighton' was Edwards' clever retort. The audience laughed and I felt a complete fool. Outside I bumped into Tim Allen, the BSkyB media chief, who expressed disquiet over the fact that a BBC journalist was running SUAM and I pointed out I was freelance. While standing briefing reporters on SUAM's view of the press conference I was regularly interrupted by Tim Bell, Lord Bell

of Bell Pottinger [of Bell Lowe lobbyists, then employed by Sky], who kept attacking what I was saying. I only wish I'd turned on him and made references to his former cocaine habit and conviction for masturbating in front of an open window twenty years ago. 'Oh, they've got you on the job, have they? Hoping for greater exposure no doubt?' or 'How's the cocaine habit?' Bell's other prominent client recently has been General Pinochet.

SUAM had a much harder job than IMUSA. They were a new organisation with few resources trying to convince shareholders that a 50 per cent premium on the share value was not a good idea. With 23 per cent of United's stock in the hands of small shareholders, a target of 10 per cent plus one share would be enough to maintain independence of the company, but a lot more was needed if the take-over was to be blocked altogether. Shareholders had to be convinced that holding on to their shares and maintaining the company's independence was more important than realising the 'investment'. This was made much harder because all the financial press were saying how inevitable the take-over was, that nothing could stop it, and the stories about United's true worth were swamped by pro-bid news items. Some of United's biggest institutional investors, such as Philips and Drew Fund, were far from happy at the prospect of the take-over. United had been a sound investment with very strong growth far outstripping most of the market, whereas BSkyB's stock was much less so. The doubts within the financial community were exploited and a document specifically targeted at the institutions was sent out, but it was amongst the ordinary individual shareholders that the battle had to be won.

United's annual general meeting was held on Thursday, 19 November. IMUSA had been an irritant at these events for the previous four years, but the 1998 meeting was an opportunity to really expose the plc board and now they had SUAM alongside. Martin Edwards had stated in the immediate aftermath of the deal announcement that he 'would argue the toss with anyone that the deal was good for Manchester United' but had refused all requests for a public or private debate on the matter and so the stage was set at the AGM to confront him. The board at Manchester United AGMs act like proprietors more than directors, ignoring questions and dismissing shareholders' concerns. Normally held at Manchester University's Armitage Centre, this AGM was held at Old Trafford and was the biggest ever with over a thousand people crammed in. SUAM members Roger Brierley and David Blatt were lobbying fellow shareholders outside when the head of United's security moved them on. Roger Brierley explains:

> We had been handing out leaflets to shareholders for some time and even Maurice Watkins, United's solicitor, had taken a leaflet.

There was no hostility, fellow shareholders were asking questions and the TV and camera crews were busy taking lots of shots when Ned Kelly asked us to move on because we were on United property. I tried to point out to him that as a shareholder I felt that the bit of ground I was standing on was owned by me but he would not listen so we moved a little further away and carried on. The scenes made all the news bulletins and United had scored another PR own goal.

SUAM arranged a briefing meeting in the Red Café, where proxy cards were dispensed to those who did not have shares and a leaflet explaining how best to intervene in the proceedings was given out. The security staff were obviously very jumpy, refusing to allow any journalists to use their tape recorders to interview Michael Crick. *Channel 4 News* managed to get a secret camera into the hall which made good footage and showed that not one shareholder spoke in favour of the deal. Sir Roland Smith chaired the meeting and tried to deflect criticism with witticisms. Most speakers were ordinary shareholders who felt extremely let down by the board but it made little difference to Smith. Edwards showed his grasp of mathematics by arguing that as 7,000 of the 28,000 had voted to accept the deal there was a clear majority in favour! But he did then go on to say that the money he was due to make from the deal was immaterial as 'once you have so much the figures become irrelevant'.

Smith refused to take a show of hands of those present knowing full well that there would be an overwhelming vote against the deal but those present from the anti-Sky campaign were nonetheless boosted by the day's achievements. Edwards even admitted under questioning that if Sky did not get at least 75 per cent of shares pledged to them, they would walk away because Sky wanted complete legal control and not just a controlling interest. After the meeting Greg Dyke was very open in declaring that he did not think the deal was a good one for the club, and not one person spoke in favour of the deal. The campaigners felt that a corner had been turned. Even at their own AGM the board had no friends, no plants in the audience and could not put up one argument why the deal was good for the club, a feat they managed to repeat in their meetings with the MMC. The only thing that they could rely on to win through was apathy.

To keep activists involved, and in preparation that the deal might be given the nod by the MMC, SUAM started writing out the addresses of the 9,000 shareholders with a holding of over 1,000 shares each. It was assumed that those with fewer than 1,000 were more likely to be supporters and less likely to sell out, but the larger shareholders needed to be convinced to hang on to their shares if the MMC did not block the bid as the bid process would start again. In the end it wasn't necessary but the exercise was useful for the next stage of SUAM's development and they continue to campaign against Smith, Edwards and their 'board of nodding dogs, woolly heads and seat warmers'!

Friends in High Places

The timetable of the bid was that the Office of Fair Trading sought submissions from 14 September; the deadline was 28 September; and the OFT had to report to Mandelson the following week. As such, the enquiry could have been completed before MPs returned from recess, effectively blocking public scrutiny. Sky were aware of the timetable and this had been the reason why they had pressed United's board so hard for a decision when they did. The last thing Sky wanted was a protracted battle, as this would expose the deal to the sort of scrutiny that would be its eventual downfall.

To counter this aim, IMUSA spent a frantic two weeks trying to persuade the world and its wife to make submissions, hoping to swamp the OFT with submissions and force them to extend their deadline beyond the parliamentary recess. With the process slowed down the MPs would return and then it would be possible to begin to build the pressure on Mandelson. Sky were doing their best to play down the number of submissions and some press reports said that only a few submissions had been received with the OFT on course to report on time. Every media company that came to mind was lobbied to make a submission, and many had already done so, although some thought it a waste of time and had to be persuaded otherwise. IMUSA lobbied academics and media analysts, persuading them of the commercial need for submissions to be made with the hope that these individuals would then speak to others in the industry. One analyst who had been particularly helpful had to withdraw from helping IMUSA formulate a submission as he had been given a job with a major broadcaster and they did not want his position compromised. This was a blow to IMUSA's own submission but at least it was a guarantee that at least one of the major broadcaster's submissions would be supportive of IMUSA's arguments.

As well as media companies it was believed that the Trade Unions would jump at the opportunity to give Murdoch a bloody nose in such a populist campaign. Julie Lawrence, a Shareholders United committee member, and a member of IMUSA, persuaded the NUJ and BECTU to make submissions but in the main the response from unions was very disappointing. The National Union of Journalists had been so decimated by cutbacks that they did not have the staff to research or write a paper, so the campaigners found somebody to do it for them for free. The General Secretary of the TUC, John Monks, was known to be a United fan so he was contacted for advice on how to rally support amongst the unions and asked for his perspective on the balance of power within the Labour cabinet. Unlike some of his colleagues he was willing to give his time – for example, on the morning of the Coventry game, and the beginning of the TUC conference, he apologised for cutting short his telephone call to Andy Walsh, but he had already kept the Prime Minister waiting long enough and thought he'd better go! At the beginning of the second week of the campaign, Chris Robinson and Andy Walsh drove to Blackpool to lobby individual unions, and although plenty of them promised help, none delivered. So at the end of the week another attempt was made, this time with David Rattee volunteering to be chauffeur for the day. Andy and David arrived in Blackpool just as Congress was breaking up; the General Council were meeting in the Winter Gardens so, having been ignored for long enough, it was decided to gatecrash the meeting. John Monks again was helpful but the lacklustre response from others illustrated why trade unionism is in such a parlous state, not even willing to listen.

Having tried to get hold of Gordon Taylor, of the Professional Footballers' Association, for over a week without joy it was decided to sit on his office steps until he arrived. None too pleased to be 'mugged', he had been away all day and was anxious to pick up his messages and get home. Like many others who had been contacted that week, Gordon was unaware of the urgency and the OFT's rapidly approaching deadline. Take-overs are usually carried out beyond the gaze of Joe Public, and without IMUSA scooting around the country and telling the interested parties what to do, the deal could well have been over and done with in that first two weeks.

The football public needed to recognise their role too and after contacting as many clubs and supporters' groups as was physically possible, hundreds more people were persuaded to make submissions to the OFT. In the end the OFT were forced to extend their deadline by three weeks in order that they could read everything. Between 350 and 400 submissions were received by the OFT in the end, an unprecedented response, and although technically the OFT were unable to pass judgement on the public interest arguments, they could not ignore such a huge number. The first target was achieved, with the three-week extension taking the time-scale into the new session of Parliament and a new arena for campaigners. The referral to the Monopolies and Mergers Commission became target number two.

IMUSA had been reliably told that, at lunch with a government adviser, the heir to the throne had privately expressed his disquiet at the prospect of Rupert Murdoch getting his hands on Manchester United. Whether the story is true or not, it did set a neat counterbalance to the clumsy 'Queen signs for United' headline run by *The Sun* as she autographed United footballs in Malaysia. This sparked an inane debate about the 'dumbing down' of the monarchy but it was difficult to see where the controversy was:

the Queen lives in London therefore she must be a leading member of the Cockney Reds!

IMUSA and SUAM needed some heavyweight legal advice if the bid were to be stopped so Michael Crick put the word out around London for corporate lawyers who might be interested in helping out. IMUSA has a good network of Manchester solicitors providing advice to fans who may have fallen foul of the police or security staff at a game, but now a commercial lawyer more acquainted with mergers and acquisitions was needed and preferably one that would work for free! On Tuesday of bid week, Yasmin Waljee of Lovell White Durrant, one of the country's largest and most respected law firms, responded to the call for assistance. Yasmin explained that she was the *pro bono* officer for LWD and that they believed they may be willing to offer IMUSA help to take the case before the Office of Fair Trading.

The *pro bono* scheme is designed to provide legal advice and assistance for clients who would otherwise be unable to afford it. Whilst demonstrating a commitment to society, the spin-off for a law firm is that they are more likely to retain staff as they are offering them a more varied and interesting selection of work than might otherwise be the case.

The first hurdle was that LWD had to make sure that there were no conflicts of interest with existing clients before they could agree to take IMUSA on. Over the course of three or four days of frantic negotiations and innumerable phone calls to clarify issues, it was agreed that LWD would act. The first meeting was scheduled for Monday, 14 September, at LWD's sumptuous London offices. To maximise the use of time, in a week when time was a rare commodity, the day was mapped out by a series of meetings with others who had rallied to the cause. As well as the legal advice, information was needed on how to mount a political campaign to keep the pressure on Peter Mandelson. Some IMUSA activists had experience of political campaigns but none had any knowledge about the political landscape at the House of Commons. The brother of one IMUSA member happened to be a director of a major political lobby firm who agreed to help. At the Charlton match on 10 September a London stockbroker had taken a leaflet and also volunteered his services. Remaining anonymous, they both contributed a great deal to IMUSA's political campaign.

The lobbyists supplied a list of influential MPs, Parliamentary Private Secretaries (PPSs), Committee Chairs and various ministerial bag carriers. This list was categorised both by the influence they could bring to bear on key decision-makers and which football team they supported! IMUSA already had some good parliamentary contacts, but this was an essential supplement. The lobby firm offered great assistance right from the word go. Whenever there was a question or any help needed, somebody only had to pick up the phone.

Meanwhile, LWD set about helping IMUSA to write detailed submissions to the OFT. As well as the *pro bono* officer, Yasmin, there were a number of senior partners led by Lesley Ainsworth and Graham Huntley, who both contributed. The bulk of the work on the submission was completed by Matthew Readings (a Liverpool fan!) with advice from Andrew Pearson (a Tottenham fan). One lawyer's comments showed how the excitement of the case even affected City lawyers:

> When the circular came round the office seeking assistance on the IMUSA case, I couldn't believe my eyes. Here was a case acting for ordinary football fans against BSkyB and Rupert Murdoch – who in their right mind wouldn't have jumped at the opportunity?

Lovells believed that tactically two papers should be submitted, one on competition issues which Lovells wrote with IMUSA assistance; and a second on 'matters of public concern', written by barrister Nick Toms and Nick Clay. A further paper was written by Nick Clay entitled 'The Globalisation of Sport' which eventually went to the MMC. The OFT submissions were completed within the two-week deadline, a massive achievement considering the burdens that everyone, including volunteers Clay and Toms, were under. Only with such dedication could the massive resources at BSkyB and United's disposal be matched.

Snakes in the Grass

The *Manchester Evening News* decided to 'stoop to conquer' in an effort to shore up public opinion behind the plc board and Sky by tapping into the well of discontent on the club's transfer policy. On 8 September, even before the deal was officially confirmed, the back page of the *MEN* ran the headline 'Treasure Chest', supplemented by advertising boards with the legend 'Ronaldo for United?' on them. The article claimed that the likes of Ronaldo, Del Piero and Zidane could be on their way to Old Trafford. It was an absolutely fantastic story, but utter garbage. Peter Spencer, Sports Editor, hadn't wasted any time weighing up the pros and cons of Sky's bid: he had a newspaper to sell and wanted to show the plc board what a good boy he was.

Spencer needed to ingratiate himself with somebody at the club because the fans had stopped trusting the paper years ago, and the manager no longer gave the kind of assistance to the United reporter Stuart Mathieson the *MEN* had come to expect in years gone by. Alex Ferguson always looked after the *MEN*'s former United reporter David Meek, giving him 'the drop' on transfer rumours and the like, but this no longer happened. The *MEN*'s problems with Alex Ferguson stretched back to 1995 when they published a poll claiming the fans wanted Fergie to leave and in the same year they also carried an article telling Cantona to go.

Fans have felt the brunt of the *MEN*'s bias before: when over 200 fans were deported from Istanbul in a mass violation of civil liberties, Spencer reported it as a 'riot' and IMUSA had been labelled as a bunch of 'pot heads' by David Meek! Some have claimed that Spencer had promised to give fans a greater voice, but this was hard to detect. Spencer himself defended the pro-bid nature of his pages by claiming that other *MEN* staff had posted more analytical and serious pieces elsewhere in the paper. Though the 'Treasure Chest' piece was not to be the last time that the *MEN* truckled up to United's board it was probably the lowest point.

They supplemented this a couple of weeks later, helpfully coming up with some old pros who believed that the deal would be good for the club. These snakes in the grass included former United star Ray Wilkins as well as Mark Hateley, who drew parallels with what they had witnessed in Italy. It didn't do 'Butch' Wilkins any favours that his comments were remarkably similar to those of Zoë Ball in *The Sun* a couple of weeks before. As a former captain of club and country he really should have known better, but instead he promised that United would be lining up top signings in the wake of the take-over. For a man who finds it extremely difficult to be so forthright when employed as a pundit for TV or radio, it was remarkably confident! Hateley was even more candid: 'Manchester United fans are mad to oppose the take-over. They will become the biggest and the best,' he claimed. For a paper owned by the Guardian group, with its long association with Manchester and support of liberal causes, the *Evening News* disgraced itself in the take-over battle.

Other venomous attacks came from more expected sources. BSkyB's Tim Allen tried to mount a Red Scare story, briefing journalists that IMUSA was a Trotskyist front organisation. Although Andy Walsh had formerly been involved with a Trotskyist group, it was a particularly ironic comment given that Michael Crick, a founding member of IMUSA, had been responsible for two books which had exposed the Militant Tendency's entry into the Labour Party! BSkyB also employed Staniforth PR, based in Manchester and responsible for some of the city's luminaries, although their attempts at feeding stories and spying on the IMUSA e-mail list were far less successful and damaging than the capitulation of the *MEN*.

Indeed, if there was a threat to IMUSA from associations with the left it came in the form of the Socialist Workers Party's activities at the home game against Coventry on 12 September. They organised a collection for IMUSA, without IMUSA's knowledge, which angered fanzine sellers and street traders, both of whom were IMUSA allies, because an illegal collection further endangered their already precarious operations. The monies collected were returned to the SWP with the promise that they would be handed on to the Tameside Care Workers' dispute.

However, despite unwanted attentions and the bias of United's local paper, the campaign was largely free from either the scurrilous personal attacks Murdoch's press is famous for or any effective subversion – sure testament to IMUSA and SUAM's solidarity and secrecy policies. The battle now moved forward to the OFT, the MMC and Parliament.

FOUR

PARLIAMENT AND THE PEOPLE'S GAME

The political implications of the BSkyB take-over of Manchester United were clear from the start. It raised fundamental questions about the further domination of the British media by one corporation; about the future of sports and TV markets; and more broadly about the place of football in British society. Ultimately politicians would have to decide what kind of game, and, following Arthur Hopcraft's assertion that 'the way we play the game, organise it and reward it, reflects the kind of community we are', what kind of country they wanted.

IMUSA had identified the need for political opposition to the deal from an early stage, including getting the backing of MPs, securing the opposition of the Department of Culture, Media and Sport (DCMS), and lobbying the Department of Trade and Industry (DTI). Politicians themselves were not slow to react as the news broke. With New Labour holding the reins, a complex equation of political loyalties and conflicts was to be exposed. Part of this lay in the nature of New Labour and its agenda in power; part in the personalities involved; and part in the increasing intersection of policy and the nation's favourite sport.

To many, even those supportive of the campaign against Murdoch, New Labour's desire not to offend big business, and Murdoch in particular, told them that it was very unlikely that the government would stop the take-over. Blair flew to Australia in 1995 to meet Murdoch and had spent considerable effort wooing the Murdoch empire, reassuring him and his executives that they had nothing to fear from a Labour government. In return, the king-maker (and de-throner) of British politics, Murdoch's *Sun*, had thrown its weight behind the Labour Party in opposition and helped it get elected. In fact, given the appalling state which the Conservative Party was in before the 1997 election, *The Sun*'s backing may only have helped the scale of victory.

Once in power, Murdoch's media had been fairly gentle on the government: one insider commented that 'the government is in fact one of the most divided in recent times, it's just that no one's reporting it'. As Roy Greenslade argued in a perceptive piece:

> On major issues such as the economy, welfare reform and law and order, *The Sun* is fully behind the government. Well, in truth, behind

Blair. It prefers the man, rather than his party . . . We should never forget that it is essentially a right-wing newspaper which has never deviated from its long-held agenda. The reason it turned its back on the Tories in favour of Blair was, first and foremost, because he would win. Second, it detected that he would not threaten the pro-market reforms instituted in the previous eighteen years. He was, in other words, a man Murdoch could do business with. [*The Guardian*, 23 March 1999]

But would Labour, and Blair, let him do business with Manchester United? Certainly, no one should underestimate that the prospect of seriously undermining Murdoch's support by stopping BSkyB's bid for Manchester United was very real.

Supporting this was the approach of the government generally – a support for the agenda of big business; a belief in the free market reforms of the Thatcher era; and backing by Gordon Brown (at a News International conference) for 'more competition, more entrepreneurship, more flexibility'. [Lee, 1999] Further, the government had seemed reluctant (despite massive public support) to vigorously regulate the privatised utilities whose fat cat chairmen had been associated with the sleaze of the previous Tory administration; so what chance was there that they would intervene in football? This political philosophy made 'the prospect of the Blair government intervening to regulate English football in a manner detrimental to the commercial interests of its principal media sponsor . . . at best remote', according to political economist Simon Lee. Jeff Powell just sneered: 'It is unlikely that Tony Blair will prevent the man whose propaganda machine swept him to power from buying his new toy.' [*Daily Mail*, 10 September 1998] What chance, indeed?

Another factor counting in Murdoch's favour was the personal and political connections of the Secretary of State for Trade and Industry and architect of much of New Labour's success, Peter Mandelson. He has a well-documented friendship with Elisabeth Murdoch, Rupert's daughter ('a gossipy relationship since they bonded at a Fourth of July party she hosted at her mansion' [*Independent on Sunday*, 13 September 1998]), and this was one cause for concern for those opposing the bid. That she was managing director of Sky Networks – BSkyB's programmers – was another. That BSkyB had invested millions in the Millennium Dome, rescuing it from financial disaster when Mandelson was 'Minister for the Dome', was a third. Even the Dome's public relations boss and friend of Mandelson, Matt Freud, had a relationship with Elisabeth. Added to all this, Mandelson was one of the few in the Labour cabal who did not parade his football allegiances – it is thought he doesn't really like the game – and as such he had no political capital to lose by offending the fans. He was, after all, hardly going to be accused of being a charlatan fan or betraying the game, as other politicians, including Blair, have been. So when United fans turned to the DTI for sympathy in their plight, they were hardly going to be invited in for tea and biscuits.

There were other Labour links which suggested that government intervention on the take-over was as likely as Ralph Milne making a United come-back. The bid had been brokered through Goldman Sachs whose chief economist, Gavyn Davies, was a friend of Gordon Brown, a Labour supporter and partner of one of Brown's staff. Indeed, Davies' children were actually 'borrowed' by Brown, who hasn't got any children, to pose for pre-Budget photos in 1998! Furthermore, Tim Allen, Director of Corporate Communications at BSkyB, fervent supporter of the take-over and antagonist of SUAM's Michael Crick, was a former Deputy Press Secretary, under Alistair Campbell, at No. 10. Blair himself had been accused of favouring Murdoch by speaking in his favour to Romano Prodi, the Italian Prime Minister, over a business deal. The web of links between New Labour and Murdoch was both substantive and detailed. Given that Mandelson was bang in the middle of the whole shooting match as head of the DTI, to whom the OFT and MMC had to report, and over whose decisions he had virtual power of veto, Murdoch and Edwards could be forgiven for thinking they had the referee in their pocket.

It wasn't as simple as that, however. Counter-balancing was another element of New Labour's make up, represented by the other arm of policy in relation to the bid, the DCMS led by Chris Smith. The change of name of this department, from that of National Heritage, spoke volumes in itself; it wasn't concerned with the old, the dusty, the rehashed past – Britain as one big open-air industrial museum – but the new, the creative. As Blair argued:

> Britain led the industrial revolution. It was defined by ship building, mining and heavy industry . . . Yet more people now work in film and TV than in the car industry . . . The overseas earnings of British rock music exceed those generated by the steel industry. I believe we are now in the middle of a second revolution, defined in part by new information technology, but also by creativity. [*The Guardian*, 22 July 1997]

One element of this was the role of sport and within that, football. Part of this was that sport was clearly important in straight economic terms: it has been estimated that sport accounts for 3 per cent of all world trade involving over half a million sports clubs in Europe; and that football accounts for $250 billion of that globally. Within this global economy, the role of television is a crucial element, with income to sport from television now standing at an estimated $42 billion world-wide. [*EC Staff Working Paper* DGX, 29 September 1998] As such, a deal which sought to unify the biggest sports broadcaster in this country with the richest football club in Europe, if not the world, was of considerable importance in economic terms to both the DCMS and the DTI. But it was also the fact that sport, and football in particular, was taking on a symbolic value, with significant cultural capital, and that partly accounted for its role in the new department's title. Whereas in the 1980s football was seen as a symbol of the country's ills, and those involved – particularly the fans – were seen as pariahs, by the 1990s everybody wanted a piece of the action.

The revolution which had been ushered in in the wake of Hillsborough (funded by the *public* purse through the Football Trust), marketed to a new audience by Sky and delivered by the new stock-market-controlled clubs, brought celebrity football fans out of the shadows. Or invented them. Now we had all been used to seeing the Alf Garnets, Elton Johns and Little and Larges of this world on our TV screens on Cup final day (or in Little and Large's case, when documentaries were being made about the decline of Manchester City). But the 1990s seemed to turn pop stars into football fans and football players into pop stars. In Zoë 'I started supporting Man United when they won the League' Ball's case, it turned a pop presenter into a hate figure for United fans.

Politicians, never ones to miss the chance of a bit of publicity, were inevitably increasingly associated with the game. Some of these had well-documented, long-standing affiliations, like Sheffield Wednesday fan Roy Hattersley and club director Joe Ashton. Others appeared more recent converts, including former Prime Minister and cricket fan John Major, portrayed at Stamford Bridge on the front of *When Saturday Comes* in 1992 in a fictitious exchange with David Mellor: 'Do you come here often?' asks Mellor; 'Only on election year,' replies Major. Although this trend was not entirely new – from town mayors to Harold Wilson, photographs next to football trophies were seen as good PR – it took on a new significance in the 1990s. On one hand it was part of the seeping all-pervasive nature of football through every nook and cranny of public life – you just couldn't escape it, especially after Euro '96. On the other it meant that there was a fertile ground – some MPs had been quietly fighting the fans' corner for years, and more recent converts also jumped aboard the bandwagon. For once, football's new popularity was to prove to the fans' advantage.

The increasing interest of politicians in football was also reflected in policy terms. Whereas the Tories had only 'firm measures' to 'defeat these thugs', Labour were to take a different approach. Of course they never 'went soft' on hooliganism (nor understood it better) – their response to violence at the World Cup in France in 1998 could barely be distinguished from their predecessors' and government support for new 'anti-hooligan' legislation was arguably more draconian – but Labour did look to go further.

Whilst in opposition, Tom Pendry, then Shadow Sports Minister, issued the *Labour Charter for Football*. This followed a series of discussions with representatives of football authorities, fans and players and sought to set Labour's agenda for the game once in office. Although partly a response to the new found profile of the game, it was also a response to a perceived crisis at a time in the mid-1990s when the game appeared to be mired in sleaze, bungs and bribery scandals. The increased commercial activity in the sport was also starting to tell, with Tony Blair warning in 1995 of the dangers a pursuit of a wholly financial agenda, and the negative impact a further removal of it from the people, would have on the sport.

The *Charter* was divided into two main sections, 'A New Task Force for Football' and 'Legislative Measures'. Under the former, the commitment was to create a Task Force 'drawn primarily from bodies responsible for the national game' and whose remit would be: restructuring the Football Association; investigating links with television; the treatment of fans (prompted by growing concern with the treatment of English fans abroad); football's finances; and the rather vague 'looking to the future'. It was, said Labour, 'widely recognised that there was a need for change' and that the Task Force would be 'focusing specifically on the need for improved administration'. Under 'legislation' were measures to deal with football violence, finance, ground safety, 'rights of fans', 'football for all', the grass roots and policing. Signed by Tom Pendry and Jack Cunningham it represented the biggest attempt an incoming government had ever made to restructure football. The wide ranging reassessment of the way the game is run, called for by Lord Justice Taylor in his Hillsborough Report, seemed as though it would finally happen.

To complement this, Labour also promised a reassessment of the Hillsborough inquiry in light of new evidence; Pendry promised to look again at the all-seater requirement in football; and Labour wholeheartedly backed the FA's bid for the 2006 World Cup. From Colin Moynihan to this: times had changed indeed. As one commentator put it: 'Where once an Old Etonian tie or a certain handshake might have gained access to a certain ear, it is now more effective to have a football scarf – especially a Chelsea one.' [*Daily Telegraph*, 29 July 1997] A large slice of this was electioneering, or credibility-seeking – 'There is scarcely a Whitehall permanent secretary or a deputy governor of the Bank of England who does not append a football club, preferably northern, to their CV' [*The Independent*, 27 July 1997] – but it did have its impact in policy terms.

In some ways it was inevitable that Labour would take a very different approach to their predecessors. The game's increased profile, its appeal across sections of the population – including a new, electorally crucial middle-class audience – and the fact that it was '"cool", cosmopolitan and utterly modern' [Brown, M. 1998] made it perfectly suited to New Labour. The fact that Labour thought it could intervene on a populist agenda, at minimal cost to the Exchequer and without upsetting its overall agenda, confirmed its approach.

Once in office, things looked a bit different, of course. The Hillsborough inquiry was never reopened, to the anger of the families and football fans; and the reassessment of the all-seater requirement was brushed aside as the government developed its obsession with securing the 2006 World Cup. Labour did set about establishing the Football Task Force within months of coming into office.

However, the first act, in the aftermath of election victory, was that Pendry got the old 'heave-ho'. Just as those First Division workhorses get jettisoned as an aspiring team get promoted, Pendry was replaced by a new signing, on the left wing, Tony Banks. Part of this was that Pendry was rumoured not to fit in with the management team headed by Alistair Campbell: a new, dynamic face was wanted. Part was that here was a government post where a risk could be taken, where a New Labour loyalist wasn't a prerequisite. Furthermore, there were considerable advantages to Banks' appointment, which few predicted: he was an outspoken football fan; he was regarded as 'Old Labour', a conviction politician, and therefore it would appease some sections of the party; he was talented and sharp; and, perhaps most of all, by bringing him on board Labour's management removed one of the most potentially vocal opponents of New Labour from the back benches where he could have caused considerable trouble. Pendry's alleged unpopularity, age, and failure to win support among Labour's senior politicians may also have been an influence.

To complement the strength on the left, and to prove Labour's Third Way credentials involving people from all political backgrounds, came a right-winger to head the Task Force, David Mellor. The former 'Minister for Fun' under Thatcher and Major, Mellor had previously been the Home Office minister responsible for exempting the Second and Third Divisions from Taylor's all-seater requirement. He had also established himself among the new football glitterati, putting aside a previous affiliation for Fulham (electorally useful, given his constituency of Putney) and renewing his Chelsea credentials (even more useful when they are the then Prime Minister's team), to become the host of Radio 5's flagship '6:06' football phone-in show. In the wake of his electoral defeat in 1997, he had also begun a football column in the *Evening Standard*.

Neither his appointment as Chair of the Football Task Force, nor the Task Force itself, was rapturously received. Brian Glanville condemned the venture: 'Showboating is all that such a committee will ever do. The government appears to have thought, but shallowly . . . The Mellor committee seems doomed to be little more than a forum for hot air.' Mellor was attacked as a 'shock jock of radio football – a sporting Howard Stern' and Banks 'little better . . . he was putting his foot in it as soon as he was so contentiously appointed Sports Minister'. [*The Times*, 29 July 1997] Citing the plights of Leyton Orient and Scunthorpe, one leader comment concluded, in a clear impersonation of some stupid, ignorant ostrich, that 'there is nothing here that need concern the government'. [*The Independent*, 27 July 1997] Who the hell did it concern, then?

The government gave the Task Force its agenda: eliminate racism; improve disabled facilities; improve the community work of clubs; 'encourage greater supporter involvement in the running of clubs'; 'encourage ticketing and pricing policies that are geared to reflect the needs of all, on an equitable basis, including for cup and international matches'; 'encourage merchandising policies that reflect the needs of supporters as well as commercial considerations'; 'reconcile the potential conflict between the legitimate needs of shareholders, players and supporters where clubs have been floated on the stock exchange'.

It gave it a membership including all the football authorities and representatives of players, managers and fans as well as local government and others. It formed a Working Group of individuals to do the graft, on which United's plc chief Sir Roland Smith sat, as well as Adam Brown. The Task Force held numerous evidence sessions in London and conducted a 'regional tour' of the country, meeting fourteen Football in the Community schemes, twenty-eight local authorities, thirty professional clubs, ten county FAs, seventy-three football supporter groups, ten community organisations, three women's and girls' teams and a variety of football researchers. It issued reports on combating racism and improving disabled access in its first year, both of which were accepted in full by the government, and on improving community relations and the grass roots, including a promise of 5 per cent of future Premier League TV income to be redistributed to the grass roots, in January 1999.

However, the meat of the Task Force's remit – the commercial aspects of the game – are what concern us here and what prompted its formation in the first place. The issue of ticket prices was an issue across the board in football, and certainly at United. The representation of fans, too, was an issue – IMUSA had been striving for years to have a meaningful dialogue with the club. The fact that the BSkyB take-over had proceeded without any consultation with fans and clearly against most fans' wishes, meant that this was something of a hot issue. Although United were well associated with merchandising – the club were the *bête noire* of the press when it came to football shirts – it was less of a concern for fans. Perhaps most importantly, a remit to consider the potential conflict between fans and directors at clubs floated on the stock exchange meant that the concerns of the BSkyB take-over should have been slap bang in the middle of the Task Force's work. That it wasn't, was to be the source of some conflict.

The Task Force at times felt like a tag wrestling ring, where different interests weigh in banging their heads and overweight bodies off each other, with the government, in the shape of the DCMS, as referee staggering around between them, trying to work out who to award the points to. Packing the Task Force with representatives of every vested interest in football, and requiring the body to come out with consensus proposals for dealing with some very controversial issues which go to the heart of the commercial revolution in English football, was really asking the body to kick uphill from the start.

So, in the middle of all this – the political affiliation with big business, the courting of Murdoch, personal links with Murdoch's family, the new agenda of government in relation to football, the web of complicated interests and negotiations in the Task Force, the personal and organisational chaos to come with the resignations in football's governing bodies, the restrictive practices case, the reform of the FA and calls for a football regulator – lands the Sky bid to take over Manchester United.

As soon as the bid was announced, Alistair Campbell, the Prime Minister's Press Secretary, sought to make it clear that it was a matter for the DTI. There's considerable evidence that Peter Mandelson saw no reason why the bid should not be allowed to proceed. He saw no legal objections and treated it as a straight business deal, we are told. There was nothing different about football. Even if there had been, the precedent had been set on the Continent at AC Milan and Paris St Germain. For a Europhile like Mandelson, what was good enough for them was good enough for us.

However, with his and Labour's well-publicised affiliations and connections with Murdoch, it was never going to be as simple as that. Compounding these suspicions was that the Murdoch press, acting on the premise that flattery gets you everywhere, had suddenly found a new darling. 'Comedy King of Conference' declared *The Sun* after Mandelson's first ever speech to the Labour Party conference, now as minister. What was an innocuous speech on the possibilities of new technology, prefaced with a joke or two at his own expense, suddenly became, in *The Sun*'s eyes, one of the great Labour conference speeches. 'He had them rolling in the aisles,' wrote David Wooding. Anyone else who was there thought they must have missed something, or been at a different conference. With supportive editorials abounding, the agenda was clear cut – butter him up, bolster him against criticism, and get the Sky bid through. The story was widely thought of as a 'standing joke on Fleet Street'. It was known that new *Sun* editor David Yelland was being heavily directed by Murdoch in terms of the paper's approach and also that Wooding (now with the *Sunday People*) was, as any *Sun* journalist, being 'spoon fed' the line. The cosy relationship of Labour and Murdoch started to appear like incestuous back slapping.

Even the more high-brow *Spectator* got in on the act, with Irwin Stelzer, one of Murdoch's key advisers and a frequent visitor at No. 10, attacking Gordon Brown and praising Mandelson's proposed reshaping of competition policy, coincidentally at the same time Mandelson had to decide whether to refer the BSkyB bid to the competition authority or not. It was contrary to all expectations, then, that Mandelson's links with Murdoch actually began to work in IMUSA's favour. It didn't appear like that at the time, but here's why.

The Labour hierarchy were fully aware that should the bid go through, Mandelson, and the government, would stand accused of favouritism, and by starting to defend against this they began to push matters in the campaign's direction. Even at the very start, Hugo Young said: 'Tony Blair should ask whether his availability to Murdoch isn't becoming an embarrassment. Even if there turns out to be no valid OFT case against the Man U sale, the social and professional entwinements between the Labour high command and the Murdoch minions will compromise the credibility of such a decision.' [*The Guardian*, 8 September 1998] For a party which had come to power as an alternative to the sleaze-ridden Tories, such accusations would be damaging. It was a lever which the campaigners began to pull on.

On 23 October 1998, Lucy Ward ran a front page story in *The Guardian* claiming that Mandelson would refer the bid to the Monopolies and Mergers Commission as a purely pragmatic way of deflecting criticism from himself and the government, but had in fact already decided that there was no reason to block the bid and no competition question to answer. She wrote:

> *The Guardian* understands that Mr Mandelson, who has the final say on whether the £623m deal goes ahead, believes there is nothing in competition law to obstruct it. He is expected to refer the bid to the Monopolies and Mergers Commission but believes that objections raised by opponents of the deal are surmountable . . . The Murdoch-owned *Sun* has recently been running a series of very positive articles about Mr Mandelson in a move which government sources believe is aimed at winning his support for the United deal. [*The Guardian*, 23 October 1998]

The story caused uproar. At IMUSA Central it appeared at first as though *The Guardian* was, rather amazingly, doing the Sky PR job for them: the campaigners were fighting hard to win a PR battle to create the perception that the bid could be blocked, and any story supporting claims that it was a hopeless task didn't help. *The Guardian* and the DTI were bombarded with complaints by fax, letter and e-mail restating fans' opposition. IMUSA got it wrong. What Ward reported was an accurate reflection of the state of play within the DTI: both she and *The Guardian* stand by her story which effectively said that a reference to the MMC was a superficial, political exercise. Although Ward will not disclose her source, the influential lobby firm working on IMUSA's behalf faxed a message to Andy Walsh the same day claiming: 'We do not believe the story initiated with him [Mandelson] . . . we suspect she got the story from comments from MPs she spoke to about the EDM; or maybe from Banks, who might have given her a bit of briefing to stir the shit a little bit.' Far from helping Sky's cause, then, its effect was to increase the scrutiny of the political machinations around the bid.

Mandelson knew this and he was furious. He has a reputation for 'bullying tactics' when it comes to the national press and has been known to call editors direct to complain. Having angrily denied the story to the paper before publication, he even went to the lengths of writing to *The Guardian's* letters page to protest as soon as it appeared:

> Your headline today, 'Mandelson to back Man Utd sale', [23 October] was complete nonsense. Contrary to what your article asserts, I have not yet considered the matter, have not yet received the advice of the Director General of Fair Trading (DGFT), and have formed no views on it whatsoever. The process in such cases is clear: the DGFT consults; he advises me; I consider his advice; I take a view; I announce my decision. It is my duty to stick to this system, and I am doing so, to the letter. The suggestion in your article that I might somehow have been improperly influenced by whatever appears in *The Sun*, or anywhere else, is absurd. I was surprised by your decision to continue with the story and headline after you had been informed that the basis of the article was wholly false. But then, that's politics. [*The Guardian*, 24 October 1998]

What first appeared like a black cloud to IMUSA's hopes at the time, suddenly revealed a shining silver lining: the bid would go to the MMC and, once there, was for five months out of the politicians' hands. It was what IMUSA and SUAM had been working towards as the best chance of blocking the deal. Although the ultimate decision still lay with Mandelson, suspicions about his closeness to Murdoch had borne fruit in seeing the bid head for the MMC. There was, however, a wider political battleground developing.

Many Labour back-benchers were fiercely opposed to Sky's proposed take-over. Many of them had clubs in their constituencies, and a deal which

All eyes on Michael. Left to right: Lee Hodgkiss, Andy Walsh, Jimmy Wagg and
Jim White listen intently as Crick outlines how Sky can be stopped
(© Paul Herrmann)

Jim White addresses the packed
Bridgewater Hall meeting,
15 September 1998
(© Paul Herrmann)

Fans work into the early hours to
send 28,000 letters out to United
shareholders
(© Paul Herrmann)

ABOVE: Duncan Drasdo delivers the Virtual Manchester petition to the Department of Trade and Industry, 27 October 1998

RIGHT: 'Dear FA, don't let smaller clubs die.' Andy Walsh addresses the audience at the Fans United 3 event at Chester Town Hall

Dressed to impress: IMUSA's team at the Monopolies and Mergers Commission. Left to right: Lee Hodgkiss, Andy Walsh, Nick Toms, Duncan Drasdo, Gillian Howarth, Michael Shepherd, Paul Windridge, Mark Southee, Nick Clay, Jon Leigh, Steve Briscoe, Mark Longden

IMUSA's message is taken to Parliament, 27 October 1998

A spot of community singing before the
kickabout outside the Houses of Parliament

A satellite dish becomes a handy
incinerator as shareholders burn
BSkyB's offer letter
(© Paul Herrmann)

The campaign trail takes its
toll: Paul Sneyd, a bottle of
Bud and a sad waistcoat,
returning from Fans United 3

ABOVE: November's pre-match meeting with L'Elefant Blau. Left to right: Joan La Porta, Jordi Moix, Andy Walsh, Alfons Godall, Lee Hodgkiss and Tony

LEFT: Andy Walsh and Michael Crick receive their final instructions before the first meeting with IMUSA's lawyers, Lovell White Durrant (photo courtesy of Peter Walsh)

LEFT: 'It's not rocket science': Steve Briscoe explains the inner workings of the Houses of Parliament to a bemused Lee Hodgkiss, 27 October 1998

BELOW: Munich meets Manchester outside a bar in Barcelona, 26 May 1999. Left to right: (back) Peter, Gregor, Dominik, Graham and (front) Andy Walsh and Martin

ABOVE: Bayern Munich's 'Stop Murdoch' banner receives a final airing

LEFT: Some took building links with other supporters too far! Mark Longden and Kevin Miles of Newcastle United's ISA at Fans United 3

ABOVE: Decision day: IMUSA's 'rapid-response team' awaits news on the Old Trafford forecourt

RIGHT: The team does its bit and makes it a quadruple victory
(photo courtesy of Joel Fildes)

threatened to exacerbate the wealth gap in football was always going to be unpopular with clubs who stood to lose. Back-benchers, free of the political manoeuvring that had pushed Labour into Murdoch's bosom, had greater rein to speak out. There was little support within the party as a whole for Murdoch, or Blair's closeness to him. Some were left-wingers, who remembered Murdoch's actions over Wapping, the miners' strike and local government cuts – 'Some of us have never forgotten the brutal sacking of 5,000 print workers at Wapping,' wrote Jeremy Corbyn MP; others, even New Labourites, recalled *The Sun's* constant sniping at Neil Kinnock. Even within the House of Lords, complaints about Murdoch's influence were voiced.

Within the cabinet itself, two distinct camps of opposition emerged. On one side was what has been described to us as the 'anti-Mandelson camp', alongside his political opponents such as Culture Secretary Chris Smith; on the other were the 'we love football' campaigners with Gordon Brown and his spin doctor Charlie Whelan as well as the irrepressible Tony Banks. Although personalities were an issue, there were serious, politically motivated differences over the deal at the core of the division.

Chris Smith had clashed with Mandelson before. Gerald Kaufman, one of the few Labour politicians to support the Sky bid, had been guided by Mandelson to write a highly critical report as chair of the Culture Committee, which attacked Smith's handling of the Lottery operators, Camelot. Thus Smith had a grievance. Although not the most popular of ministers with the back-benchers – not least because of his love of opera, ballet and the high arts – here he found common ground. Smith was also close to Blair and began building bridges with those on the back benches also opposed to the bid. One insider told us that he became a 'very, very effective' opponent of Mandelson.

Tony Banks was not only a football fan, but also had reason to be aggrieved at Mandelson's behind-the-scenes story-spinning. Soon after coming into office, Banks had made a couple of gaffes. One of these, at a fringe meeting at the 1997 Labour Party conference, was Banks' description of the Conservative leader William Hague as a 'foetus'. The statement was caught on video but even so was largely ignored for twenty-four hours. However, it surprisingly shot up the media's agenda the following day. One of the alleged reasons for this was that it was an expedient means to deflect attention from Mandelson's failure to get elected to the National Executive of the Labour Party. He'd used Banks' gaffe to deflect bad publicity on his own failure.

Banks became outspoken on the Sky bid. In one interview with Liam Hallaghan of the *Financial Times*, he warned of the threat of multi-club ownership, insinuating that football matches might be rigged if the same owner owned two or more competing clubs. This is an issue which is now on the agendas of both UEFA and the EU, as we have seen in chapter two, but Banks' linking of the Sky take-over to corruption in the game was unprecedented. The *FT*, sceptical that there were any competition reasons to stop the bid and supportive of both Mandelson and the commercial agendas in football, downplayed the quotes and the story.

However, Banks got the Parliamentary Labour Party on side very quickly and established himself as the 'football' champion of the back-benchers within the government. As such, the Sky bid for United was being attacked from both ends of the culture spectrum: the friend of Blair and opera-going Chris Smith on one side, and man of the people, former GLC stalwart and football wag Tony Banks on the other.

Supporting this opposition was also Gordon Brown. Now Brown and his ally Whelan were no friends of Mandelson either: the two heavyweights of Labour's first term had fallen out big style, with Mandelson's camp accused of fuelling press speculation about splits between the Exchequer and No. 10. Blair, acting the schoolmaster, had banged heads together and put them both on probation and as such Brown's opposition was understandably muted, with both trying to keep a lid on disagreements. However, it is alleged that they were keen for links between Mandelson and Murdoch to be exposed during the take-over procedure.

No. 10 was playing a very straight bat in terms of public pronounce-ments on the take-over, referring to it as a matter for the OFT and DTI. From the moment the bid was announced, the Prime Minister's Press Secretary, Alistair Campbell, was trying to hold the various different factions within the government together. Whereas the issue for campaigners may well have been 'the future of football', as Rachel Sylvester wrote, in Whitehall it 'was about cronyism', and specifically how to avoid charges of it. [*The Independent*, 13 September 1998] Given the breadth of opposition within Parliament, the party and the cabinet, in hindsight it started to look as though it would have been very difficult for the government to let the bid proceed on any grounds. The political opposition was just massive: it was an issue which was uniting New and Old Labour, bringing the cabinet, junior ministers and back-benchers together, and the most PR-sensitive government for years was desperate to avoid charges of favouring Murdoch.

Crystallising this opposition within parliamentary procedure was the All-Party Football Group of MPs. The Group was established in 1982 by Labour's Tom Pendry and Tory Jim Lester, with Pendry chairing it from 1982 to 1992 and Joe Ashton from then until now. Its monthly meetings regularly discuss football matters, meeting administrators, players, fans, referees and legislators. The meetings are private but questions are raised in the House and the Group takes a leading role over legislation, for example playing a key role in relaxing the Taylor requirement on all-seater stadia and recently supporting the Premier League against the OFT.

The Group met on several occasions to discuss the take-over, which was overwhelmingly opposed from day one. Here was an issue it could really get its teeth into. Joe Ashton MP appeared on *Newsnight* as soon as the deal was announced, outlining the damage it would do to football as a whole. Ashton, who had previously defended Sky's role in football, stuck his neck out and was to feel the wrath of the Murdoch press later.

A parliamentary campaign aimed at getting the proposed take-over referred to the MMC was mapped out. Part of this was done through the Early Day Motion described below, but the Group also lobbied with other members of the back benches, to junior ministers within departments and tabled questions to Smith, Banks and Mandelson. The pressure began to tell from within as well as from without the corridors of Parliament. BSkyB responded by lobbying hard, employing the leading PR company Lowe Bell. BSkyB had enjoyed a good relationship with the Group, sponsoring its Labour conference fringe meeting, but made very little headway on this issue, later withdrawing sponsorship at the 1999 conference. Manchester United sent Martin Edwards and Maurice Watkins to speak to the Group, along with Wakeling and Booth from Sky, but faced a barrage of criticism which left them very taken aback. 'There has never before been an issue which has so united the Group as this,' one insider said. 'A paper drawn up by Adam Brown found much favour with the Group. It was used as a briefing document which formed the basis of the Group's submission to the MMC, a powerful testament to the strength of MPs' feelings. Amazingly, nothing was leaked, illustrating the strength of feeling on this issue and both Joe Ashton and Joan Whalley gave evidence direct to the MMC.'

Some members became key players. Terry Lewis, MP for Worsley, United season ticket holder and IMUSA member, turned up at IMUSA meetings to give the low-down on the latest news from Parliament and to advise how to proceed. Not part of the New Labour set, he became an important ally. Whilst much attention was being focused on the lobbying of the OFT and getting the bid referred to the MMC, one way in which the mounting parliamentary opposition was put to greatest use was the launching of two Early Day Motions.

IMUSA had acquired the services of a top parliamentary lobby firm to advise and act on their behalf. They suggested the idea of an Early Day Motion. Although EDMs were rarely even given time to be debated, let alone make it to legislation, they were a superb way of illustrating back-bench support on an issue and getting press attention. The lobby firm drafted a motion which was passed to Terry Lewis. He then presented it to the All Party Group and got Joe Ashton to second it and other leading members of the Group to support it. They then set about getting other MPs to sign up. EDM 1675 read:

> . . . that this House objects to the agreement where BSkyB Television will purchase Manchester United plc; feels that this will create an unacceptable situation where BSkyB becomes both the biggest purchaser of televised football and also the owner of Europe's largest football club; is certain that this is not in the best public interest of fans, clubs or television viewers and sport in general; and calls upon the Secretary of State for Trade and Industry to refer the proposed take-over to the Monopolies and Mergers Commission in addition to setting up a full inquiry into the funding of football by television, in all its aspects.

IMUSA and SUAM set about co-ordinating pressure on MPs to sign the EDM, including massive letter-writing, fax and e-mail campaigns, as well as a lobby of Parliament. To aid this IMUSA managed to secure a parliamentary database which included all MPs' home numbers and constituency fax numbers, providing direct contact with every MP in the country. EDM 1675 achieved incredible cross-party support with over 150 MPs signing, and massive backing from Labour's back-benchers. It is thought that only two MPs ever publicly supported the bid during the whole process, Graham Stringer and Peter Lilley. Stringer was lobbied by Andy Walsh and Steve Donohue and later accosted by Mark Longden at an FSA parliamentary reception, but maintained his backing for the club's board.

The lobby of Parliament itself was a huge success. IMUSA's barrister, Nick Toms, had suggested it as a way of focusing the attention on the political process.Taking place on Tuesday, 27 October, a coach-load of IMUSA activists travelled from Manchester to be joined by other IMUSA members, leading lights in SUAM, and representatives from over twenty other clubs from the Premier to the Conference. On the journey down it was reported that Sky had only managed to secure 44 per cent of shareholders agreeing to the merger. Take away the holdings of the directors and Sky's holdings and it meant only 16 per cent of the shareholders had voted for the take-over: campaigners were ecstatic. Fans poured into the parliamentary committee room to air their views to the collection of MPs. As Paul Windridge recalls, 'I was surprised to see so many IMUSA and SUAM members outside the gates – we'd taken over! It was full inside, so I was drafted into playing an impromptu football match on St Stephen's Green!' Jackets were thrown down as goal posts in the pouring rain, there was fly-goalie and 'the press clamoured around us for comment as the Westminster traffic pounded around us. If somebody had suggested this scenario a few months previously I would have thought them worthy of committal!'

Over fifty MPs gave their views against the bid, from the Labour stalwarts to Conservative MP Roger Gale. 'That football fans were in the unlikely position of being transported to the corridors of the House of Commons, to a meeting in one of the many grandiose rooms, saw the lengths to which this had become a major issue within Parliament,' recalls Barney Chilton. 'One MP after another entered the room to hear honest and passionate speeches and there was a growing sense that BSkyB may have bitten off more than they could chew. When Mr Bell the white-suited man of Tatton himself arrived, I knew the fight had entered war stages.'

Once the meeting was over, fans descended to lobby their own MPs. Duncan Drasdo:

> I remember Andy trying to address the committee room and getting upstaged by Joe Ashton, who didn't want a lowly fan controlling proceedings as he was perfectly capable of running things himself! While at the lobby we had to rush round to the DTI to deliver a print-out of the thousands of names on the Internet petition which Virtual Manchester had been running. We got bollocked by security for trying to photograph the handover to a Mandelson secretary.

Others had even more interesting encounters. Mark Longden, queuing to get back inside the Commons for the lobby, spotted Peter Mandelson leaving from the same entrance. Melissa Moore tried to sell him a T-shirt, which slowed him down just enough. 'I thought right, let's have a word and leapt over the barriers that separate the "proles" entrance from the MPs' access. I put my arm around him and said, "You are going to knock this bid back, aren't you, mate?" Mandelson mumbled something non-committal that he was considering it. He looked a bit frightened, to be honest, whereas I was getting cheered from those queuing!' With a Radio 5 microphone for company Mark escorted Mandelson back to his offices. The threat of Mark returning the following week may have swung it – but we will never know for sure!

Given that members of the government – including all ministers, junior ministers and Parliamentary Private Secretaries (PPSs) – were not supposed to sign EDMs, it was a huge success. Indeed, government members were not even supposed to comment on the bid. Highlighting the inter-departmental Whitehall opposition to the bid were in fact a number of PPSs including Ian Pearson, a leading Blairite back-bencher and PPS to Geoffrey Robinson; Rhodri Morgan, chair of the Public Administration Committee; Clare Wood, another Blair loyalist; and Gerry Sutcliffe, then aide to Treasury Chief Secretary, one Stephen Byers. Although the lobby did not receive the expected press coverage, due to Ron Davies' Clapham Common encounter, Mandelson began to look like a very lonely figure.

Sutcliffe was also a member of the All Party Group and a supporter of reform in football's administration. As MP for Bradford he knew about the issues surrounding smaller clubs, he was captain of the MPs' football team, and is reportedly a rather talented goalkeeper. A football man, he was to follow his support for EDM 1675 with a private member's bill in May 1999 calling for independent statutory regulation for football, something which the Football Task Force was in the middle of negotiating.

The first EDM, designed to get the bid referred to the MMC, was followed in the new session of Parliament after Christmas with EDM 266. This moved the target from a referral to the MMC to getting it rejected. In particular it highlighted the core concern for the MMC: 'That this house . . . believes that the possibility of BSkyB Television acting as both a bidder for television rights to the Premier League as well as the owner of its most high-profile club is a matter of serious public interest and anxiety.' In all, over 200 MPs signed either one or both motions. Given the restrictions on government members, and the sympathies which campaigners knew existed among many of them for IMUSA's cause, the government hierarchy could not have got a much clearer message about how Parliament and its own party felt. Thus, despite Mandelson's influential position in government, and his role as architect of New Labour, he faced absolutely massive political opposition if he were to allow Sky's take-over of Manchester United. The role of IMUSA had been central in co-ordinating support, in leading the campaign and in directing matters, but the response from Parliament could hardly have been more satisfying.

Next stop on the political trail was the government's Football Task Force. Set up to consider issues in football which included involving supporters in the running of clubs, and reconciling the potential for conflict between supporters and plc boards, the take-over of Manchester United appeared to some to be as central an issue as was likely to arise during its deliberations. David Mellor, instructed to speak in a personal capacity only, reacted to the announcement of the bid in bullish fashion, claiming that it would be very damaging to the game to have the country's monopoly live broadcaster of Premiership football owning the biggest club. Campaigners were further encouraged when Mellor spoke to Adam Brown: 'Are we going to fight this thing, Adam?' he asked. 'I already am,' he replied.

Although it was clear that there would be some serious support for the take-over on the Task Force – Sir Roland Smith sat across the table from Adam at meetings of the Working Group – many fans thought that this issue was something the Task Force should show a clear line on, potentially disastrous as it was for the whole of football. It was hoped that, with the commercial aspects of the Task Force looming, an unequivocal message could be sent to the government. It was something of a forlorn hope.

The Task Force had 'met' IMUSA before and it had hardly been love at first sight. On its Manchester regional visit in February 1998 the meeting, held in Manchester Town Hall's Great Hall, bedecked with portraits of the city's fathers, was dominated by Manchester United fans, including a huge representation from IMUSA. Co-ordinated by IMUSA, fans ignored the government's remit for the Task Force and refused to talk about anything other than the reintroduction of terracing. At times chaotic, always highly charged, and clearly completely frustrating for *some* panel members, it was the most politically heated of all the Task Force's visits. 'We're absolutely buzzin',' said one IMUSA committee member afterwards. 'They hijacked the whole meeting,' said a Task Force member.

The first meeting of the Working Group since the bid was lobbied by IMUSA's unofficial 'London branch', which included actor Roger Brierley from SUAM and Barney Chilton, editor of United's longest running fanzine, *Red News*. To the Task Force's credit, the lobbyists were allowed in to address the meeting about their concerns, Barney outlining why they thought it now inappropriate to have Roland Smith remain on the body and that they wanted the Task Force to make an unequivocal statement against the deal. Given the strength of feeling it was a curiously polite affair, and markedly different from the hostility which had been on display at the Manchester meeting. As Barney recalls: 'The amazing campaign route took in a visit to a Football Task Force meeting, a convivial enough occasion where we were allowed to voice our fears and disagreement to the bid to the large working group, which included David Mellor amongst many and, somewhat bizarrely, the chairman of the plc which had negotiated the deal, Sir Roland Smith, whom we asked to be removed from the body – no offence, like.' Brown recalls:

> Once they had left, I put forward the arguments about the threat the deal posed for the whole of football – that it would be totally subjugated to the interests of television – and why I saw it as central to our deliberations. I thought that the take-over arguably represented a greater threat to football than the RPC. Indeed, the Task Force went so far as to specifically back the Premier League in its RPC case, but no such support was forthcoming over the OFT and MMC's investigation into United.
>
> I was first told that it would be inappropriate for the Working Group to comment, but if I could demonstrate enough support on the Task Force's main body, it would be discussed. I wrote a two-page statement and started the lobbying, receiving support from the FA's Graham Kelly, Gordon Taylor, John Barnwell of the League Managers Association, the Local Government Association, supporters' groups and other individuals. It was a big majority. The Premier League were furious, though. Both Peter Leaver and Mike Lee telephoned me and Leaver, in his bellicose manner, accused me of trying to hijack the

Task Force, immediately getting the DCMS to reiterate that they did
not think it appropriate for the Task Force to comment.

It was difficult to understand this logic. The issues were about the representation of fans (the clear majority were against); about the role of plcs (the
take-over would reshape the organisation of English football); and about
the future financing of the game. How could it be more relevant to the Task
Force's remit? The fact that two months later the Task Force saw fit to issue
a report which backed the Premier League in the RPC emphasises the
political nature of this decision. On that there was a consensus, on this the
Premier League would be isolated. In the RPC case, the Premier League had
a vested interest in getting the Task Force to support it. On this they did
not. It was suggested that the lack of a clear public line from the Premier
League about the Sky take-over was about keeping Sky on board in their
RPC case. The government's willingness to keep the Premier League happy
also boded ill for the rest of the Task Force's work.

One other push was made with politicians, and that was a meeting
IMUSA had with Tony Banks. IMUSA had written asking for a meeting and
had received no response. Not satisfied, Nigel Krohn set about phoning
Banks' office until he agreed to meet. Andy Walsh, Julie Lawrence (an
IMUSA and SUAM member), and Roger Brierley met Banks, in his
ministerial attire of black shirt and black tie on 12 October. Banks outlined
that he couldn't be seen to be prejudicial to the bid process which was why
he hadn't commented publicly. He inquired as to IMUSA and SUAM's views
about the possibility of other take-overs and about the specific complaints
about Murdoch. Brierley outlined the complaints of shareholders and
Walsh asked for Sir Roland Smith to be removed from the Task Force as
well as calling for greater regulation of football. Banks reassured them that
he would be speaking to other members of the cabinet about issues and
would pass on IMUSA's views. As they left the meeting, which had run over
time by forty-five minutes, who should be there waiting but Graham Kelly
from the FA!

Whether it was the 350-plus submissions the Office of Fair Trading
received on the take-over, the political pressure within Parliament and
government, the arguments of almost all organisations in football or the
massive public opposition, the Press Association made the following
statement on 29 October 1998:

> BSkyB's bid to take over Manchester United was today referred to the
> Monopolies and Mergers Commission by Trade and Industry
> Secretary Peter Mandelson. Mandelson was acting on the advice of
> the Director General of Fair Trading, who said the acquisition raised
> issues of competition over the TV rights to football. The Director

General also noted the wider concerns of public interest related to the proposed deal. The BSkyB offer will now be subject to a full investigation by the MMC which will report its findings next March. In its statement issued on Thursday, the Department of Trade and Industry was careful not to take sides over the deal. 'The decision to make a referral does not in any way prejudge the question of whether or not the merger would be against the public interest. It is for the MMC to report on this after its investigation,' the statement said.

What is almost certain is that without IMUSA and SUAM, who had co-ordinated, cajoled and concentrated opposition, the referral may never have taken place. Andy Walsh pointed to the wider implications which their acceptance of 'public interest' implied:

> I am absolutely delighted. This is what we've been working for over the last two months and it's exactly what we wanted. The referral to the MMC will give football fans from Manchester United and other clubs the opportunity to discuss for the first time how football should be structured in this country. Our concern has been that somebody spending £2.40 on a share in Manchester United plc has a greater share in the way the club is run than somebody who spends £300 to £400 on a season ticket. That disparity needs to be addressed. We expect the MMC to look at all aspects of the game, not just the BSkyB–Manchester United take-over, and hopefully they will ensure the situation caused by the Sky attempt to take over our club is a thing of the past.

It was greeted with euphoria by the campaigners:

> The joy when we heard there had been a referral to the MMC could not be quantified. In a sense a large portion of the hard work had been done. Sheer weight of numbers – not through a mass campaign, but by co-ordinating the numbers and striking at the right time and at the right place. Guerrilla tactics, terrorising the club and no doubt causing Martin Edwards a few sleepless nights. Murdoch must've turned puce! I can almost imagine him screaming at the fuck-wits at BSkyB in utter disbelief. [Nick Clay]

In fact the tensions between the bid process, Labour and the Murdoch press were soon to emerge. Murdoch threw a wobbly at a Sky press conference to announce company results at the time the bid was referred to the MMC, exposing his obvious involvement in the take-over, which up to that point had been strenuously denied by Booth and Edwards.

Allegations about a gay Mafia in the cabinet, including Ron Davies' extra-curricular activities on Clapham Common, suggested that Murdoch's press had cooled on the government by late autumn, as Mandelson referred the bid to the MMC. Mandelson himself was 'outed' at this stage. Other players, such as Joe Ashton, were to feel the wrath of *The Sun* in exposés about his private life, clearly linked to his outspoken opposition of the take-over. When stories began to emerge about Mandelson receiving an undeclared loan from Geoffrey Robinson, the press were even less sympathetic. The paper which had been singing his praises in October, *The Sun*, pushed him on to his sword.

Mandelson went on 23 December 1998, as the MMC were in full swing. For someone who had set so much store on being incorruptible, accepting a £373,000 loan from Geoffrey Robinson, Paymaster General, and then failing to declare it, was a calamitous cock-up. Whether Brown and Whelan (of whom Robinson was an ally) were behind the revelations, or someone connected with Paul Routledge's biography on Mandelson, or Mandelson himself, remains unclear. That Whelan was to follow soon after suggests tit-for-tat, as the Mandelson–Brown feud imploded. What the resignation of Mandelson did for the prospects of the BSkyB bid for Manchester United was no less dramatic, however. It removed the one person in the cabinet sympathetic to the merger. True, as a take-over 'wet', Mandelson had been well and truly hung out to dry by his cabinet colleagues and the rest of the party; but he still held the trump card as Secretary of State. Murdoch's chief ally had suddenly gone.

The second phase of this was that Mandelson was replaced by Stephen Byers. Byers was a northern MP and, although not one of Labour's football crowd, had hinted that he was sympathetic when approached at the Labour Party conference in the autumn of 1998. His PPS, of course, was Gerry Sutcliffe, who although not in a position to advise on this matter, was a football man through and through. The attitude at the DTI towards the take-over was said to have cooled considerably as soon as Byers was in place. Should the MMC suggest that the take-over was a bad idea, the 'obstacle' that Mandelson represented was now gone.

FIVE

UNITED FOR UNITED:

FROM CHESTER TO BARCELONA

At one time football fans turned up, paid their money and departed, complaining that the ref was bent and the centre forward had no left foot. Occasionally they stayed away in protest, sometimes they organised fund-raising to save their club or build a new stand. Mostly, they fought between themselves. As with so many things in football, the 1980s changed all that. By the time the BSkyB bid for Manchester United appeared, fan organisa-tions existed across the country and the notion of 'politicised' supporters was very well established. What became important for those in the campaign was garnering as much cross-club support against the deal as possible. But football is a tribal business, so for IMUSA to get backing in its campaign, a widespread and deep-seated hatred of Manchester United had to be overcome.

Bournemouth, Northampton, Brighton. In each case, the only saviours or potential saviours of these 'clubs in crisis' were the supporters, who organised protests against chairmen, dug deep to stave off bankruptcy, formed supporters' trusts and campaigned for a better distribution of income within the game. At each turn pleas were made for other fans to help, to stand together for the good of all football, to stand united. Now it was Manchester United's turn. Easily the most disliked club in England, securing support from fans of Chester City and Bournemouth was not going to be easy, especially given the club's role in the demise of football's wealth distribution.

But get support they did. At the lobby of Parliament, over twenty clubs were represented. E-mail messages and letters were received from across some pretty deep divides – Liverpool, Leeds, City. At a national level the FSA supported lobbies within the Task Force and directly to the Football Association. The FSA and IMUSA were also instrumental in establishing the Coalition for Football Supporters, an attempt to get all the various fans' groups to speak with one voice. Internationally, support came from Bayern Munich fans, who brought a huge 'Stop Murdoch' banner to their Old Trafford fixture, and from Barcelona, whose L'Elefant Blau organisation had their own battles to tell of. With United fans from every corner of the globe joining in, the ranks of the opposition were swelling.

In terms of organised fan opposition, the oldest national group is the National Federation of Football Supporters' Clubs (NFFSC). Although some independent groups are members, the NFFSC is mainly a federation of the official club supporters' groups. In 1985, the Football Supporters' Association became the second national fans' body. Forged in the wake of the Heysel tragedy and playing a key role in both the aftermath of Hillsborough and the battle against Thatcher's ID cards, it has an individual membership, organised on regional, not club lines as well as having a number of independent club organisations (including IMUSA) as affiliates. However, although by the mid-1990s both national organisations had regular meetings with the football authorities and could get considerable exposure in the media (especially the FSA), membership and participation remained low and a meaningful role in decision-making in the game often seemed as distant as ever. The new commercialism in football seemed to place another obstacle – corporate priorities which viewed fans as customer fodder – in their way.

As well as the FSA and NFFSC, a number of Independent Supporters' Associations (ISAs) have grown to prominence at club level. Some, like IMUSA, have become well established and active on a range of issues. The majority have been formed on single-issue campaigns – at Arsenal and West Ham over the bond schemes, for instance – and have disappeared almost as soon as they appeared once the burning problem has been doused. Other club groups, such as at Bournemouth and Northampton, have become involved in the running of clubs. Added to these, during the 1980s, the football fanzine began to make its mark with articulate and witty critiques of how the game and clubs were being mismanaged and fans treated badly. Over 2,000 titles are estimated to have been in existence in the last fifteen years, giving fans a means of expression and acting as both mouthpiece and sounding board.

At Manchester United, the official supporters' club, run by David Smith, was wound up in 1987 to be replaced by a money-spinning membership scheme. The FSA were active in Manchester for many years, particularly effective in highlighting the mistreatment of United fans in Istanbul in 1993, when hundreds were detained and six imprisoned. United have also been blessed with three long-standing fanzines of high quality: the London-based *Red News*, the oldest; *Red Issue*, irreverent and radical; and *United We Stand*, started by the then sixteen-year-old journalist Andy Mitten and now enjoying national distribution. Following the fledgling HOSTAGE campaign, IMUSA has stepped into the breach as a sustainable and fiercely independent fans' organisation at the club. With IMUSA, these three fanzines and newcomers *Red Attitude* and *Red Army* all preaching from the same hymnbook, United fans have found themselves well served in recent years.

Thus, by 1998, the idea of fans organising to protest at something as fundamental as the ownership of their club was not a surprise; it was to be expected. Although not funded from anything but membership fees, dependent on the voluntary work of dedicated individuals, and run on the fuel of commitment, there was nevertheless a network of supporters' groups on which IMUSA and SUAM would have to draw. The acid test would come in the approach and reaction of other fans.

Financial Problems and Clubs in Crisis

For many, football has never been in ruder health. But scratch beneath the surface and there is a game running on empty. In the Premier League, total wages rose by 36 per cent, exceeding 50 per cent of income, which rose by £105m (23 per cent) to £569m for the first time. [Boon, 1999: 4] Even the phenomenal rise in ticket prices can't mask that this is a situation no other industry could tolerate. At the bottom – well, to be honest, from the top of the middle downwards – there is a financial plight such as the game has never seen. Thus there is now a situation where one club's turnover is greater than that of one of the divisions of the Football League.

Part of this is down to the Premier League and television: their break-away meant that the 50 per cent of TV income redistributed from the old First Division to the other three divisions has dried to a trickle. At a time when football has never had so much money coming in, and therefore should be in a position to make sure everyone at least survives, 'collectively, the game is far from proving that income growth can be converted into sustained profitability'. [Boon, 1999] More money may come in, but more goes straight out in wages, share dividends, directors' salaries and transfer fees abroad. It's like a Third World country which strikes it rich in oil or some cash crop and suddenly has currency flowing in; without democratic structures, the wealthy few prosper with obscene riches while the majority starve.

During the year of the bid, Hull City faced obliteration after being bought by sports entrepreneur David Lloyd and unceremoniously dumped when his proposed super-stadia with the local rugby team didn't look like a goer. They were within a day or two of going bust. Chester City were unable to pay the wages of a skeleton staff as Mark Guterman's disastrous tenure as owner ground to what seemed like oblivion. Then Crystal Palace, bought by Mark Goldberg from Ron Noades, unable to deal with the magnitude of the task, catapulted into receivership and is currently struggling not to be wound up. Also on the casualty list were Portsmouth, Luton Town and Lincoln City clinging to survival. There were big clubs, not long from the Premiership, like Sheffield United, who were unable to hold on to players given the financial pressures, jettisoning managers who couldn't work with such restrictions. Also, Doncaster Rovers, betrayed by their chairman Richardson, who burnt down his own club's stand to make personal profit from the sale of the land, were relegated to the Football Conference. To sacrifice a football club on the altar of greed, for the sake of a few square metres of brownfield real estate – could it get any more desperate than that?

Some clubs – Brighton, Northampton, Bournemouth – had clawed their way back from the brink by leading imaginative, community-based campaigns and installing supporters into the ownership and decision-making process. Northampton Town's Supporters' Trust, with their elected director Brian Lomax, became a by-word for how a football club should be run – involve the supporters, give them a stake and you'll reap the rewards. Lomax is an evangelist for this approach: supporters on club boards should be democratic, accountable, entrenched and have a meaningful role. As these have blazed a trail in the lower leagues, however, the prospect was, and is, that more and more fans would face the same battles, though not all would prevail.

But so what? In the context of the corporate world in which the BSkyB take-over was planned this was the natural selection of the market place. The strong and rich will survive and prosper, the rest will disappear. As Sir Roland Smith commented in an ominous statement to one Task Force meeting before news of the bid broke (paraphrased), 'The future of football isn't with your Northampton Towns and your Rotherhams! The future's with people like Rupert Murdoch and he isn't interested in that. He's interested in getting AC Milan against Manchester United broadcast across Europe!'

What this logic says is that a football club is a business, and as a business you make yours as strong and powerful as you can. This means making it commercially powerful, so if a company twenty times bigger than you offers to buy you out, you go with it. Expand the business, expand your assets. Move into new areas of competition and don't be so damn romantic about the old ones. And certainly don't go giving away the money you have earned through TV deals and the like to small fry competition. Some of them will fail. They won't be able to keep up with you. When that happens, they just go. Bye-bye.

But for a fan, for a town or city, losing a football club can be traumatic. Fans can't just decide to get on a different bus and go somewhere else. It's not like a supermarket blowing a corner shop out of the street – at least then the same product can be got somewhere else. With football, the product is the team you support, not live football as an abstract concept. British football and British football culture (not to mention Italian, Spanish, German, South American . . .) has been created by the place and importance of clubs within localities. Its strength lies in the closeness of a club to the place in which it is situated and the importance in terms of people's identity and attachment with it. The 1990s have seen that fabric, those interwoven threads of society, begin to unravel. And once it goes, it doesn't come back. Not like it was, anyway. Ask Accrington. Ask Maidstone. Ask Doncaster.

Ironically, this argument that football is a sport first and a business second – too important to be left to the strict laws of the market – is precisely what the Premier League found themselves arguing in the restrictive practices court and they won some sympathy for it. To fans of lower-division clubs, they could be forgiven for thinking that the Sky bid was just another nail in the coffin of a collective football identity. Like the Premier League formation, the TV deals which cut them out, Bosman and the spiralling wages, the changes to the Champions' League, it was just another move by the rich to isolate themselves from everyone else. Some turned their backs: it had nothing to do with them; United were getting what they deserved.

Support From Far and Wide

What IMUSA began to do, had to do, was highlight what the take-over meant for smaller clubs and the English game as a whole. It had to be demonstrated that this was a battle which had implications for everyone, big and small. For one thing was sure: if Sky owned Manchester United, sooner or later they would have an individual TV deal from which Sky would be the sole profiters and the trickle-down of money, little as it is, would dry up completely. It would widen the wealth gap and spell disaster for some.

For Arsenal or Newcastle, corporate ownership in the shape of Carlton and NTL waited in the wings. For Coventry or Southampton, the heroic battles to stay in the Premier League would be that much harder with less of the collective TV pot. For a well-run or well-financed First Division club, such as Huddersfield or Wolves, breaching the Premiership wall would be that much further down the road, and, once achieved, a return to whence they came was that much more likely. Blackpool or Bury or Preston faced the prospect of being eclipsed forever by a gargantuan club on their doorstep. For Brighton or Bournemouth or Northampton, their valiant struggles for survival and regeneration under new ownership would be jeopardised if the threadbare rug of TV income redistribution were pulled from under their feet. The battle to stop the bid should have been a battle in which everyone had a stake.

At times this wasn't easy. Overcoming an inherited, ingrained hatred of anything 'Man U' would take some work. It was the ABU factor – Anyone But United. It would mean saying, 'Forget that this has anything to do with

United, this is about the future of your club, your football.' Some of the reaction was pure hatred: 'I wouldn't spit on anything to do with Man U if it was on fire. What I say is KILL OFF MAN U. I'M ALL FOR THE TAKE-OVER,' read one message. Some entered into a dialogue, had some intelligence that pushed prejudice aside, and turned the corner.

But it was a double-edged battle, because the perception within United ranks – certainly the hard core who travel away, who see what it means to other teams to beat United on their patch – is a growing one of 'no one likes us, we don't care'. That siege mentality, exacerbated by their own club's hierarchy being against them, selling it off under their nose, had to be overcome as well. The arguments had to be made within United circles that the message had to be carried out, to all those people at all those clubs who would support anyone but United. IMUSA had to dispel the notion that they were an arrogant bunch who couldn't care less about the rest of football. That IMUSA's fight was their fight, and theirs IMUSA's.

However, things started better than anyone could have hoped very early on. The FSA had a press statement out on the day of the IMUSA press conference offering support. The NFFSC had voiced their concerns to one or two nationals and both were to make contributions to the MMC. It's not to belittle either of them to say that their support was expected. What wasn't expected was some of the others who fell in at first light. The number of people who were bang on from day one, ordinary fans sending messages of support, just took campaigners' breath away.

Liverpool fans, for instance:

> Obviously the involvement of Murdoch is anathema to me, but the wider issues of media ownership will affect us all . . . we should forget about rivalries etc., and unite against this threat to the game. [Sam]
>
> I never thought I would come out and support Man United fans in anything, but this issue is so serious and the consequences will involve the whole of the football world. [Liz]
>
> Much as I detest Man United and all that it stands for, this fate is too ghastly even for your club. A quick, clean death would be preferable to the long, lingering half-life of commercially dictated TV slavery that awaits any club weak and short-sighted enough to sell its soul to the media. [Mike]

Some of this was clearly to do with the hatred of Murdoch after *The Sun's* disgrace following Hillsborough – 'All genuine Liverpool fans hate Murdoch after the disgusting *Sun* reports of the Hillsborough disaster (and we thank you for the support shown by the Man U fans)' – but to overcome one of the fiercest rivalries in football was still something.

Then there was Millwall:

> Whilst I can't say that Millwall fans have any love whatsoever for
> Man United, and many might say that they deserve all they get (and
> frequently do), I think most of us appreciate that BSkyB's
> involvement may well represent the thin edge of the wedge as far as
> football is concerned. You have the support of my fanzine, *Tales from
> Senegal Fields*.

. . . and Manchester City:

> As a City fan, I'm quite enjoying the turmoil United is in at the
> moment. On a more serious note, though, and leaving aside such
> rivalries to think about the good of the game as a whole, I, too, am
> horrified by recent events.

Darren Foreman, of Wimbledon's Independent Supporters' Association,
who are fighting to actually keep their club in this country, never mind who
owns it, signposted the links between campaigns (the possibility of United
being moved was one of the fears about Murdoch's ownership):

> There seems to be quite a bit of support for you. Hope it all goes
> well; one of the side effects that we've seen is that Joe Kinnear came
> out and said something along the lines of 'Well, with all this BSkyB
> business going on that no one could ever have predicted, who's to
> say that our move to Dublin can't happen after all?' Not something
> we're happy about!

And those with access to the Internet waded in, from the Premiership –
'Cheers, m8. Best of luck in the fight against Murdoch. Choosing from two
pricks, I prefer Martin Edwards' [Christian Jahnsen, Guardian of *The
VillaWeb*] – to the Conference:

> Greetings From *Shine On You Crazy Diamonds*! We are the Fanzine
> behind Rushden and Diamonds FC who have the distinction of
> being called the MUFC of the Conference! We have put together a
> page supporting you on our website! Please have a look at what we
> have put and let us know if we have wrote anything that the
> Australian B*stard can sue us for!

Some appreciated that, big or small club, fans still had an uphill battle.
They saw the need to offer what help they could, even as a lonely voice,
such as Ray Brown, AFC Bournemouth e-mail list administrator:

I have cancelled my Sky Sports subscription over this affair and am urging members of my AFC Bournemouth e-mail list to follow suit – so far with no success . . . It's depressing me . . . the 'I'm all right Jack' mentality of some of our fans, that is. When you think about the fantastic moral and financial support we received in our darkest hours in early 1997 I'm sickened by the pro-Sky stance of some of our e-mail list members. Good luck in your battle.

Kev Miles, of the Independent Newcastle United Supporters' Association, promised their help in a prophetic statement:

> This is not simply a catastrophe for Manchester United fans, it is a threat to the whole of football. It is vital now that all fans put their prejudices against Manchester United to one side, look at the long-term effects, and realise that our game as we know it is being destroyed in the interests of multinational corporations. It may be Manchester United today, but it will be the likes of Newcastle United and others tomorrow.

All these arrived in the first week or so of the campaign and showed campaigners that this was something far bigger than the concerns of a few obsessives who hung out in Old Trafford too much. To the campaigners it was a massive boost to know that there were so many fans who would normally wish any of a thousand curses on them and their team, who were prepared to take the time to write and let them know that they were not alone and that this was more than just their fight.

Some did remain beyond the pale, ignorant of both the implications of the Sky take-over for them and IMUSA's beliefs about what the plc had been doing in the club's name over the last decade.

> You didn't mind money coming before football when Man Utd *et al* formed the Premiership, did you? You're just taking the piss now by whining to us fans of small clubs. If Murdoch bought up Man United and shut them down, he'd be a hero to most of us. Stop whining, and accept the taste of your own medicine. [David Stephenson, Yeovil]
>
> If you all stopped paying mugs' prices for trashy souvenirs and shirts, the likes of Murdoch would not be convinced you are daft enough to pay per view etc. You are making (have made) your own bed. Lie in it and stop bothering the fans of teams who are not concerned with such issues. [Christopher O'Neil, club withheld]

United fans may not have been vocal enough in opposition to the

Premiership or even the club becoming a plc; sometimes such opposition only manifests itself when the outcomes of such decisions begin to affect fans. Having said that, there was and still is a huge contingency of United fans who are utterly alienated by the changes in football over the last ten years and have always been in total opposition. What is sad about the above comments is that if a member of IMUSA had sat down with one of 'them' and talked about the state of football, about the inequality of wealth, about how the Premier League was divisive, about what reform was needed to protect smaller clubs, about bringing back the dream factor which money was destroying in football, about it being a sport first – something to devote your life to – and a business second, about it not being something to be traded and exchanged like so many barrels of oil, if all this discussion took place, without either party knowing which team the other supported, they would probably have agreed with each other. Put Manchester United into the equation and it all goes pear-shaped with some people. They presume all United fans like and buy the merchandise. They think every IMUSA member was a fan of the Edwards regime because they were opposing Sky. They think that just because United fans celebrate when United win the League, they are somehow responsible for the Premiership's existence.

When dialogue was possible, some people came around to see the bigger picture of what the deal meant. Richard Murphy, writer of Brighton fanzine *Seaside Saga*, began by announcing that 'This is all about European Super Leagues and the like. Our club won't get near it. This isn't going to affect proper football supporters, just the fancy Dans in the Prima Donna League.' After a heated series of e-mails, he was putting the 'e-mail conversations' with Adam Brown in the fanzine, including details of how to give support to IMUSA, and saying: 'Ultimately the Murdoch take-over could deprive the Albion of vital cash. As he [Brown] says, "Even if you can't think about the Reds' interests, think of your own."'

One of the most satisfying things for many at IMUSA was the contact made with Chester City's Independent Supporters' Association. Having seen their club head for oblivion under Mark Guterman, the PFA were now paying the players' wages, manager Kevin Radcliffe was paying the water bills and supporters were involved in the organisation of the club, which was in serious financial peril. The concerns of a club with millions in the bank and – a common, massive misconception, this – about to 'receive' another £600m seemed distant and, to one fan at least, offensive:

> While your fight to stop a media magnate from pumping countless millions into your already super-rich organisation may be vital in some quarters, here at Chester City FC there are far more important issues at stake. Unless Chester can find a buyer by the end of the year, we will go out of business . . . Just half a million would help us

to secure our future . . . Shouldn't it be your shower supporting the Chester battle?

So when IMUSA received a message in December 1998 saying that Chester had been given a live Friday night game on Sky, which would pay them a lifeline of money, and to which they wanted fans of whatever persuasion to attend, IMUSA took up the challenge. 'Due to the precarious position of Chester City and Brighton's previous threat of extinction, it is a fitting match to highlight the plight of clubs in the lower divisions. [We] believe it to be the ideal opportunity to designate the day as the "Third Fans United Day",' they said.

IMUSA organised a minibus of fans to go down, to demonstrate on Chester's behalf that what was happening to them was against the interests of all fans; that IMUSA sympathised with their plight because, apart from anything else, what had happened to them had happened because they weren't being listened to and they weren't being involved in decision-making, just as IMUSA weren't. It was also decided that, because Chester desperately needed the cash from Sky and this was their protest, IMUSA would not use the occasion to further its own cause, either through attacks on Sky or by displaying banners against Murdoch and the take-over. In fact, IMUSA members were in the bizarre position of standing adjacent to Chester fans displaying placards that read 'Thank you Sky'! It was impossible not to feel that both the divide in football and the common purpose of fans had rarely been greater. Mark Southee describes the evening:

> On finding Mark Howell, the chair of the Chester City ISA, we were signed into the social club and were soon reminiscing about 1983 and all that with the Seagulls. With kick-off looming we made our way to the home terrace and found a gap for ourselves. We were joined by the chair of the Bar Codes ISA [Kev Miles] and a Yorkshireman who claimed to have a non-bleating girlfriend.
>
> During the half-time break, the banner of scarves donated from all ninety-two league clubs was paraded around the ground. To be fair, the Seagulls probably deserved something just for the massive (and vocal) support they brought. After the game we went to Chester Town Hall, where Andy Walsh gave a speech as well as Mark Howell, the MP for Chester and Attila the Stockbroker from Brighton. The passion on display was in marked contrast to the attitude of some Megastore bag carriers at OT – shame we can't do a swap!
>
> It is ironic that when the top end of the game is awash with cash, the lower league clubs are left out to dry. The FA couldn't care less, happier to spend thousands trying to get the World Cup here (and by whatever means possible it would appear) than worry about the roots

of the professional game. With the attitude of clubs like Villa (over the Barry transfer from Brighton!) not exactly helping, it's no wonder that people give United fans a slagging. You may think that as a United supporter what happens to Chester, Oxford, Portsmouth *et al* doesn't affect us, but consider this: Rupert Murdoch is more than capable of doing to United what the likes of Guterman have done to Chester. Same attitude, just more money involved. You have been warned!

Towards a Coalition for Football Supporters

Another sign of increasing co-operation across club divides were the moves in which IMUSA were heavily involved to create a single, national voice for supporters' groups, the Coalition of Football Supporters (CoFS). Authorities had long used the fact that there were two national fan groups to divide and rule, to pretend that they didn't know what fans wanted and to get out of funding fans' organisations. The hypocrisy of the fact that authorities themselves had spectacularly failed to unite into one body never broke through the dust at Lancaster Gate. The FSA made the first moves in a 1998 conference motion which called for a new body to represent all fans. IMUSA's Mark Longden became heavily involved in a Steering Group which included the FSA, ISAs and the NFFSC and which worked around the country building support for an umbrella body which was eventually constituted in June 1999.

Despite scepticism within IMUSA's ranks, in some ways the Sky deal proved the point: fans couldn't exist in isolation. Although the threat of Sky and the dangers it posed to United fans were first and foremost a United matter, fans were now playing in a bigger league, part of a much bigger picture. The CoFS process has led some to conclude that a wholly new organisation is needed, replacing the FSA and NFFSC, to unify fans' interests across the board.

Mark Longden, a CoFS radical, took on the role of IMUSA's CoFS supremo with gusto. He linked the urgent need for proper national representation across clubs with the anti-Sky campaign.

> Throughout the campaign I was continually haranguing other supporters' groups to write to the OFT, the MMC or their MPs. The response was fantastic and I feel we owe these people a debt of gratitude. I received newspaper cuttings from around the country on things written on the Murdoch deal. The CoFS process was under way while the battle was raging and the issues of the campaign provided a vital kick up certain people's arses to get their act together and to try to move the process further along at a faster rate.

At certain times the cross-club support was very effective. The National Federation was instrumental in getting a wide range of fans' groups to attend the lobby of Parliament. This not only saw united opposition to the Sky bid, reinforcing the pressure on MPs to sign the first Early Day Motion, but heard numerous calls for greater co-operation between fans' organisations, something wholeheartedly supported by MPs present. It was the small clubs' attendance, and the force of their arguments, which particularly impressed Longden, however.

> I contacted my large, and getting larger, phone list of ISAs to try and get as many people as possible to attend the lobby of Parliament. This was also my first contact with the national federation. They proved vital in turning out the troops from the lower League clubs, whose attendance was in my opinion a major eye opener for MPs and could have been a major factor in the final outcome. The only disappointment for me was the no show from some of the big London clubs. 'Big Time' Bernie (Tottenham ISA), who'd said 'of course I can't make it', and Chelsea ISA's Mark Pulver's refusal to return my calls made me very, very angry. However, despite that lack of commitment, this was the day that I knew we would win.

The lobby of Parliament was an extremely powerful demonstration of the strength of unity amongst supporters from vastly differing backgrounds. It illustrated that the questions of ownership, control and involvement of supporters in running football were paramount whether you were talking about the top of the Premier League or the bottom of the Third Division. By the end of the 1998–99 season, and partly as a result of the unity of purpose among fans over the Sky take-over, fans' organisations were closer and more united than they had ever been.

A Different Kind of Campaign

There was something very different about the campaign against Sky, though. Brighton had had pitch invasions and organised the massively impressive 'Fans United' days; Burnley fans turned their backs on the pitch during play; Man City fans attacked their chairmen; and numerous others demonstrated with the ubiquitous 'sack the board' chants, banners and abuse. IMUSA's campaign had very few public signs of the unfolding, mounting protest.

The lobby of Parliament was one instance, but apart from the football match on St Stephen's Green, most of it was behind closed doors and, let's face it, it was hardly raucous. The plc's annual general meeting, too, had the 'usual' signs of protest in that campaigners stood outside, leafleting, lobbying. But once again, as soon as you passed through the SPS security blanket, it was a matter for those inside – apart from Channel 4 sneaking a camera in, of course! IMUSA's visit to Chester was much more what you expect from football fans' protests: at the match, the club scarves paraded around the pitch at half-time, a public meeting and social at the Town Hall afterwards, but that was their protest which IMUSA were supporting. Life as a campaigner against Murdoch wasn't quite like that.

It was a tactical decision, really. The at times fragile, and certainly muted, support from some sections of United's fan base meant that IMUSA had to tread carefully. In a season which would see United tilting at the treble, the board and Sky could have made major PR capital out of any disruption to the team's performance. Nobody wanted to save the club from Sky by jeopardising the team's performance. IMUSA even took the step of promising Ferguson and the players that they wouldn't be distracted from their jobs. The match was what the match always was: the escape from the mundane, losing oneself in what was happening on the pitch. It didn't quite work like that; at times the worry about the take-over battle and the sense that some of those who were considered fellow brethren couldn't care less brought a depression to going to the match which was unusual. But that was mostly private; the protest rarely intruded in a public, physical sense into match day proceedings.

The nature of the campaign, the political process which it inevitably involved, lent itself to this approach anyway. The lobbying of the OFT, representations to the MMC, the work of City lawyers and parliamentary lobbyists, the letter-writing to MPs and shareholders, the debates within the Task Force, the constant relationship with the media, the work of the MMC itself: none of this required mass public protest. The public relations issues, getting the message across time and again in the media – this was the public face of the campaign. Appropriately for a club with which most people only have a relationship through the media, the public face of the campaign was through the same papers, TV stations and radio phone-ins. The down side may have been at times that it was harder to make fans, of United and other clubs, feel involved, but it was a situation dictated by limited resources, circumstances and best options for blocking the take-over.

This isn't to say that large numbers of people weren't involved. Nothing could be further from the truth. The volume of calls, letters, e-mails and verbal support was massive. Whether involved with setting up websites, writing e-mails, sending letters to MPs, writing to their far and distant family and friends getting them to act, going to meetings, speaking with other fans, the numbers certainly turned out. Doing their bit. Making the difference. Just in a different way. For those who were not as well informed or involved in what was being orchestrated from the small terraces and labour clubs of Stretford, who like David Mellor after the Charlton game bemoaned the lack of 'dogs I was expecting to bark that didn't', were looking for the pitch invasion and attacks on the club's premises, the *sensation*: for those people, it must have seemed a strange business. Holding secret meetings with London lawyers, co-ordinating the writing and propositioning of Early Day Motions, organising lobbies of Parliament, advising MPs on what to say, being on first-name, home-number terms with half of the national press: this just wasn't what football fans do. This was a fan protest that wasn't.

. . . And the Cry Went Up: 'To Europe!'

Bayern Munich were to play a big part in the 1998–99 season. A *big* part. It began on 10 September – the day after IMUSA's press conference and three weeks before United's first Champions' League game against them, in Munich – when an e-mail was received from Gregor Weinreich, a Bayern fan. It read:

> Hallo from Munich!
> First of all: Sorry for my terrible English, but when I went to school, following FC Bayern to away-matches was more interesting than English lessons. We already wanted to contact you a few days earlier, because we thought, we maybe could organise a protest against the planned EFL at the match ManU–FCB together. Now we've all been shocked by the news about the deal with Murdoch . . . So our offer: if you want to organise any protest at the match in Munich, we can help you . . . So if you want to get e.g. a protest-banner or something like this in the stadium, we maybe can help you. We have also just in the moment very big problems with our club . . . In my opinion especially fans of all the big European clubs must start working together, because if not, there won't be any football in a few years . . .
> We would be glad, if we can help you.
> Gregor Weinreich, CLUB NR.12

Another Bayern fan wrote simply: 'Fight Murdoch!!!!! Reclaim the game! Stand together against the enemies of football! We are looking forward to 30/10 and 18/11. Sebastian.' So, within days of the campaign starting, the idea of setting up a European fans' network, something to challenge the top clubs' G14 grouping, was mooted. It was like that, this campaign – from a handful of people in Stretford Labour Club to a European fans' network in three days.

In fact the European angle had its roots in a campaign called Eurostand. Originating in Denmark, this was an attempt to co-ordinate a protest against UEFA's policy that all matches in UEFA club competitions should be held at all-seater grounds by the 1999 season. Although in England this would not have made any difference – all the grounds were all-seater anyway – the campaign struck a chord with the growing unrest on the standing issue. With fans being ejected from Old Trafford for standing up in seated areas during games, there was a great deal of sympathy with the aims of the organisers, and it matched the aims of IMUSA, the FSA and others to get a reintroduction of terracing. Organised totally through the Eurostand website – in itself a powerful signal to IMUSA and others of the effectiveness of co-ordination and contact through the Internet – it called for a day of action on 11 September:

> During the first half: all fans will be seated, keeping quiet and will only applaud when goals are scored, similar to a tennis match. This will be a symbol of how boring football will become in future. Imagine yourself as the boring football fan UEFA wants you to be. Be creative (ties, cigars, suits, bowlers, stock-listings, cellular phones etc.). During the second half: all fans will stand up and give full vocal support. This will symbolise how much standing and singing supporters mean for football, and be a symbol of how it ought to be.

Although a stand-up protest was planned at United, the timing could not have been worse. With the Murdoch deal fresh off the boardroom table, everybody's attention and efforts had switched. Standing and terracing just wasn't an issue when the very future of the club was at stake. As such, Eurostand never had the impact it could have done, in Manchester at least. What it did do was supply a nascent list of contacts across Europe. Adam Brown issued a circular e-mail to all on the Eurostand list in the first week of the campaign against Murdoch: the first point of contact between Bayern's fans and IMUSA.

In fact, given the pressures everybody was under at IMUSA and SUAM – the priority at that time was to lobby the Office of Fair Trading and politicians as hard as possible to get a referral to the MMC – there was no protest at United's match in Munich. The first meeting between the groups of fans was when Bayern visited Old Trafford on 18 November. Formed in July 1997, NR12 describe themselves as 'not another Fan Club, but the independent supra-regional association of active FC Bayern Munich Fans,' defending the rights of fans, supporting the retention of standing areas in the stadium, and trying to prevent the influence of groups whose only concern with football is profit. Andy Walsh describes the meeting:

> Myself, Lee Hodgkiss and Steve Briscoe arranged to meet Dominik and Gregor from Club NR12 in the Copthorne Hotel before the

Champions' League home game. They were very keen to assist IMUSA in stopping Murdoch but a little unsure what help they could give. We discussed ways that we could strengthen the ties between the fans of both clubs for the future. Both IMUSA and Club NR12 agreed that the best way to combat Murdoch and others like him was the establishment of a pan-European fans' group. It was agreed that we start with Barcelona and then look to establishing links with other groups similar to our own.

One thing they did do was bring a huge, plastic red and white banner which they unfurled before the match, reading simply, 'STOP MURDOCH'. For opposition fans in a Champions' League match to have gone to such effort on IMUSA's behalf was both astounding and a recognition by them that, given the European Football League debates just a few weeks earlier, this battle was as much about the future of their club and what competitions they would compete in as it was United's. Still, the knowledge that the message was being carried across Europe and resonating with like-minded fans was a huge boost.

The banner, which they donated to IMUSA, had an interesting life, not least when it was taken to Inter Milan by Mark Longden and Monica Brady on 17 March for United's quarter-final tie, second leg. Getting it there was one thing, into the ground quite another matter, as Mark Southee describes:

> There was a top atmosphere in the bar before the game, which contrasted greatly to what greeted us when we got to the ground. The 'official' United gates were a nightmare, with the cops seeming to enjoy their games of letting two in at a time and then shutting the gates again. Mick, Vinny, myself and the 'Stop Murdoch' banner managed to get through, but for some reason offence was taken to Vinny's bright green shirt and he was being hauled off by the blokes with guns. Once rescued we made for the entrance as quick as we could.

Television's love of football has given many fans the chance to air their grievances to huge audiences, vocally or visually, and audiences don't get much bigger than the Champions' League quarter-final. There's a neat irony, too, in using a television-driven spectacle to further your campaign against a media mogul taking over your team. This time however, the luck of the ticket draw meant that the banner ended up near the top of the stadium – good for avoiding 'the oranges, plastic bottles, lighters, coins and "fluids" that were being "offered by our hosts"', as Mark puts it, but bad for TV. At any rate, 'the poor banner then spent the rest of the first half being used as the resting-place for Gordon, who had overdone the pre-match warm-up'!

After the Ginger Prince had done his stuff and the stadium was empty of all but United fans, Mark made his way to the first aid section, to the right of the United fans at one end of the ground.

> I couldn't resist a peek out at the pitch and was surprised to see all the Reds staring back to us at the side of the pitch! I thought, 'sod it' and unravelled the banner in full view of IMUSA's 'constituent audience' to a big cheer. With too many dibble and stewards around we couldn't keep it up for long, but then a photographer came legging over and demanded it be shown again for his benefit, so up it went.

Following the match, an attempt was made to fold the banner properly outside a bar close to the ground.

> We had just got it rolled out when I see this Italian charging towards me, along with others, brandishing what looked like a big black dildo! I didn't have time to wonder what he wanted to do with it, and spun round as he caught me a couple of times across the shoulder. At this point I selected 'Italian gear' and made a retreat back to the bar door, closely followed by Dunc who had to deploy a handy table to keep one Italian off him. The bottles rained down, but amazingly the banner survived and after checking the coast was clear, Dunc ventured back to retrieve it.

The other main international contact came with another of United's Champions' League opponents, Barcelona. Now, Barcelona is almost unique when it comes to European football. The club is a non-profit organisation. It is owned by its 120,000 members, who have the opportunity to vote in their president every five years. Barcelona also has an identity deeply rooted in the history of the Catalan region. The magnificent Nou Camp stadium was the only place where Catalan could be spoken without fear of arrest, or worse, under the Franco regime; the team is regarded as the Catalan national side; and the Barcelona shirt is so highly valued that sponsors' names have never appeared on it. As such, the club appears to embody much of what IMUSA, and other fans' groups, strive for. A democratic structure in which fans have a real say; the symbolic importance of the club placed before commercial interests; the club as a sporting institution rooted in the community; and a club where profit is reinvested, not pocketed or paid out in dividends to shareholders.

However, all has not been well and not as perfect as it seems. Entrenched club President Nunez is being fiercely opposed by a group called L'Elefant Blau who not only want to provide an alternative but also challenge what they see as a creeping commercialism in the club. The group fears that Nunez wants to use the club's centenary celebrations – Barcelona 2000 – to float the club on the stock market. The fact that Barcelona 2000 is itself a commercial venture has heightened the perception that flotation will come through the back door.

L'Elefant Blau is a new type of organisation in Spanish football, organised more on the lines of an English supporters' group, appealing to all fans and on a campaigning model. One key difference, however, is that they have a democratic structure – of sorts – to work within. Nunez may have a grip on power, an ability to pack meetings and votes with his sympathisers, and the power of the club machinery at his disposal, but at least there are mechanisms for his removal. L'Elefant Blau set about organising a vote against Nunez at around the same time as Murdoch was moving on United. The group wanted to hold a ballot of Barcelona members on Nunez's regime. However, using his institutional powers, the President refused the group access to the club database, making it difficult to contact members. They needed 5 per cent of members to force a vote of no confidence, and they achieved this by getting 6,000 fans to sign a petition at a stall they organised on Las Ramblas. In the end Nunez survived the vote by getting enough of his loyalists to support him, but only just. L'Elefant Blau are now involved in building support for the next scheduled vote on Nunez's presidency, which, if successful, should be in time to block Barcelona going the way of Manchester United.

There were clear sympathies between the two groups which Murdoch's bid for United highlighted, not least the problems of plc status and a self-belief in the ability to overcome huge odds through uniting fans' forces. A delegation of IMUSA members first met L'Elefant Blau at United's Champions' League match in Barcelona in November 1998. Andy Walsh describes the meeting of fans, and minds:

> Lee Hodgkiss and I went on a wing and a prayer to Barcelona with hotel accommodation but no tickets. IMUSA member Mick Meade had lined up an interview on Radio Barcelona's sports show the night before the match. The show's presenter, Bernard Soleh, had been at the Bridgewater Hall meeting in September and was so impressed by what he had seen that he wanted to do an interview live on air. Bernard put us in touch with L'Elefant Blau. We left the radio studios and made our way to L'Elefant Blau's offices where six of their committee members met us to explain what they were trying to achieve and express solidarity with our fight to stop Murdoch.
>
> They were obviously following the Sky deal very closely as demonstrated when the President of the group, Joan La Porta, showed us a file of Spanish and Catalan newspaper clippings

detailing IMUSA's campaign back home. L'Elefant Blau were using our fight to illustrate to Catalonians what could happen to Barca should Nunez get his way. It is a very real possibility that Joan could be elected to replace Nunez in the not too distant future, securing the future independence of one of the world's great football institutions.

One of the ideas being discussed at the time in IMUSA was to hold an academic conference on the running of football, to bring together the learned and the practitioners to highlight the alternatives which football had to choose from. SUAM's Jonathan Michie, a professor at Birkbeck College, University of London, took up the challenge and a two-stage conference was planned for 1999. The first stage was an invite-only 'pre-conference' organised for 3 February. L'Elefant Blau and IMUSA had got on so well in November that a delegation of the Catalans came to London to dispel some myths. Barcelona had been talked about increasingly as a model European club and L'Elefant Blau set about outlining the problems they faced and the intrusion of commercial priorities at the club. One of those in attendance was Armand Caraben, former general manager of the club, who had been responsible for signing Johann Cruyff! Having Tommy Docherty opposing the Sky deal in the media just didn't seem quite the same, Lou Macari or no Lou Macari!

Although contact was maintained, the next time the groups got together was in the euphoria (and, for the Bayern lads, agony) of the European Cup final. Where once rival fans may have fought, NR12 came prepared to declare their intentions on the eve of that historic match:

> Football supporters all over Europe should co-operate in solidarity to protect the football as well as the supporters' rights. [This] we did at our Champions' League match at Manchester when we unfurled a banner with the writing 'Stop Murdoch' on it, to demonstrate our solidarity with the Man U supporters in their fight against their club's take-over by Rupert Murdoch's BSkyB. This is why we are looking forward to joining a coalition of supporters' groups from Barcelona and Manchester with the aim to build up a European supporters' organisation.

Andy Walsh recalls:

> Returning to Barcelona was a sheer joy. It's one of the best football stadiums in the world and one of the most wondrous cities in Europe, and my team were playing there in the European Cup final – a football fan's nirvana. With the links IMUSA had developed during the season it could not have worked out better, the fan

groups Club NR12 of Bayern Munich and L'Elefant Blau of Barca were now close allies, sharing a similar outlook on the game and vision of the future. Another radio interview was lined up for Tuesday night with Bernard at Radio Barcelona but Dominik and Gregor from Bayern had to organise the huge mosaic. Literally a ton of paper had been transported in three cars from Bavaria for the match the following night. The effect was witnessed right around the world. So we arranged to meet them on the day of the game on the Wednesday afternoon. After that amazing win, like most United fans we headed straight for the bar to celebrate and met Joan – Club NR12 understandably didn't join us! Dominik did send a message a few days later asking if IMUSA knew any Gillingham fans as they were interested in 'establishing a suicide pact'!

The prospects for and development of an alliance of supporters' groups across Europe, cementing such ties, has now become one of IMUSA's priorities for 1999–2000.

There is a common thread, from Doncaster, to Hull, to Chester, to Brighton, to Palace, to Portsmouth, right up to Southampton, Newcastle and Manchester United. In each and every case the problems stem from the question of ownership. Whether they wanted to sell the land the ground was on, or wanted to cash in on their plc status, the anger of fans was brought about by the decisions of the clubs' owners. Not only that, but in England, had the FA's rules on ownership – designed to prevent profiteering from clubs – been updated and upheld, and had fans been key elements of the ownership equation, the problems would have been far less likely to occur. This must be the lesson for the future of fans' involvement in running football. If clubs are to be run in the interests of fans and football as a whole then supporters must have an ownership role.

The same appears to apply across the water at Bayern Munich and Barcelona. The forces of darkness are gathering in front of fans' noses. The G14, who, like so many horses of the apocalypse, are likely to reach the bottom of their current trough and be looking soon for pastures new to feed their bloated stomachs. The time for a European network of supporters, to lobby, protest and voice opposition, has never been more needed. The Sky take-over bid saw what may be the beginnings of this. As the world gazed into the media glare of some of 1998–99's most glamorous European fixtures, in the side streets and bars around the grounds, out of range of arc light and microphone, fans of these great European clubs were saying to each other: 'enough is enough'.

By the end of October 1998, the unity which supporters' organisations had demonstrated against the BSkyB take-over of Manchester United was beginning to tell.

SIX

THE MONOPOLIES AND

MERGERS COMMISSION

However well things seemed to be going, however wide support was becoming, the serious business of making submissions to the Monopolies and Mergers Commission was, by mid November 1998, the crux of the matter. Time was short. The MMC was to report by 12 March, with the Trade Secretary given another four weeks to deliberate and make his verdict on the MMC's report. But submissions to the MMC had to be in before the end of November, with face-to-face hearings to be held through December and January.

It was here that IMUSA and SUAM's ability to draft in academic, legal and financial help paid off. Their detailed submissions, combined with those from academics, accountants and lawyers, raised the public interest issues to the top of the agenda and put both BSkyB and Manchester United on the defensive. The advantage was hammered home by other third parties, including the All Party Group of MPs, the Independent Television Commission and the National Union of Journalists. This was make or break time; the chance was there; performance, persuasion and watertight argument were what counted. With just about every interested party coming out against the take-over, and only BSkyB and Manchester United seemingly in favour, the proposers faced a tidal wave of opposition. How much that counted at the MMC, though, was unknown.

The MMC panel was chaired by Dr Derek Morris, Emeritus Fellow in Economics of Oriel College, Oxford. With him were Nicholas Finney, Managing Director of the Waterfront Partnership; David Jenkins, General Secretary of the Welsh TUC; Roger Munson, a Chartered Accountant from Coopers and Lybrand; and Dr Gill Owen, Chair of the Public Utilities Access Forum and an environmental consultant. A formidable bunch, and about to decide the future of Manchester United.

That the future of England's biggest football club, and by implication, the future direction of the game itself, had come to this was a pretty dire indictment of English football's ruling bodies. The FA had let the powerful and wealthy dominate the development of the game since the 1980s. They had let clubs bypass the FA's own rules of membership so that clubs became a source of profit. They had let some become so powerful that they were dictating to the rest; and they had let television's dollar shine so brightly it mesmerised and blinded the clubs' chairmen. As such, the FA had invited the corporate take-over into their home, like a senile old duffer showing a burglar his family silver.

So now everything rested on the MMC. The campaign had come further than many had dared imagine back at the beginning of September; the deal had gone to the OFT; the OFT had been bombarded with submissions calling for an MMC referral; a massive PR campaign had been mounted which eclipsed that of two organisations many, many times as wealthy and powerful as IMUSA and SUAM; an alliance of forces crossing every social class, political persuasion and profession had been mustered; fans had lobbied, argued, persuaded, written, e-mailed, cajoled and worked so damn hard that the campaigners' lives weren't the same anymore. Now supporters had to go and give the performance of their lives. The Cup final had been reached, and nobody was going to remember the losers.

The network of those making submissions was by now extensive and well connected. Time was very short and people were tired. However, boosted by what campaigners rightly saw as a 'stage victory' in the referral itself, things moved quickly. Information about what arguments to make and how to approach the subjects was shared quickly. E-mails flew around the IMUSA list and submissions were posted on IMUSA and SUAM websites. IMUSA's *pro bono* lawyers, Lovells, were unable to provide the resources for the MMC inquiry – they had done enough already – and they confirmed that the OFT submission needed no revision. In order to get a second opinion, Nick Toms and Andy Walsh went to see Conor Quigley QC, an expert in European Competition Law and yet another United fan who was willing to offer his services for free. Conor confirmed that the OFT submission was well argued so the invitation to appear before the MMC itself was awaited.

A decision was made to keep the competition arguments confidential so that the opposition didn't have advance knowledge of the issues being put forward. However, the process was different from the OFT consideration in that it would be the strength of argument, as opposed to the strength of public disquiet, that counted. As such, there was no wholesale assault of the MMC in the way that the OFT had been targeted. 'In this case it's going to be quality and not quantity which swings our case,' argued Jon Leigh. 'So we should not all write – we should help IMUSA put together our evidence and then IMUSA should write and present.'

Thus, there were two parts to the process: the arguments put forward on the issues of competition and public interest; and the presentations themselves.

The Written Submissions

Things started looking good pretty early. The MMC terms of reference had included both competition and public interest issues, which in itself was good news, but, having received all the submissions, they took the unprecedented step of outlining the questions their inquiry would address. In a press release on 8 December, the MMC said, 'the group believes that it would be beneficial to the inquiry to make public its thinking on what issues it has to address'. Within the Fair Trading Act of 1973, the public interest is defined as 'maintaining and promoting effective competition'; 'promoting the interests of consumers, purchases and other users of goods and services . . . in respect of prices charged for them and in respect of their quality and the variety'; and 'promoting, through competition, the reduction of costs and . . . facilitating the entry of new competitors into existing markets'; and 'maintaining and promoting the balanced distribution of industry and employment'. [FTA s.84(1)]

The first question for the MMC was the nature and definition of existing markets within which BSkyB and Manchester United operate; what market power the companies had and the likely impact of the RPC case, digital broadcasting, PPV, ownership and organisation of football. Second were the reasons for the merger, Murdoch's motives. Third were the various scenarios should the bid go ahead, including its likely effect on: BSkyB's advantages over other broadcasters; breakaways as a credible possibility for United; MUTV; preventing other broadcasters buying rights to United and others' matches under individual negotiation; the rules of the Premier League; inducing other media–club mergers; and its effect on media access to players and barriers to growth. Fourthly, they wanted to know the effects on consumers regarding: price for matches, BSkyB channels and merchandise; the supply of PPV; the removal of free-to-air coverage of matches; the rescheduling of matches; possibilities for reducing or increasing spending on players; the effect on competition between teams; the conflict of interest between sporting and televisual priorities; the possibility of exacerbating the wealth gap to the detriment of poorer teams and fans; and the choice of ground location and competition. Fifthly, the group wanted to know if other aspects of football might be affected, including the authority of the game's ruling bodies, the overall ownership of English football, further loss of supporters' influence and whether News International's interests would be paramount. Finally, the MMC wanted to know about what remedies might be possible.

Thus, there were two core areas: competition within the pay-TV market and the threat to the public interest. The first of these encompassed concerns about both the pay-TV market and competition in football; the later issues included the effect of the deal on the consumer and the wider future of the game.

Competition in the Pay-TV Market

It was widely established that football was a key area of the premium pay-TV market. Indeed, in the OFT's 1996 *Review of BSkyB's Position in the Wholesale Pay-TV Market* it had stated: 'We were satisfied that there were no close substitutes for live Premier League rights. On a hypothetical monopolist test, live Premier League football would constitute a separate market.' As such, the power of Premiership football in getting people to subscribe was regarded as sufficient to designate that area of pay-TV as a discrete market. In this BSkyB clearly had a monopoly: 'Therefore, exclusive control of live rights to Premiership football forecloses a relevant market because live Premiership football constitutes a discrete market.' [IMUSA (b) 5.6; references in this chapter refer to MMC submissions, unless indicated.] The importance of sport to selling pay-TV had been well established, not least by Murdoch himself, and as IMUSA argued, 'The fortunes of BSkyB itself are a case in point. BSkyB saved itself from financial ruin effectively by securing live Premiership football on an exclusive basis in 1992.' [IMUSA (b) 3.7]

How would the merger affect this situation? There were effectively two scenarios. One was where the Office of Fair Trading win their restrictive practices court case and clubs have to sell TV rights individually; the other was if the existing collective selling arrangements continued and where Sky would be in competition with others for all the Premiership's TV rights. In both cases, argued the campaigners, Sky owning United would give them an unfair competitive advantage.

> [In the first case] BSkyB's ownership of the club . . . would ensure that they were able to acquire the rights to televise Manchester United matches and subsequently dominate the whole market. This is a clear case of market distortion which eliminates competition from other television companies to acquire rights to Manchester United – BSkyB would effectively be negotiating with themselves . . . In [the second] case BSkyB would still be in a very powerful position to ensure that they get the contract. Although Manchester United have only one vote in twenty at the Premier League, BSkyB's ownership of the club could mean that, for instance, the threat of withdrawal . . . would be enough to make sure that BSkyB are given the contract. Given Manchester United's dominant position within football, and their importance to the television football market . . . the threat of a United breakaway would undoubtedly be very powerful. [Brown, A. 3.2.2]

> If the RPC were to bring an end to the current bargaining arrangements, then other broadcasters would be at a competitive

disadvantage *vis-à-vis* BSkyB in attempting to secure television rights, since the biggest and most popular club would already be owned by one of the other broadcasting companies . . . The proposed acquisition would decrease competition through the vertical integration of the supplier and broadcaster of Manchester United football matches. [Michie *et al*]

If collective selling were to be maintained, BSkyB would have a 'seat at the table' when the Premier League Chairmen voted on who should be awarded the new television rights. They would, argued campaigners and rival broadcasters, not only have privileged information regarding the terms the Premier League were looking for but also, informally or formally, have detailed financial information about the league. Added to this was the importance that Manchester United had enjoyed historically in the organisation of football and its sale of rights:

In 1983, away teams were deprived of any share of gate receipts in league matches, to the obvious advantage of those, like United, who attract large home crowds; in 1988, a TV deal with ITV was agreed which gave the bigger clubs a much greater share of TV revenue; in 1992, the Premier League was formed by the FA. Such changes have generally been forced through at United's instigation. It is not thought that the other major domestic clubs have sought to force through any major changes with which United disagreed. [IMUSA (b) 4.1]

If BSkyB were to acquire United, the balance of power in negotiations for Premiership rights would change in a way that could only reinforce BSkyB's position of strength . . . thereby reinforcing BSkyB's dominance throughout the pay-TV sector. It is self-evident that a BSkyB-controlled United would object to live Premiership rights being awarded to any broadcaster other than BSkyB. [IMUSA (b) 5.8–5.9]

But how would they enforce this? Sky and United countered that the club would still only have one vote in twenty in deciding the future sale of rights and that bidding was undertaken on the principle that offers were sealed (secret) and final (they could not increase their offer). What they failed to do in their submissions was convince the MMC that information would not be passed between parent and club. Even so the possible abuse of their power was real:

United's influence over the Premier League, and indeed the FA and UEFA, has been greatly strengthened by Media Partners' proposal for a new European Super League. This proposal would enable United to leave the Premiership and to join a separate European football league comprising other major European clubs such as Juventus, Ajax and Bayern Munich. Since Premiership football would lose much of its appeal if United were no longer involved, the Premier League almost certainly has the need to keep United on-side. [IMUSA (b) 4.28]

Another argument was that their ownership of the club itself would deter others from bidding for rights and this was supported in testimony from OnDigital and Cable and Wireless. Further, the informal flows of information – a knowledge of the terrain on which bids were being made – could not be prevented. A third was that Manchester United's audience was singularly powerful within the pay-TV market and as such BSkyB could use their market power to ensure other clubs backed their bid, by offering either incentives or threats.

> Twenty per cent of all Premiership games shown live by BSkyB involved United; these United games accounted for 26.6 per cent of total viewing of live Premiership games; and average viewing of United games was 33 per cent greater than average viewing of Premiership games generally. [IMUSA (b) 5.1]

As such, the interests of football as a whole would also be jeopardised:

> Manchester United could be used to push for an acceptance of the BSkyB offer. They might do this even if the deal were not in the interests of the football industry taken as a whole, provided it was in the interests of their parent company, BSkyB.' [Michie *et al*]

In the scenario where clubs sold rights individually, the case was open and shut: if BSkyB owned United, they were not likely to sell their TV rights to anyone else. This might not prevent other broadcasters getting other clubs' rights, but the market as a whole would be distorted by the dominant position of both BSkyB and Manchester United as outlined in the viewing figures and market share. If BSkyB entered the market to sell subscriptions, they would be at a competitive advantage by owning the most watched club. What this also meant, therefore, was that BSkyB would be in a better position to obtain the rights to other clubs because of their stronger market position; they could offer more and would be a deterrent to others entering the market, in a clear breach of the Fair Trading legislation.

There was also the issue of ensuring that there was sufficient competition in new markets. The main area of concern was the digital pay-TV sector in which BSkyB's main competitor was OnDigital. It was argued by many who gave evidence that, should BSkyB be in a position where they could dominate the Premier League pay-TV market, through ownership of Manchester United, they could use this to achieve market power over OnDigital.

> The ability of BSkyB's competitors to mount a serious, long-term, competitive challenge to BSkyB in the retail market would be significantly undermined if they are dependent upon BSkyB for the supply of premium sports channel(s). [IMUSA (b) 5.3.1]

Lying behind this reasoning was a knowledge of the strategic reasons why Murdoch wanted to buy the club. As an internal memo submitted to the MMC outlined, the main one was to help secure the rights to live Premier League football.

> BSkyB are buying Manchester United so that they can ensure their position as suppliers of the best live football. Further evidence to support this is the fact that the proposed offer of £623m is a considerable amount of money to pay for a club which at present, even in its dominant position, turns over £90m a year, with a £20 to £25m profit margin. Unless the purchase is intended to make money elsewhere – i.e. through the sale of television subscriptions – it would take BSkyB many years to recoup the investment. It is, and must be viewed as, a strategic purchase to control the acquisition of television rights and as such is a threat to competition in that market. [Brown, A. 3.2.1]

The vertical integration of content and supply – the fact that one company owned the means to broadcast as well as what was being shown (Manchester United) – raised concerns about a conflict of interest. This conflict of interest existed on two levels. The main one was an immediate concern that what the parent company wanted – exciting content, cliff-hanger seasons, a variety of winners – was not what the fans wanted or what the club were obliged as a fair sporting institution to attempt to do, which was to win everything. This conflict was exposed using quotes from Sky themselves. As one IMUSA member, Paul Windridge argued in his submission:

> If BSkyB bought the club, would they really want United to win everything all the time? Of course not – that would be bad business. Vic Wakeling, MD of Sky Sports, said, 'What we don't want to happen in English football is perhaps what's happened in Scottish football, where Rangers won nine titles in a row.'

Such an attitude contrasted sharply with Mark Booth's assertion that 'Man U fans want to win the Cup – we want to win the Cup', and exposed the attempt to sit on two stools. A market distortion of this kind was not in the industry's or the public interest. The other conflict was the possibility that a Sky-owned United could be competing against other teams in which the parent company had an interest, either as the company who owned their TV rights or another club they part owned (the Canal Plus merger was still on the cards at the time). Both the European Commission and Sports Minister Banks had alluded to the problems this would create in maintaining the credibility and integrity of the sport.

The take-over also threatened competition because it threatened the existing structure of domestic and European football. On one level BSkyB could use ownership of the club to push for the individual sale of TV rights, whatever the RPC ruled, by persuading or enticing six other clubs to vote with them to stop any collective deal, enhanced by their commercial strength. On another level was the possibility of a breakaway. Again the votes of other clubs could be 'bought' with promises of TV coverage.

Another threat to the existing structures, which embodied the redistribution of TV income, was the likelihood that if this merger were allowed to proceed it would soon be followed by other clubs being bought by media companies. Such a situation would certainly destabilise the Premier League (each media company would own the rights to their club, precipitating individual selling), threatening the viability of smaller clubs. This line of argument led to a debate about the football industry and competition within it.

Competition in Football

Testimony on the question of how the merger would affect the football market – the 'live' market as opposed to the televised – centred on a number of points.

The premise of these concerns was that football was a different kind of business from others. One might expect market concentration in most sectors of business and, indeed, the entertainment industry. In the popular music industry, for instance, five multi-national record companies account for something like 80 per cent of global sales, and when one company buys another (Seagram/Universal's purchase of Polygram) or is vertically integrated at all levels (Sony) there are few questions raised. So what is different about football?

One is the dynamic between club and 'consumer' (supporters).

> The crucial difference in understanding the dynamics of the football industry is that, for the vast majority who pay to go to games . . . the

motivation is an emotional 'support' for a particular team. The prime
motivation for the consumer then – the football fan – is not which
supplier offers best value for money for the given product (either live
or televisual football); nor is there the normal competition between
suppliers of the same product. For the consumer of 'live' football,
each company – football club – within the football industry is itself
the sole supplier of the product they wish to purchase, competitive
football played by 'their' football team. [Brown, A. 1.1]

At the base of the industry, the main dynamic is not a market battle between
companies to provide the best value for money for the same product, but
the purchase of different products from different suppliers. 'Football is not
just another product like a soap-powder, car or washing machine,' IMUSA
argued, 'but entails an emotional investment by the consumer, or fan.' This
was supported by various studies of the football market:

> The relationship between a team and its supporters is exceptional in
> the sense that the customers do not need success . . . fans can
> therefore constitute for some teams a real asset of truly intangible
> nature. [Salomon Brothers 1997: 9]

Although success for football clubs will usually bring bigger audiences, a
club's market potential is also constrained and defined by its geographical and
socio-economic location (Leeds United have a bigger potential audience than
Oxford). However, what is also true is that the 'audience' is not transferable –
the football fan will not start supporting another team if either the quality of
the product declines or the price increases – and the more people there are
wanting to see a particular team, the more dominant the club is over its fans.
In this sense Manchester United possess market power, as the MMC eventually
concluded: 'All football clubs with a strong supporter base will have a degree
of market power. Because it is particularly well supported, Manchester
United's power is greater than that of most other clubs.' [MMC 2.73]

Another factor marking football as a different kind of business is the
historical nature of football clubs as companies.

> Football clubs started off as local community organisations . . .
> Manchester United evolved from a team of railway workers from the
> carriage and wagon department of the Lancashire and Yorkshire
> Railway's engine shed at Newton Heath. [IMUSA (a) 2.2]

As such, they had a role over and above that of making money. One, they
were sporting institutions and only became limited companies with the
professionalisation of the game, mostly in the late nineteenth century. Two,

these companies operated under strict conditions which meant that clubs were not seen as a source of profit, enshrined in the FA's Rule 34 (see chapter two).

This rule, together with a redistribution of both gate and television income, meant that the normal concentration of capital in a business was restricted, a balance was maintained. The 'success' of the English football industry historically is that as a business, football has ninety-two clubs able to compete with each other in a relatively meaningful manner. Although, of course, there have been some teams which have dominated periods of time (Arsenal in the 1930s, Liverpool in the 1970s and '80s, Manchester United in the late 1960s and '90s) and as such have been the more successful businesses, this position has not been entrenched and failure has followed success. The determinant of this success or failure has remained largely on the field of play.

With the introduction of more normal commercial imperatives in the 1980s, 'League football's communal character [which] was maintained by redistributing money from gate receipts, sponsorship and television from the big clubs to the small' [IMUSA 2.4] has been diminished. No club exemplifies this more than Manchester United, who have dominated the 1990s to an extent rarely matched. Combined with the success on the field, the club has out-performed in a commercial sense as well. Deloitte and Touche stated that: 'Manchester United could claim to be the biggest club in the world in financial terms,' and at the domestic level, they concluded that, 'Manchester United dominated the financial performance of all clubs; their pre-tax profits exceed the whole turnover of Division Three; and the club's operating profit is about 30 per cent of all total Premier League operating profits.' [Boon, 1999] As the All Party Group of MPs argued:

> The sheer size and strength of Manchester United means that they are already four or five times bigger than their average opponents in the Premier League and compared to foreign teams they are already bigger than Inter Milan and Juventus put together. [APFG 22]

The MPs further commented that checks had always existed in football to safeguard against one or more clubs becoming too powerful and therefore unchallengeable: wage restraint, the transfer system, the dividing of gate receipts, and controls on directors' income and share dividend payments. 'Now all these checks have gone. Remorselessly the bigger clubs have got richer and the smaller teams struggle against bankruptcy.' [APFG 46]

The proposal, that the dominant force in television sport buy the dominant force in English football, threatened to exaggerate this division of wealth. Manchester United had already led the way in getting a bigger share of the football pot than others and the deal offered two more drivers for increasing this financial dominance. One was that Manchester United would benefit from having the backing of a very powerful company, eight times the size of the existing plc. This would give the club the power to bankroll commercial and playing developments. Second, the bid threatened to restrict the supply of TV income to the clubs' competitors, other football clubs.

It was a double whammy for any club not likely to be snatched up in a rash of media take-overs, which included most of football. The leaders disappear into the distance, at the same time as cutting off the fuel supply. It posed an acceleration of United's domination, to the detriment of competition within football. How could you have a repetition of the Wimbledon example where a non-League club was able to rise to the Premiership, against such financial odds? Such a reorganisation of business may be acceptable in some industrial sectors, but such an approach does not take account of the peculiar nature of the football industry, and football as a sport, as the Professional Footballers' Association outlined:

> The element of competition in professional football has declined during the last two decades as earlier principles of equal distribution, for example, of commercial and television income have been eroded . . . Whilst it is appreciated that certain clubs in big cities would naturally gravitate toward the top, nevertheless professional football has managed to maintain the 'dream factor' so essential in sport, making it possible for clubs such as Wimbledon to come from outside the four full-time divisions into the top level . . . Sport needs a competitive atmosphere in order to thrive whereas, of course, business often looks to remove competition. [PFA]

Public Interest

This links to the issues that campaigners had advocated on the basis of the public interest. One fear was the implications the take-over had for a sport which has proved itself unique in British society. As IMUSA argued: 'this is a case where it is appropriate that wider considerations should be taken into account in addition to any adverse effect on competition. This is very much a test case. It is clear that if this merger goes ahead it will be followed by the take-over of other football clubs by media/communications companies.' [IMUSA (a) 1.3] It would set a precedent which, sure as one plastic pitch followed another, would blight the game. As soon as the bid was announced, Arsenal were linked with Carlton; Aston Villa with Central TV; and NTL made an agreement to take over Newcastle United. With a plethora of other broadcast and media interests owning other football clubs, the overall prospect was that football's future would be determined by the priorities of a handful of media companies.

'Very soon,' argued Jon Leigh, 'there could be no more than half a dozen English clubs monopolising football.' The national game would be in the control of global TV. Paul Windridge highlighted the positive opportunities which an appraisal of the bid provided: 'This has now become a real opportunity for change, to set the game of football back on its true path. A path that supporters want to walk . . . football does not need . . . to be dominated by the media.'

That football, and football clubs, should be allowed to determine their own future was a core argument. The sale of Manchester United to BSkyB would mean the sale of the country's football club to an American-owned multinational. The government had blocked certain sales of key UK businesses to foreign companies before – would the MMC accept such public interest here? The importance of football within society was a crucial element: it was an economic, social and cultural asset. No other pursuit has captured the imagination of such a large proportion of the British for such a long time as football. The 1960s football writer Arthur Hopcraft was quoted in one submission:

> The point about football in Britain, is that it is not just a sport people take to, like cricket or tennis or running long distances. It is inherent in the people. It is so much a part of national life, it is not a phenomenon; it is an everyday matter. There is more eccentricity in deliberately disregarding it than in devoting a life to it. It has more significance in the national character than theatre has. [Hopcraft, 1969]

To let such an important part of the nation's life be jeopardised by putting television interests in the driving seat, particularly at a time of such uncertainty about the game's future, would be the greatest folly, argued campaigners.

Football clubs had always remained independent entities. Many of them have been owned or controlled by individual or consortia of local businesses. The flotation of clubs on the stock market opened the way for corporate control to move in, as in the BSkyB take-over, which would make football clubs a small part of a much bigger concern. This raised issues both about the role of clubs in the local community as well as the ability to determine its (and football's) own future. 'It will mark the end of Manchester United as an independent entity,' argued IMUSA.

> Up until now the football club has been a largely self-contained operation. Even when it became a public limited company the

football club remained the core of the business. This will not be the case once Manchester United plc become just one small part of News Corporation's global media empire. [IMUSA (a) 2.2.7]

The global performance of the brand would be as important as the performance of the team on the pitch; the priority would not be footballing success (though this might coincide at times) but what the subsidiary football club could deliver to the parent company. 'It is essential,' Michel Platini was quoted as saying in one submission 'that football remains in the hands of football people.' [Windridge, p7]

It would also remove the club yet further from its roots as a Manchester institution. Given that one of the criteria of the Fair Trading Act is 'maintaining and promoting a balanced distribution of industry and employment in the United Kingdom', there is also a concern with the public interest at a local, city level.

> Manchester United is undoubtedly one of the city's biggest assets, attracting visitors and investment from across the world . . . its symbolic significance to the image of the city and subsequently the local economy should not be underestimated . . . Such a reputation is not built on economic performance on the stock market, but on a footballing reputation and tradition. Clearly BSkyB wish to exploit this reputation . . . given the nature of the company [BSkyB] – largely owned and certainly controlled by a foreign multinational – how can anyone expect them to be sensitive to such intangible, yet vital, local concerns which ultimately have an enormous impact on the region's economy? [Brown, A. 4.1]

There were further public interest concerns for the MMC, in terms of how the deal would affect the consumer, the football fan. This concern was on two levels – the consumer of pay-TV football and the consumer of live football. BSkyB had already used its position as sole supplier of live Premiership football to steadily increase revenue from its retail sale. Campaigners said that Sky was already abusing its position: Premiership football had cost no extra to the basic subscription in the beginning; within seven years this cost jumped to £22 per month, an increase of 300 per cent. They had also created more than one sports channel, with separate additional subscriptions on the other channels. Even for 'communal' subscribers such as public houses – a means by which those who cannot afford the individual subscription can still watch the national game – the cost has risen way above the rate of inflation, suggesting that BSkyB was already abusing its market dominance.

But Sky's impact has been on more than prices. The introduction of live matches on Sundays and Mondays; the late 'booking' of live games which are particularly attractive and the use of morning kick-offs, have all contributed to a manipulation of live fixtures with little or no consideration of the consumer. Manchester United faced mid-week fixtures at Southampton on two consecutive seasons, meaning fans had to take time off work and do a 500-mile round trip to see the fixture.

Given that one of News Corporation's priorities was the Far-Eastern market, the threat of kick-off times and fixtures being arranged to suit that audience highlighted the perils of the take-over for the match-going fan. For instance, should News Corp find that they were actually making much more money from viewers in another part of the world than in England – and more than they were getting through gate receipts – it is perfectly feasible that matches would be arranged accordingly. For most fans, the detail of how TV rights were bought and sold was not exactly a top priority. What did matter was the impact which ownership of those rights had on matches, fixtures and the competitions clubs were in. The integration of one market (TV) with another (football) was looking particularly unfavourable for the match-going fan.

IMUSA also highlighted that the limited influence fans have on decision-making at a club level would be further diminished, as the club moved from one with football as its core business, to a multinational-controlled TV company. 'The views of supporters will be further marginalised; the exploitation of supporters will be increased; and the heritage and traditions of Manchester United will be jeopardised.'

Other concerns for public interest were raised. One was that Murdoch's global empire was a complex web of companies, yet was particularly strong in the UK, with major media interests. Jonathan Michie highlighted the dangers in the particular context of Manchester United, raising yet further competition objections:

> The proposed acquisition would risk an abuse of cross-media promotion. There would be a continual danger of BSkyB as well as *The Sun* and *The Times* newspapers promoting Manchester United, MUTV, Manchester United magazine, Manchester United radio, Manchester United videos and other Manchester United related outlets at the expense of the competitors to all these publications, products and services. [Michie *et al*]

It also meant that the UK exchequer would not benefit in terms of the balance of trade and tax revenue, by putting ownership and control of Manchester United into the hands of a global media empire. By the end of the MMC's 'third party' hearings, they could hardly have been getting a very positive spin on what the bid meant. Whether or not it was in the public interest, it certainly wasn't what the public wanted. The weight of opposition was huge.

The Removal of the Middle Ground

One of the options which both the MMC and the Secretary of State for Trade and Industry would have to contemplate was the possibility that the bid could go ahead, but only if conditions were placed on the activities of the company. A genuine fear of campaigners was that certain restrictions would be imposed, which Murdoch had proved elsewhere very adept at slipping out of. The strategy was to remove the middle ground. Make it clear to the MMC that no conditions would do, that safeguards and Murdoch went about as well together as Alex Ferguson and tea cups: sooner or later they'd get broken.

Murdoch had been here before, and had not showered himself in glory. When he bought *The Times* and the *Sunday Times* in the early 1980s a referral to the MMC was avoided on the promise that ownership of the company would not be transferred to News International and that there would be no interference with editorial policy. Within a year the flagship papers were part of News International and the editor, Harold Evans, sacked. Campaigners dug up the following evidence that Murdoch didn't just break conditions, he revelled in it:

> One thing you must understand Tom, you tell these bloody politicians whatever they want to hear, and once the deal is done you don't worry about it. They're not going to chase after you later if they suddenly decide what you said wasn't what they wanted to hear . . . they just stick their heads up their asses and wait for the blow to pass. [T. Kiernan, 1986: p238]

'So what if Sky guarantees that they would not withdraw United from competitions; that they would sit out of negotiations on TV rights; that they would not get exclusive rights to broadcast?' asked the MMC. Evidence was cited of Murdoch's willingness to break up existing structures and risk the very future of a sport to stop competitors in his handling of the rugby league saga in Australia and his track record in America, where he had shown little sympathy to the traditions of the Dodgers baseball team. Combined with all this was the uncertain framework in which Sky would be operating. No one knew what the structure of English and European football was going to be, or the mode in which rights were to be sold, and thus, it was argued, it would be foolish to put conditions on the deal when they may be totally inappropriate in a few years' time. In particular the suggestion that no information would be leaked between the club side of the business – details of Premier League meetings, for instance – and the television side had to be undermined.

> First, it would be virtually impossible to be confident that a behavioural undertaking would continue to remedy a particular concern in the future when so much uncertainty exists. Secondly, it would be very difficult in practice to monitor any undertakings to check that they continued to be effective. [IMUSA (b) 6.5]

The MMC, time and again, faced the argument that there was no safeguard. In the middle of that middle ground, those making submissions attempted to dig a great big hole into which it was hoped the bid would fall.

Finally, Jonathan Michie sought to address the contradiction in the take-over business and highlight the peculiar nature of publicly owned football clubs. This was an issue that was to resurface once the process was over. What sort of club do supporters want? What role should shareholders have? How do you organise things?

> The peculiar nature of the football industry can, finally, be illustrated with reference to one of the consequences that the proposed acquisition would have . . . namely that several thousand shareholders who have a keen and passionate interest in the future success of the company in which they have a stake (as owners as well as supporters) will be forced by law, against their will, to part with their shares . . . BSkyB have made clear that their aim is to acquire the 90 per cent of shares which would then allow them, by force of law, to require all remaining shareholders – which in the case of Manchester United plc would consist of several thousand fans – to then part with their shares in their club. As one shareholder put it at the November 1998 Manchester United plc AGM, his share certificate is displayed proudly on his wall at home; he will not be replacing it with a share certificate in BSkyB. [Michie *et al*]

The Presentations

Once papers were prepared, experiences were shared by those known to be sympathetic, so others would be ready for the ordeal. Sky and United would be doing everything in their power and they had the expensive, professional help to get them through it. Although confident in the arguments, knowing the deal to be wrong, it was still necessary to perform. The MMC's statement on the issues it would cover was hugely encouraging.

This occurred on 8 December, four days after Adam Brown had been before them, but before IMUSA and the FSA on 11 December and SUAM and Jonathan Michie *et al* after Christmas.

The MMC panel goes through the evidence put down on paper with a fine-tooth comb and they then question witnesses on it for hours. It's about as far from the experience of going to a football match as it is possible to get: a different world for many of those involved. Adam Brown was first up in their London offices:

> Addressing the MMC is a bit like going in front of a tough job-interview panel, but without the freedom to bullshit. You're faced with professors of economics, industrialists, financial experts, trade unionists and their back-up. I was kept waiting for half an hour – apparently they were in the middle of a debate about what constituted the 'market' in this case. Having not resolved that one, they clearly decided they'd better hit me with it almost as soon as I'd sat down. A curve ball, as the BSkyB execs would say. You're there, on one side of a fine old, U-shaped oak table, and across the way there's four MMC members [Nicholas Finney was not in attendance] and a staff of ten or so.
>
> I just remember being very hot and really wanting to take my jacket off but not wanting to get distracted by anything. The discussion was very intense and in your mind was always: 'you've got to get this right; this really matters'. Afterwards I didn't feel like I'd given it my best. Munson had seemed most hostile and has a bit of an off-putting manner when he clearly disagrees with you; the union chap, Jenkins and Gill Owen, most sympathetic; and Morris, the chair, played it like a firm-but-fair school master – a straight bat. Difficult to know what they were thinking at that stage, but at least they were tackling all the right issues.
>
> Once outside I looked at my watch and realised that what was supposed to be an hour-and-a-half session had been over two and a half. I was jiggered. Re-reading the transcript, it doesn't seem that bad – a working over of the issues we had all been talking about for weeks. Who knows whether it made a difference at the end of the day? They must have heard the same arguments from so many people. At least I did my bit.

The Football Supporters' Association made their submission on the same day as IMUSA, early in the morning. Represented by Alison Pilling and Tim Whelan, the nature of the whole event had struck the pair as somewhat bizarre, as Alison Pilling recalls:

Tim and I met the MMC in a hotel off Piccadilly Gardens which was quite plush, although looking like it had seen better days, very colonial. Appropriately, I felt a bit like one of the native servants who had been asked to see the Master about someone stealing the family silver or something, with the kindly old Master gently quizzing us about points in our submission. I find one of the most intimidating things about official functions is the little details. Everyone in the room had a neat pad of paper in front of them and a newly sharpened pencil alongside a glass and a bottle of Perrier water. I can't help thinking that I would have been much more relaxed with a pint of lager and a blotchy biro.

The 'biggy' in many ways was IMUSA's time before the panel. Having led the campaign against Murdoch from day one, now was the time to show that this supporters' organisation had grown up. It was all well and good being on hand to offer a sparky quote to the media every time United courted controversy, and it had been another step to handle the press in the unbelievably professional manner the organisation had done, but it was quite another still to prove yourself in front of the combined forces of the MMC. Mark Southee, pen at the ready as always, was on hand:

When I joined IMUSA I volunteered to help out in any way I could. But not even in my wildest, Guinness-fuelled fantasies did I imagine it would involve sitting in front of the Monopolies and Mergers Commission explaining why Rupert Murdoch should keep his print-stained hands off our club. But this is exactly the position we found ourselves in. This was the day we had been working towards almost since our campaign began, but it still took some grasping of what we were about to try and do. As no one (apart from ourselves) had given us a chance of even getting this far we were determined to show that behind the 'raggy arsed football supporter' exterior we knew what we were on about.

The previous Sunday we had met up with our legal eagle to discuss how we were going to handle our meeting. We had already had some feedback from IMUSA member Adam Brown that didn't make any of us feel any easier. Adam had been invited to the MMC in his role as academic/football writer and Task Force member and reported that he was given a bit of a grilling by the panel. As we had no idea how the meeting would run we decided to stick to specifics. We all knew the arguments inside-out, but getting them across clearly in such situations would be the hard part.

The arrangement was to meet in Wetherspoons at 1 p.m. before the meeting at the Piccadilly Hotel. Three of us – Nick 'Shellsuit'

Clay, Duncan Drasdo and myself – decided to meet up earlier for some last-minute swotting in a coffee bar. I don't think much sank in, but at least the caffeine intake would keep us alert! Meeting the rest at the allotted hour, the mood was very businesslike. Even Mr Briscoe was quiet (for Steve anyway!). With everyone assembled IMUSA 'went to work'. On getting out of the lift at the hotel we were surrounded by a media scrum. It is a shock to find cameras and microphones pointing in your direction and being expected to come out with something sensible, so the rest of us left the 'media whores' to it and waited to be summoned. This was the worst bit. If you can imagine a combination of your worst exam, your driving test and a dentist's waiting room you will get some idea of how I was feeling.

Eventually we were led into the room. Far from the instruments of torture I was expecting, the tables had bowls of sweets on them! Andy Walsh's opening speech was excellent and set the tone for the whole meeting, being serious, but not too much. We explained why IMUSA had come into being and some of the other issues that we had been involved with since its inception. At no time were we stuck for plausible answers. Far from being a torture session we were able to put ourselves across as confident and knowledgeable about what the panel were trying to find out. The ninety minutes seemed to pass in no time and we were deep into injury time when proceedings were stopped. We could have gone on for much longer but we had obviously tired the opposition, who ran out of questions!

With a promise to do some research and report back on some specific issues, we departed to the waiting media circus. With interviews completed we went for a 'debrief' in the Edwards bar, of all places! The consensus of opinion was that we could not have handled ourselves any better, we had done what was asked of us and a lot more besides. Edwards, Booth and co. may have dismissed us as irrelevant; the MMC most definitely did not. Whatever happened in March, at least we had given it our best shot.

Nick Clay had been heavily involved in the campaign, not least preparing IMUSA's written submission with the *pro bono* lawyers, Lovells.

Though not quite the finishing post, the MMC hearing was something of the high water mark for most of us . . . I kept telling myself it wasn't the be all and end all, but it was close. If we could come out with our credibility and arguments intact . . . we could pull off what had seemed impossible three months ago. All we had to do was convince a selection of the great and the good in a forum none of us had ever experienced.

All I can say of the hearing is that Andy Walsh led from the front. He had worked his butt off for three months on this. The passion and the certainty came through every single sentence he uttered. When one of us got into trouble, Andy was there with either a different perspective, or some rhetoric to steer us out of choppy waters . . . I really don't think the MMC were expecting, despite the depth and force of our written submissions, a group of football fans to come out with such powerful arguments.

Afterwards Andy had gone off to do some TV; the rest of us were absolutely buzzing. We raked over the embers and recalled some of our answers and insights – Andy's blinding insight into the way in which Mexican football had been taken over by media companies, and how we all nodded in agreement when none of us had the slightest idea what he was on about! There was only the Mandelson hurdle to clear now! The campaign had drawn those involved that day closer together . . . It was most definitely a unique set of circumstances, and however we may drift apart that day will remain unique.

Duncan Drasdo recalls:

I was surprised how much I had to say but actually enjoyed the experience in the end. A bit like after finishing an exam you thought was going to be much harder. My only disappointment was on reading the transcript – my best contribution, which even had the accountant [Munson] nodding in agreement, was attributed to Briscoe! One comment enjoyed by all was Nick Clay's attempt to paint a picture of going to the match after the MMC delegation had 'bought tickets' and attended the Leeds home game: 'Walking down Sir Matt Busby Way, the sights, the sounds, the smells – watching all the fans on the forecourt "interact" with each other.'

'I remember being in the lift with two other IMUSA members and three of the MMC panel,' says Paul Windridge. 'I looked them in the eyes and said, "Okay, you're not getting out of here until you promise to dump the bid."

'"No, don't do that," they replied humorously, "we've got to get home to our families tonight!"'

SUAM went before the MMC in January. Michael Crick describes:

We had been called to the MMC at their London HQ for Tuesday, 26 January . . . Our team was: me, Hytner, Nick Towle, Lucy Burns, Andrew Salton and Peter Crowther. We had a two-hour session in Peter's office a week beforehand – 20 January – and Peter had arranged a dress rehearsal the night before the MMC, with a serving member of the MMC as interrogator. Peter said he would also arrange for an academic colleague to come along too, and I was astonished when it turned out to be Stefan Szymanski, a good friend of mine who is an economist at Imperial College.

One area I elaborated on a lot was the question of whether it was realistic for United to break away from the Premier League if BSkyB lost the collective TV contract, an area IMUSA were asked about but never really answered in my view. I argued that this was a realistic threat, given: one, United's historic involvement in threatening breakaways; two, the Murdoch experience with Australian rugby league – noting how Mark Booth was then chief exec of Foxtel; three, the fact BSkyB could financially underpin United quite easily during a breakaway; and four, the growing alternative possibilities in Europe, which may soon make it quite difficult to fulfil Premiership fixtures anyway! Far more likely than United breaking away from the Premier League itself, I argued, was that United would refuse to fully honour a TV deal if it was with some other TV company, and the Premier League would then be unlikely to expel them. I pointed to the discrepancy between Tim Allen's statement on 9 September that the first thing Sky would do is have a price freeze – quoted in the *Manchester Evening News* and the *Evening Standard* – and Edwards' *United We Stand* interview statement that there would *not* be a price freeze.

I was surprised and pleased at how interested they were in arguments that Murdoch/News Corp have a terrible record of broken promises on take-over deals. They asked for more detail on this . . . Roger Munson wanted evidence that Murdoch had ever said he saw United as an insurance policy, in case the BSkyB–Premier League cartel was busted. We sent them an *FT* article from 3 October which said Murdoch indicated this . . . Finney wasn't there. Munson was hostile; Morris neutral; Owen quite sympathetic and Jenkins very sympathetic. We all felt they genuinely hadn't made their minds up yet and were really interested in what we had to say, all of which was good.

Following IMUSA's session, Andy Walsh posted the following e-mail message, reflecting the sentiments of many:

> I felt that today's meeting went better than we could have expected, you cannot help but get a tremendous sense of pride in our achieve-ments so far in this campaign but today was the culmination of not just three months' hard graft but three and a half years of tireless

work by dozens and dozens of dedicated Reds . . . If we do lose this fight, we can all look ourselves in the mirror and clearly state that we did our best and could not have done any more – but we ain't gonna lose, are we? We're gonna stuff the bastards, then the real fight starts to wrestle control of the club from Daddy's boy and create a club regime worthy of the supporters. Well done for today; just a few more months to go . . .

In a list that reads a bit like a Christmas carol – and a famously repetitive festive terrace song in honour of one Eric Cantona – by the end of the whole shooting match the MMC had seen the following: twelve broadcast companies; seven football authorities; six Premier League clubs; six fans' organisations; five local authorities; three Nationwide League clubs; three trades unions; seven other groups; three MPs and Manchester United and BSkyB.

They had also received testimony from over 300 individuals, every single one of whom was against the merger. Indeed, of all those who made submissions to, and appeared before, the MMC, the only ones to support the merger were the six Premier League clubs (all of whom, it was rumoured, were likely to follow United into media ownership) plus Manchester United and BSkyB. Whilst a handful of submissions were somewhat equivocal, believing that commercial restrictions, Chinese walls, or behavioural restrictions could work, the overwhelming majority of the testimonies were whole-heartedly against the merger.

This in itself was a fantastic victory for those who had been campaigning. True, some of the opposition was well-rooted self-interest, such as the rival TV companies, but most of the arguments centred around the issues which IMUSA, SUAM and the others had been banging on about from day one. Some campaigners had secondary evidence to prepare; corrections to statements made in the evidence sessions and further arguments against the bid. But apart from that the job was done.

As January 1999 drew to a close, a weird sense of calm descended as far as the take-over was concerned. There wasn't a great deal anyone could do now. Campaigners had pushed it this far, they'd argued the toss a thousand different times; they'd talked and talked and talked on the media, hammering home a phenomenal PR battle. Then they'd badgered and harried people and called in favours; gone to Parliament and got the MPs on-side; sat down and written a long and difficult testimony on the future of the broadcast industry. The fears for football and the importance that this case represented had seen fans delve into the murky past of the club's would-be suitor. Finally they had put it all on the line in a forum nobody had ever expected to be in and ended up central to a major commercial and political enquiry.

On the pitch things were anything but calm as United's season took off. From the defeat at home to Middlesbrough in December, the team didn't look back and weren't to lose again. Rising to the top of the Premier League at the end of January, the lads on the pitch had matched the sterling efforts of the fans off it, by putting themselves in contention. In the Cup, United saw off Middlesbrough and then produced the first miraculous comeback of the season defeating Liverpool in injury time with an Ole Solksjaer goal, having trailed since the fifth minute. The delirium and relief which that victory produced put concerns about the take-over temporarily out of everyone's minds as United fans lorded it in front of the demoralised Scousers.

The future of the season was in the players' hands now. The future of the club rested with the five members of the MMC: an economics professor, a trade unionist, a managing director, a chartered accountant and an environmental consultant. They had until 12 March to write their report and reach their conclusions; then it was all down to Stephen Byers. After all the activity and the work, there was nothing to do but wait and worry.

SEVEN

DECISION DAY

It wasn't as if things weren't interesting on planet football in the first few months of 1999; it was just campaigners couldn't do much about any of it. Like a shipbuilder pushing his latest creation out to sea they could do no more now to control events, in terms of influencing the MMC report, than watch it drift out to sea. IMUSA and SUAM had charted the course they thought it should take, given the stern a hearty slap with a bottle or two and sent it down the ramp. Which direction the captain and crew decided to follow was as yet unknown, and what storms it had to sail through were beyond them. And storms there were aplenty.

First to get washed overboard were the guardians of English football, FA Chair and Chief Executive, Keith Wiseman and Graham Kelly. Ostensibly it was for an unauthorised loan of £3m to the Welsh FA in return for the Welsh FA's support of Wiseman in his attempts to get on to the FIFA Council. The English FA was pursuing its target of staging the 2006 World Cup and felt that a seat at FIFA was a prerequisite. The two were found guilty by an FA Council sub-committee in December 1998 and Kelly resigned immediately. Wiseman, who had already been accused of profiteering at Southampton, needed a little more encouragement along the plank before he toppled over the edge of the good ship Lancaster Gate in January 1999.

Although 'cash-for-votes' was the immediate cause, many observers recognised the resignations as a *coup d'etat*. Modernisers within the FA had long been anxious to remove Kelly – who was viewed as a poor public 'face' for the organisation and resistant to change – and his ally Wiseman. They wanted a wholesale reorganisation, including a separation of the organisation of the amateur and professional game. Public Affairs boss David Davies has been cited as the eye of this revolutionising storm – one FA insider talked of him 'wining and dining as many FA Councillors as he can' over a year before the cash-for-votes scandal. There was certainly conflict between the departments of Public Affairs and Chief Executive, including clashes over Task Force roles. However, it was soon clear that although there was a coalition of forces involved in removing Kelly and Wiseman, there was much less agreement on what to do next. The second stage of the revolution – election of the new rulers – was to come at the FA's Annual General Meeting in June 1999.

At this meeting a valiant bid by Ipswich Town's David Sheepshanks, considered one of the more youthful and liberal contenders, was defeated by the Premier League's own champion and long-standing FA council member, Geoff Thompson. Although Ian Stott of Oldham was elected vice-chair, giving the Football League something to cheer about, it was widely recognised as an assertion of the Premier League clubs' power within the game's ruling body, particularly with the consolidation of a possible five out of six places on the professional clubs committee.

The second big name into the drink was Peter Mandelson, also in December 1998 (chapter four). Given his by now well-publicised belief that there were no competition issues to be resolved in the BSkyB deal, it was something of a relief. Although feelings were mixed at the time – some felt that his links with the Murdoch empire had worked in the campaign's favour – the thought that he would have the ultimate say over what to do with the MMC's final report sent a shudder down spines. Stephen Byers, who was brought aboard in his place, would prove more sympathetic. So a boat home for Christmas for Mandy; a bit of a shock for Byers, called to the captain's bridge; and a happier one for the life guards at IMUSA and SUAM.

Next, following a final loss of patience by the football world and the tabloids with the eccentricities of the England manager, Glenn Hoddle was sacked. Hot on his heels came the last but by no means least to sink to Davy Jones' locker, the twin heads of the Premier League, and once again financial issues were at the centre of matters. As their lawyers fought their corner in the RPC, and as the MMC geared up to deliver its verdict of the Sky take-over, the Premier League's chief executive, Peter Leaver QC and chairman, Sir John Quinton were busy promising private fortunes to two consultants. That these were former BSkyB executive Sam Chisholm and former BSkyB deputy managing director David Chance, and that they were to get vast sums of commission for negotiating the next Premier League TV deal, jarred with the concerns being raised about the game's future at the time. The pair were promised an annual consultancy fee of £600,000, a 5 per cent commission on improvements to the existing contract, a 5 per cent cut of pay-per-view deals and between 5 and 10 per cent of equity if the Premier League floated its own TV company. Nice work if you can get it.

Leaver and Quinton were on dodgy ground on two counts. One was the obscene sums being promised to Chisholm and Chance. The possibility of them making literally tens of millions offended chairmen of clubs who were struggling to meet rising salary costs for players, and it appalled the football-going public. Given that several clubs in football were bordering on extinction and the Premier League had promised the Task Force that it would give just 5 per cent of TV revenue to the whole of the rest of football (£120m over ten years was promised in June 1999), the deal was greed gone mad. Secondly, in an echo of the FA scandal, Leaver and Quinton had brokered this deal without consulting the rest of the Premier League.

The arrogance and avarice on display was astounding and drew the anger of supporters: 'The FSA believes that individuals amassing personal fortunes from the game is wholly unjustifiable and against principles of fair competition, redistribution of income and the health of the game.' [FSA Press Release, 12 March 1999] In a vote of confidence the Premier League overwhelmingly opposed Leaver and Quinton and they resigned on 11 March 1999. Given that BSkyB were in the dock at both the MMC and RPC, it was an amazing lack of judgement to have involved two former BSkyB executives in such an excessive remuneration package, without the consent of the League chairmen. Leaver was not popular anyway: considered highhanded, arrogant and rude in meetings he had offended many, including some on the Task Force, with his abrasive manner. There was hardly a well of sympathy on which he could draw to retrieve his position, and, with acting chairs and chief executives at both the FA and Premier League and an acting England manager, a vacuum opened up in the leadership of the English game at a time when it needed leadership most.

One side issue which is relevant here is that it emerged that Leaver had spoken to the MMC on behalf of the Premier League. In his evidence he said the merger 'would discourage others from bidding' for Premier League TV rights; would enable BSkyB to get confidential information to 'tailor its bid'; and that any remedies, in the form of ring-fenced business dealings, undertakings about confidential information being passed from United to the parent company, or preferences given to show United matches, would be 'difficult to enforce'. [MMC 6.105] It was a powerful message to the MMC against the take-over. Martin Edwards, who thought there was an agreement that the Premier League would remain neutral, was furious and was going to call Leaver to account at the March meeting. Unfortunately for the butcher's boy, by the time he came to the chopping board, someone had stolen the bacon.

By mid-January the Restrictive Practices Court was in full swing, with the Premier League and its allies desperate to protect the collective sale of TV rights. Campaigners started to hear some familiar arguments coming from unfamiliar mouths. Fans' groups had long argued that football had to be seen as a different kind of business, that it could not be legislated for in the same way as supermarkets, given the emotional ties of fans to clubs. Indeed, such a viewpoint was also supported at the 3 February conference at Birkbeck College hosted by Jonathan Michie, when business and economics experts from around the country outlined the different make-up of the football industry and the need for revenue sharing of TV income to maintain sporting competition.

It was odd, then, to hear a vigorous defence of the interests of smaller clubs from the very organisation which had plummeted them into crisis in the 1992 breakaway. Charles Aldous, the Premier League's QC, said that an abolition of collective selling

> . . . may be fine for one or two of the top clubs but it would be divisive and disastrous for smaller clubs. Independent licensing would result in a free-for-all with the Premier League being run for the benefit of the major broadcasting companies, who will acquire major stakes in clubs. It would result in bigger clubs playing at various times for the benefit of the broadcasters. [*The Guardian*, 13 January 1999]

The overlap with the deliberations of the MMC were startling and, for an organisation responsible for blowing a hole in the concept of redistribution of wealth, the hypocrisy was astounding. It was therefore encouraging to the campaign when the Football Task Force issued its third report, *Investing in the Community*. In it the Premier League got unequivocal backing for their court case, centred on the importance of redistributing money. As a *quid pro quo* they promised better redistribution. What was important for the campaign was further evidence that football had to be seen as a special case.

The Task Force's report actually saw another casualty: the PFA's Gordon Taylor resigned as the report was launched. Ostensibly about an invite to the launch itself, the resignation had a history dating back to a row between Mellor and Taylor over the commitment of players, Taylor's members, to community work. Although the PFA's own figures confirmed that players' community commitments were often not met, Taylor was right that such evidence, submitted in confidence, should not have appeared in the media prior to the report. The upset that had caused blew up in January, and the progressives on the Task Force had lost a vital ally.

Further shenanigans in the Task Force included a second attempt by Adam Brown, on 18 February, to get a statement against the Sky take-over from the body. Although unsuccessful, there was a silver lining. Both the FA and the Football League made it clear that their considerable evidence had highlighted the problems that the take-over represented. Although predecessors Kelly and Wiseman had been prepared to make this opposition public, it was comforting to know that the MMC had received another powerful broadside against the merger. In fact the FA and League argued that 'the proposed merger would inevitably lead to distortions of competition contrary to the public interest', and that 'there was unlikely to be any remedy short of prohibiting the merger that would be effective in eliminating anti-competitive effects'. [MMC 6.86; 6.87]

Having delivered their 'community' report, the Task Force set off to reach a consensus on the commercial aspects of its remit, including the thorny questions of controlling ticket prices, resolving the conflicts in plcs and the creation of a regulator for football. At the time of writing, the fleet appears divided and heading in different directions, with one half supporting an independent regulator and the other resisting any interference. The failure of the FA and Premier League to come up with proposals to adequately address the concerns initially raised in the Task Force's remit – reform of the game in the interests of fans – has merely polarised these divisions. Task Force destination: unknown.

A very encouraging sign came from the Independent Television Commission on 12 February. Chief Executive Peter Rogers led a delegation which argued that the MMC 'should stop such take-overs because they would impede the sale of broadcast rights'. Further, they 'told the MMC that acquisitions of sporting teams by broadcasters would distort the free market in broadcast rights to matches . . . [affecting] the price paid by television companies and the quality of coverage'. [*Financial Times*, 12 February 1999]

At this point in the story, February 1999, three of those involved were hit with a bombshell. A very reliable inside source first hinted to Adam Brown and then let slip to Andy Walsh that 'you will be very happy with the final report of the MMC'. They couldn't believe their ears and sat, each on one end of a phone call, in dumb silence. Chris Robinson was with Andy at the time and was in on it. With two months to go before the decision would eventually be known, they had to decide what to do. The instinct was to shout it from the rooftops; the reality was that it had to be kept quiet. Adam didn't even know that Chris knew until he dropped a hint at the Coventry away game – 'Looks like a nice little victory,' he said. Not sure whether he meant the game or the take-over, and with a thousand flapping ears around, little else was said.

The secrecy policy initiated at the start of the campaign faced its toughest test. Like little boys who had peeked under the wrapping paper before Christmas, they thought they knew what the present was. And what a present! But they weren't supposed to know; if they spoke out they could be proved wrong by events and look foolish; and the public campaign had to be kept on track, as before. What the ever-present media scrum would have given for that scoop made the mind boggle!

Knowing you are in sight of land and actually making it ashore are two slightly different things and these three campaigners didn't want to capsize at the last minute. It was played completely dumb for around two months, and it was very hard. With mounting speculation as the decision day drew closer, with contradictory reports in the press, and with people with whom they had worked so closely and passionately in daily contact, keeping it quiet was no easy task. How good it would have been to relieve the concerns of people battling to save their club, but to have done so would have jeopardised everything. As it was, optimism was raised elsewhere.

Mellor had commented that he thought the deal would be blocked; another was a source inside government who said that he thought at the very least there would be strict conditions imposed, which, however unsatisfactory, was more than campaigners could have hoped for back on 9 September.

In fact, when you hear something as important as the MMC coming down in your favour over such an issue but are unable to do or say anything about it, you stop believing it. It becomes unreal, a dream or mirage not to be trusted. Combined with the knowledge that Byers had the power to over-rule anything the MMC came up with anyway, you put it out of your mind, forget that you have heard it. When you can.

Sky and United must have known by this point the serious concerns the MMC had about the take-over, but continued to counter in their evidence sessions. Sky changed tack on their reasons for the merger offer, claiming to the MMC that the early strategic reasons advocated – of 'buying a seat at the table', of giving 'significant leverage' over domestic and European TV rights, of 'being in position to influence decisions for a European Super League' – were now somehow 'flawed and not borne out on a full examination of the legal and factual information'. [MMC 5.37] They were desperately trying to distance themselves from any notion that the purchase of United was to secure TV rights, a position which had been blasted by all and sundry and which clearly raised competition and conflict of interest issues. As such, Sky started talking about the merger assisting 'BSkyB to take advantage of impending developments in the digital world', of 'expanding the value of the Manchester United enterprise [sic]' and 'having an ownership stake in more of the content of all of its channels'. [MMC 5.38] Whether these reasons were true or not, none of them came close to the prize which everyone knew Murdoch was after, his battering ram of live Manchester United games.

They also started a charm offensive with the MMC, claiming that 'it intended to behave sensitively in dealing with Manchester United and its many supporters', but then almost immediately contradicted itself by deny-ing there were any 'tangible public interest issues'. [MMC 5.41] Given that the MMC had just heard chapter and verse from the 'sensitive' supporters, and it had received reams of evidence from a broad spectrum of those concerned highlighting public interest issues, this was a tactical error. BSkyB and Manchester United both refuted allegations that United might break away from the Premier League, saying it was unworkable, and BSkyB distanced itself from the activities of News (Foxtel) in Australia over the Rugby League Super League fiasco. Furthermore, BSkyB argued that prices would not go up, although they claimed United's current policy was a 'very successful commercial formula', not recognising that this strategy was fiercely opposed by fans. They also said that rescheduling of matches, in particular the Monday night games, was done sensitively, with 'no question of asking fans from Southampton to travel to Newcastle on a Monday night'. [MMC 5.72] So Manchester to Southampton is fine, but not Southampton to Newcastle – what reassurance! Edwards added another pearl by saying that pensioners stood to lose if the deal was rejected, because the share value of pension fund holdings would fall!

What the MMC thought of all this would be in their report, delivered to the DTI on 12 March. The date was etched into many diaries and many minds and a sense of expectation grew during the week, but there would be no news about the report until the Trade Secretary gave his response up to a month later, the statutory deadline for a final decision. The only activity for frustrated campaigners was a constant reading of press speculation and hypotheses around the MMC report. From what government inside sources said, the report was being delivered to the relevant people in three sealed security bags and no one, but no one, would have any information before Byers' decision.

Andy Walsh had been given Stephen Byers' home phone number early on in the campaign and decided to call him on Saturday, 13 March, the day after he would have received the report from the MMC. Although it risked antagonising him, if the report wasn't unequivocal an extra nudge might help. In the end he compromised and left a brief message, reminding him of the importance of the decision and imploring him to jump the right way. His wife, Sarah, knew he had been on the phone and wanted to know who to. She hit the roof when he told her. 'That is absolutely ridiculous! You have gone too far this time. What is he going to think of you phoning him at home on a weekend?' There had been a few crazy moments in the campaign up until then, but she clearly thought that phoning the Secretary of State at home was just about the worst. At least he knew IMUSA were concerned about his work!

The sense of anti-climax after 12 March was palpable. Everyone knew a decision had been made by the MMC, but did not know what Byers would decide. However, far from things going quiet, the pace now began to quicken. Gradually at first, but quicken all the same.

First came the Budget. Now, in normal times, the Budget is about as far from the concerns of your average Manchester United fan as it is possible to get, save for complaints over the price of ale. However, this time Byers declared he was changing competition policy and 'announced the independence of Britain's competition authorities . . . to remove politicians from the merger regime'. [The Observer, 14 March 1999] The aim was both to avoid the controversies which mergers generated, and with it political embarrassment, as well as to provide a more consistent approach of competition authorities to business.

Oddly, this small but significant change in the way the country was going to decide whether corporate mergers could take place or not made ears prick up. What it meant for the take-over was that, should the MMC advocate blocking the bid, the Secretary of State could hardly then allow it to proceed. You don't alter years of competition policy by saying you are going to remove political decisions and politicians from the process, and then turn round and stick your mitts in the middle of the biggest hornet's nest the MMC has seen in donkey's years. Arguably, Byers already knew the gist of the MMC's report when he announced the change in competition procedure and it might have one side benefit – deflecting the wrath of Rupert by making accepting the MMC report a 'non-political' decision. Whatever, the feeling now was that what the MMC said would go.

However, there was always the fear that the MMC would tilt the rudder in Sky's favour, and no matter what tip-off you had had weeks before, how much your head told you it was solid, or that the campaign had won the arguments time and again, no one was going to believe anything until they saw Stephen Byers telling the world that the decision was the fans'. And now, if the MMC report went in favour of the bid, there was little Byers would or could do in campaigners' favour.

These fears were enhanced when the *Daily Mirror's* Harry Harris, having a bit of time off from harassing England managers, took a punt on 13 March. The bid would be allowed to proceed, he said, but with conditions attached. *The Guardian* backed up the story. What was particularly worrying was that here were two newspapers with an interest in stopping the take-over saying it would go ahead. This was a blow. IMUSA knew Murdoch could never be trusted; that once he got his hands on the club, things would never look back and that sooner or later he would get what he wanted from United. After all the efforts that had been put in to removing this 'middle ground', after all the arguments about how Chinese walls and voluntary conditions could not work, were they really going to trust the future of the club and the game to such a man, in such uncertain times? IMUSA rightly responded by dismissing the stories as 'idle speculation', which Harris later admitted it was, but you couldn't help worrying. The effect of the story on the share price seemed to suggest the City was thinking along similar lines: 'Manchester United shares soared earlier this week in the belief that the deal would be approved with minimal conditions. The shares peaked at 248p on Monday before easing to 244p, up 5 per cent and above the 240p cash offer in the original BSkyB bid.' [Press Association (PA), 17 March 1999]

However, in a month when emotions would swing violently from one extreme to another, in an uncanny mirror of many of the titanic struggles on the pitch at the time, it wasn't long before another story emerged. On the day of Manchester United's European Cup quarter-final second-leg tie against Internazionale in Milan, the *Daily Telegraph* proclaimed that they had information that the bid would be blocked. 'Citing sources close to the

Department of Trade and Industry, the newspaper said the commission had ruled the £623m take-over was not in the public interest.' [PA, 17 March 1999] What was particularly encouraging about this report was that for the first time it was being rumoured that the deal was out on public interest grounds, rather than on competition issues, ground campaigners were confident of.

Having been otherwise engaged in the city of Milan for all of 17 March, some never heard this rumour until after the fantastic draw, and quarter-final win over Inter. The share price fell faster than the fruit, bottles, coins and bodily fluids which had rained down on United fans at the San Siro that evening, plummeting 10 per cent at the news and signalling that the City – a crucial barometer all the way through this saga – was taking it seriously. After a scintillating match, Scholes' equaliser and this news, United embarked on an unbelievable two months, both on and off the pitch.

In a piece entitled 'Murdoch's United bid faces curbs', *The Guardian* returned to the theme which had dogged the government all along – its relationship with Murdoch:

> Tony Blair was poised last night to intervene in the official vetting of Rupert Murdoch's bid for Manchester United Football Club. The Prime Minister's intervention is aimed at ensuring that a take-over, if approved by the government, is hedged by guidelines to prevent the media mogul using his new leverage over the game to benefit his broadcasting interests. Downing Street's move came as shares in football clubs fell sharply after an unconfirmed report that the Monopolies and Mergers Commission had advised the government that Sky TV's take-over attempt should be blocked. If the government halts the £623m deal, relations between Mr Murdoch and Mr Blair's administration could come under huge strain. [*The Guardian*, 18 March 1999]

The *Financial Times* was less convinced that the MMC was to deliver this message, however: 'This would be hard to justify on competition grounds. After all, why should sports rights be treated differently from other must-have content?' [*Financial Times* 31.3.99] They went on to warn: 'And the MMC would lack imagination if it could not think up workable conditions to manage conflicts of interest when Premiership broadcasting rights are next auctioned.'

The increasing speculation started to strain New Labour's relations with Murdoch. Ben Wegg-Prosser, Mandelson's political adviser at the DTI, was offered a job with *The Sun* in January, after Mandelson's resignation (for which *The Sun*, for whom Mandelson could do no wrong before the MMC referral, offered little sympathy). SUAM had complained about the appointment to the DTI. As Prosser was leaving in March to take up his new post, *The Sun*'s editor David Yelland withdrew the offer. The intense speculation focused on Labour's relationship with the Murdoch empire and the likely outcome of the MMC inquiry.

> Early leaks from the DTI suggest that the MMC inquiry has not gone in BSkyB's favour. Even if allowed, Murdoch would be required to give undertakings which would undermine his deal. Clearly, Murdoch's executives have a shrewd idea already about the report's recommendations. So Murdoch – and, by extension, *The Sun* – could well be facing a showdown with Tony Blair's government in the coming months . . . Given Wegg-Prosser's relationship with the DTI, and his Labour affiliations, Yelland, Murdoch and [Les] Hinton [News International chief] questioned the wisdom of having him on board. On balance, they decided, the conflict of interest would be too great if the going got hot . . . That's why the coming Manchester United storm could be spellbinding stuff . . . All we know is the man who got the game's first red card: Benjamin Wegg-Prosser.' [*The Guardian*, 23 March 1999]

Hard on the heels of these revelations came Manchester United's half-term pre-tax profits, down to £11.08m from £15.39m for the six months to 31 January. Claiming the loss was to do with increased players' wages – up by £3m – the club also had to acknowledge that they had spent a whopping £1.7m on the BSkyB take-over and had sustained big losses – 20 per cent – in the sale of merchandise. [*Financial Times*, 31 March 1999] The merchandise bubble may have burst, players may be getting more greedy, and the club may have been pursuing a corporate strategy with which few agreed, but it was to be the fans who had to pay. In a move which angered the football world, the club announced ticket price increases of up to 15 per cent, five times the rate of inflation. Of course other clubs were doing the same – Southampton were to be landed with an extra 20 per cent charge – but none of them had pocketed £11m in six months with a European Cup to play for.

For a brief moment, minds returned to more familiar ground. Price increases were the meat and drink of supporter protest at United and elsewhere – it was after all one of the issues around which IMUSA first rallied. The media did their usual stuff and IMUSA were inundated with requests to comment on the increases. A balancing act had to be performed. On one hand the ticket prices were unjustifiable for a company making £11m in six months and this was the core message. On the other, part of the reason for the fall in profits was the money spent on a take-over no one wanted, and fans were being made to pay for it. This brought the issue back to the greatest concern.

However, there was more to do with the take-over than this. Did it mean that, as campaigners were hearing, the club was expecting a defeat in the MMC battle? Was the price rise a recognition that the profits which the directors were about to accrue were not on their way, and they had to make something back? IMUSA's Mark Longden was convinced this was the case: 'Martin Edwards finally buried the deal for me when he announced ticket price rises for the next season.' However, some were less optimistic. Sky had promised that they wouldn't increase prices for two years, should they take over. In pessimistic mood some concluded that this was an arrangement between Edwards and Sky, confident of victory, to get price rises in place before the take-over was allowed to proceed. The new owners would have two years' grace and could justifiably say that they were not responsible for these increases.

Life became like that Guinness advert with the surfers. The heart beats faster. You have to take the plunge. But good things come to those who wait. You ride the crest of a wave. Soon you'll be home and dry. Land appeared in sight when Patrick Wintour, 'a highly respected political journalist with good contacts in New Labour', claimed in *The Observer* on 4 April that the bid would be blocked:

> Rupert Murdoch's controversial take-over of Manchester United will in effect be blocked . . . the MMC report, which will be published in the next fortnight, questions whether undertakings that United would not inform its parent company about details of bids from rival firms for broadcasting rights would be enforceable in practice. [*The Observer*, 4 April 1999]

The acceleration was really beginning to tell when, following this revelation, the news broke that BSkyB had written to Stephen Byers offering a series of conditions and undertakings they were prepared to make to allow the take-over to proceed. By now they must have had wind that they were losing the battle. Indeed, the club and BSkyB were given the MMC's report at least five days before publication so that they could remove commercially sensitive material. So they knew what the MMC was saying: the question was what would Byers do about it?

The situation seemed finely balanced; much more so at the time than it really was. Byers had the freedom to do one of three things: accept it in full; reject it (if it recommended blocking the bid, but not if it recommended proceeding); or impose conditions. There were two contradictory tensions. One was the Labour establishment's concern to keep Murdoch on-side – they had already seen a moderation of support over Mandelson and Wegg-

Prosser. The other was Byers' decision over future competition policy, removing the political role, which suggested he would accept whatever the MMC said.

BSkyB went straight for Byers. In a letter they offered three conditions. One was that they would agree to exclude Manchester United from the Premier League vote on any new TV contract. The second was that it would 'prevent it gaining access to confidential information about rival bids for broadcasting rights'. The third was that it agreed that it would not initiate any breakaway from the Premier League. [*Financial Times*, 7 April 1999] In fact these conditions were already outlined in BSkyB's evidence to the MMC. That they were appealing to Byers directly, illustrated that that they knew what the MMC had thought of them.

For campaigners this was the middle ground that was so feared. Conditions and Murdoch didn't work. Could BSkyB swing it? One aspect which was seized upon was that within this offer of conditions was a caveat: if another club was taken over by a media corporation then they had to abide by the same conditions; and if there were three or more of these, the restriction would be withdrawn. Given that it was widely accepted that the merger would soon be followed by others (NTL were already waiting in the wings), these conditions were about as solid as a sandcastle; sooner rather than later they'd be washed out to sea.

For one final time, the DTI became the focus of campaigners' attention and Byers' fax machine had one more hurdle to climb before it would be left alone. Adam Brown highlighted another weakness in a hastily faxed letter:

> If the proposed conditions were imposed, they would be entirely meaningless if the RPC rules in favour of the OFT and outlaws the collective selling of TV rights. Given such a situation, BSkyB would have exclusive access to the rights to televise the biggest club in the country and, indeed, Europe. Furthermore, even if the Premier League win their Restrictive Practices case, the maintenance of collective selling of rights is by no means secure, particularly if media interests are allowed to own other football clubs. It would take just seven clubs to veto any collective Premier League sale of rights and allow those clubs owned by media concerns to establish their own, exclusive deals.

On 27 March, Andy Walsh disappeared on a well-earned two-week holiday to France and Spain with his family. Just before leaving he had given an interview to *The Guardian*, which took up most of the sports page on 30 March. Once again steering the interviewer away from concentrating on the personal, the figurehead, he did, however, leave himself open to one charge: 'Although Andy Walsh has helped marshal grass-roots opposition to BSkyB's bid to buy Manchester United for £624m, that does not mean to say he can organise lunch in North Wales [where he was working that day] for under a tenner.' Andy then outlined what the campaign had meant:

> People were willing to risk their jobs and even their relationships at home. They put their whole lives on the line because of how important the issue was. There has been no football campaign anywhere in the world which matches this one . . . It may seem trivial to many people but the bond that exists between football fans transcends many others. [*The Guardian*, 30 March 1999]

At the time, 'there were indications that the Secretary for Trade and Industry Stephen Byers [would] make an announcement on Thursday' (1 April). With Andy suddenly out of reach, a frantic series of e-mails and phone calls followed as all the rumours about a decision date, tactics of how to handle the decision and press reports were relayed to campaigners. At one point Andy was conducting telephone conversations with Adam Brown whilst sitting on Mont Juic overlooking Barcelona. Eleventh hour victories and Barcelona were to become acquainted again that season, but that particular good omen wasn't known to anyone at this stage.

The 1 April deadline came and went, and another source claiming it would be 2 April proved unfounded. Campaigners started wondering whether Byers would leave it until the very last day, and if he did, what that implied. These false dawns came and went as if they were any ordinary day. They were, but for those who had been waiting so long it was agony. With the *Observer* report on Sunday, 4 April, and the *Financial Times* report of BSkyB's offer of conditions, the speculation became intense. Andy Walsh, out of the frying pan, tried to bring some sanity to proceedings, not helped, it has to be said, by an Antoine de Caunes impersonation:

> Bonjour my British chums! The issue [of Byers negotiating conditions with Sky] is a red herring. Neither Byers nor the MMC will enter into negotiations with Sky or United over the deal . . . Let us all keep a clear head, this next couple of days are going to see a heightening of activity from the rumour mill, we need to remain focused on what we know to be fact. [E-mail to IMUSA committee, 8 April 1999]

BSkyB wrote to Byers at the start of the week beginning 5 April. It was known that Byers had to make a decision by Tuesday, 13 April – the statutory one-month deadline from delivery of the report. It was the final week of the long battle and all the indications were that now, finally, events were going the campaign's way.

On Monday, 5 April, Andy Walsh was told by a parliamentary

correspondent that the MMC report was in the House of Commons Votes Office, meaning that publication was imminent. Lee Hodgkiss had another tip-off that the decision would be on Thursday, 8 April. Adam Brown then received a telephone call from a contact within football with a 'very, very reliable source' that it would be 'the end of the week'. Another leak to him from the government said Friday. Everyone was on tenterhooks. Andy was away in France; Mark and Monica were in Scarborough; Adam was supposed to be at a Task Force meeting on the Friday, which he cancelled once it was clear that 'the end of the week' didn't mean Thursday. The frustration for Andy, heading back up the French motorways, was tangible:

> I hope Byers waits until Monday but if he doesn't, good luck with the media stampede and make sure that the press enquiries are shared out but that the same message is given . . . Bonne Chance, I will be back around midnight Saturday, probably too late for the first volley, if Adam's snout is correct, but I will have my mobile switched on at *all* times and will be itching to be kept informed. [E-mail to IMUSA committee, 8 April 1999]

Chris Robinson was, on the surface at least, calm: 'Look, you can't put your life on hold waiting for it. It'll just come when it comes.' The trouble was, that was what many people had been doing for the last seven months. Although things would never be the same again, at least they could get back to normal life once it was over. It also didn't mean that IMUSA and SUAM shouldn't be prepared. The press frenzy would match, for a short period at least, that which had been dealt with at the start of the campaign. The line was this:

> Don't allow yourselves to be bullied by a journo who wants more than you are willing to give. Talk to each other about the sorts of questions that are being put to you so that you are all aware of the tripwires some of these bastards can set and be extra careful with journos we don't know . . . be courteous and firm . . . As sure as eggs are eggs we will be asked to demand Edwards' resignation: this is not the time; he must first be given a final chance to talk to IMUSA and respond to fans' concerns. Any new bidder that may emerge must be made to feel that they can only hope to succeed if they respond directly to our questions, but we don't want this to be explicit or else we will start to put people's backs up; we don't want anybody thinking we are a bunch of arrogant Mancs now, do we?! [E-mail to IMUSA committee, 8 April 1999]

Michael Crick and other SUAM members were in London ready to handle the media there, with three press releases at the ready covering the potential outcomes, except for Jonathan Michie, who was returning from work abroad, and Oliver Houston, who was in Manchester. Lee Hodgkiss, Steve Briscoe, Jon Leigh, Duncan Drasdo, Dave Kirkwood and Adam Brown were on hand in Manchester. By Thursday night everyone was ready. If it wasn't now, it was going to be a long weekend of waiting.

There's a Second World War film about the Normandy invasion where a German officer in his bunker on the French coast is scanning the blank horizon, incredulously sceptical about the rumours of an impending battle. 'Nothing, nothing,' he says, 'not even a seagull.' Suddenly, he screams: 'Hilfe! A British invasion fleet!!' and the first mortar crashes down. It's *Boys' Own* stuff. The morning of Friday, 9 April, was a bit like that. Lee Hodgkiss was expecting some press enquiries (there were always *some*). At the very least he thought some of the more sussed journalists would be wise to the rumours. But it was deathly quiet. Then, at one o'clock, Stuart Mathieson from the *Evening News* called to say that the club had confirmed that there would be an announcement by Byers at 3 p.m. Blood rose. Stomachs turned. This was it. Action stations.

'It was a bright cold day in April, and the clocks were striking thirteen.' So goes the eerie start to George Orwell's novel *1984*. 'Even by 1.45 nobody had got there,' says Steve, 'and we were ready to chuck in the towel.' But gradually they came. Lee and Steve had been at Old Trafford early doors, as Big Ron would say. 'Eddie Taylor was wandering around there like some nomad,' says Steve. Adam Brown had been in an almost deserted university building trying to work, but, unable to concentrate, he finally gave up and headed up to the ground. Why fans do this is a bit odd, really. Campaigners were far more likely to hear news and information remaining by radios, TVs and computers than standing in a football club's car park, but it's always the same: Eric's ban, Eric leaving, title wins when United don't even play, the take-over announcement – fans always end up standing in the car park. Soon they were joined by Jon Leigh, Oliver Houston and later Chris Robinson, Duncan Drasdo, John 'the Chef' Wroe and others. Beneath the Munich clock at Old Trafford a handful of those involved in the campaign against Murdoch from the start were gathering along with about as many radio and television broadcast vans. These few knew that with two more 'strikes' of that clock, it would bring either freedom or Room 101.

The time was mostly spent pacing around answering the odd call – the phones had finally warmed themselves up, like some tired old pro getting ready for his last shot of glory. 'The journos hadn't got a clue which way it was going to go,' recalls Steve and preliminary interviews were arranged: BBC, ITN, GMR, Radio 5, MUTV and Sky News. It was a strange and reassuring fact that the journalists associated with the last two of these stations were usually fair-handed; indeed, one of them was practically jumping for delight at the prospect of fans winning. It made you feel that the battle for the freedom of the press wasn't quite lost yet.

Then, all of a sudden, it was three o'clock. Steve's phone went and there was a flurry of activity towards the BBC radio van. Everyone huddled round, journalists and fans together, no more than fifteen in total.

> I have therefore announced to the stock exchange that in order to protect the public interest I am blocking the proposed merger between BSkyB and Manchester United.

Byers had barely got the words out, before the rest was drowned by whoops of joy. 'It's blocked! *It's blocked!*' Others came running down the forecourt. The cameras and microphones whirled into action as we hugged and punched the air. 'We've done it. We've bloody done it!'

But no one had heard if there were to be conditions:

> I agree with the MMC that none of the alternative options which they have considered would provide an effective remedy. I also agree with the MMC that the adverse effects of the merger . . . are very serious. I therefore accept the MMC's recommendation that the merger should be prohibited, and am asking the DGFT to seek suitable undertakings from BSkyB that it will not proceed with the merger.

He had blocked it outright. However confident campaigners were, whatever they'd been telling everyone, they couldn't believe it. That he stopped the deal both on competition grounds and because it would 'damage the quality of British football by reinforcing the trend towards growing inequalities between the larger, richer clubs and the smaller, poorer ones' was the icing on the cake.

Steve was straight into the Sky van and on air: 'Can you categorically tell me there are no conditions?' he asked. Kay Brady confirmed it. Fighting her company's corner she said, 'But you must agree that Sky has done a lot for football?' Steve decided now was the time for dishing out the Briscoe charm, overtaken with euphoria: 'They've done dick for football! The presentation may be quality but they've done nowt for the grass roots, smaller clubs or youth football!' 'Thanks, Steve,' the producer said, 'that's nearly lost me my job!' No one could help but laugh, you couldn't blame him, but it was hardly the 'courteous and firm' response Walsh had called for!

Duncan Drasdo was still in his house when the decision came through. He recalls it this way:

> Message from the Doctor [Brown] – decision due at 3 p.m. Two radios on, GMR and 5 Live. Trying to listen simultaneously. Pumping the air, running up and down the landing. Jumping up and down, standing on the toilet seat, purple-faced, veins a-bulging,

orgasmically shouting yes, yes, yes – à la *When Harry Met Sally*! Er, you're not getting mixed up with another incident here, are you? Everyone on phone and e-mail going mental. Up to OT; met up with Jon Leigh and all. Round to The Trafford and Dog and Partridge to buy some champagne. Champagne at the D and P? I don't think so. None at The Trafford either, so we had to settle for a crate of Boddingtons draught – much moaning from the lager monsters. Celebrating on the forecourt. Got caught out once or twice gooning in front of the cameras – until the Press Officer whipped us back into line! Shining, happy people.

It was ironic. Here was a campaign whose aim was to stop a media mogul taking over a football club, and thus erect the first barrier in the forward march of television into football, to say enough is enough. Yet it was also one which had been waged in the media, in the glare of the TV, radio and papers. Now, at the final act in the drama, there were more media present than campaigners. Supporters were suddenly swamped. From Lee, to Oliver, to Briscoe, to Adam the scrum moved around, gobbling up the glee; taking it down; chopping it into bite-sized pieces.

It didn't last long, though, and soon they were waiting around to give the more measured reactions to a schedule of interviews which went on into the early evening. Unfortunately one or two comments drifted into the dreaded 'Edwards should resign' territory and that would be picked up heavily by the papers in the following days: 'If he really does want to make £80m, he must sell his shares to the people that care – the fans. And then he must go for the sake of our once great club.' [*Independent on Sunday*, 11 April 1999] It may have been what everyone wanted, but the tactic was to put pressure on for a meeting, however unlikely. SUAM had a letter asking for a meeting through the letterbox almost as soon as the bid was blocked, although at the time of writing this has never happened. They also issued the following statement:

> SUAM will now rename itself Shareholders United, and campaign both to preserve United's independence and to maintain one of the aims of the 1991 flotation 'to allow as many fans and employees as possible to own shares in Manchester United'. The best way to keep United out of the clutches of people like Murdoch is for every ordinary fan to buy as many shares as they can. [Press release, 10 April 1999]

With Edwards ensconced in the stadium's offices, the club did eventually issue a statement, a few lines typed on to a white sheet of paper, copied and handed out on the forecourt. It read:

> The board of Manchester United today note this decision. Although disappointed by the outcome, the board is confident that Manchester United will maintain its record of success and secure its objective of achieving consistently outstanding playing and business performance for the benefit of its supporters, employees and shareholders.

The question which immediately sprang to mind was that if the club could so easily maintain its success, what good would the take-over have done? It was the question neither Sky nor United ever answered.

For Sky's part, Vic Wakeling said that now they would be concentrating on their 'core business' of 'making great television' and they would continue to be involved in football. 'It is not a blow to Sky,' he said, 'it is a blow to football.' In this he gave the game away and proved the fears that the club would be a small part in a much bigger machine, correct: TV was their 'core business'; United a peripheral concern. The man from Sky who had been prepared to meet IMUSA right at the start, who had sat down and proved his reputation for straight talking, also paid tribute to those involved in the campaign at IMUSA and SUAM: 'There are certain groups who are going to be happy with this because they have campaigned very vigorously and very effectively against this deal.'

Mark Booth, BSkyB's Chief Executive – the man who, as vice-chair Steve Briscoe argued in one piece, 'couldn't name our right-back; he couldn't name the players on the plaque who died at Munich; he doesn't know the history of the club' – was less admiring: 'This is a bad ruling for British football clubs who will have to compete in Europe against clubs who are backed by successful media companies . . . We would also like to thank the silent majority of fans and shareholders who have recognised the benefits which BSkyB would bring to their club.' [*The Independent*, 10 April 1999] That damned silent majority again – if only they'd speak up!

Once the interviews had been dealt with, it was off to town to celebrate and the professionalism the campaign had shown clearly took a matter of hours to disintegrate! Duncan Drasdo describes:

> We met up later at The Pevril of the Peak for a celebration, joined by most of the committee, before the North Manchester lads pussied out leaving the hard core to head for Bar Aqua. My last memory of the evening is rolling out of this bar and having a three-way drunken hugging competition with Dave Kirkwood and Mark Southee. This caused alarm with the bouncers – especially when we staggered and fell on the pavement in a heap, breaking Dave's hip (nearly).

Once the euphoria was over, it was possible to study the Trade Secretary's statement more closely. The fact that the MMC Report had said both that the merger was against competition within the pay-TV market as well as against the interests of the future of British football was hugely significant. They took on board arguments that clubs are effective monopolies given the peculiar nature of football custom:

> We have . . . noted that all clubs have considerable independence in setting the ticket prices of their home games because many of their supporters have no substitute for these games. All football clubs with a strong supporter base will therefore have a degree of market power. Because it is particularly well supported, Manchester United's power is greater than most other clubs. [MMC 2.72]

However, their core argument was about the market power of BSkyB and the threat to competition the deal posed in the pay-TV market. The MMC considered four scenarios: the merger in the context of collective selling of TV rights, and the merger in the context of individual selling (if the OFT win the RPC case), both of which could occur where this is the only merger *and* where other clubs are sold to media companies. [MMC 2.219] In the first and second scenarios – collective selling – they concluded that BSkyB's chances of securing those rights would be 'substantially higher' if it were allowed and this applied even if other clubs were taken over by media companies. [MMC 2.220; 2.222] In the third and fourth – individual selling – they would 'still have substantial advantages over other broadcasters competing for the rights of Premier League clubs' by dint of their ownership of Manchester United and their existing market power. [MMC 2.221]

However, significantly, they went on to say that:

> Although we have based our conclusions mainly on the effects of the merger on competition, we have also looked at wider football issues. We have concluded that the merger would reinforce the trend towards greater inequality of wealth between clubs, weakening the smaller ones. We have also concluded that the merger would give BSkyB additional influence over Premier League decisions relating to the organisation of football, leading to some decisions which would not reflect the long-term interest of football. On both counts the merger may be expected to have the adverse effect that the quality of English football would be damaged. This adverse effect would be more pronounced if the merger precipitated other mergers between broadcasters and Premier League clubs. We were unable to identify any public interest benefits from the proposed merger. [MMC 2.228]

This was dynamite. Not only had they implicitly accepted arguments that the football industry was different and the role of the support unique, but they also concluded that first, the growing inequality in wealth in the game was wrong; second, that media companies owning Premier League clubs would exacerbate this; and third, that there was no benefit to the public of the merger. Given that the government accepted these findings in full, the implications were huge: what would the government and its Football Task Force now do to prevent the widening wealth gap in football?

There was more. The MMC considered the issue of undertakings or conditions in the operation of a merged company. Again they were unequivocal: any undertakings could not 'prevent informal flows of information'; Manchester United's influence, whether they voted on Premier League rights or not 'would be unaffected by the undertaking'; other bidders would still believe the undertakings could not work, making them ineffective; and 'if collective selling were to break down, the undertaking would be overtaken by events'. [MMC 2.233] Any Chinese wall would be 'difficult to police', they said and the MMC 'were not convinced [it] would work'. Further, undertakings about not initiating a breakaway 'could not be monitored and enforced'. [MMC 2.237–2.239]

It was a fantastic victory: the MMC just did not trust the club or BSkyB. Whether the arguments IMUSA and SUAM had been pushing about the dangers of Rupert Murdoch and his record of breaking conditions had any influence or not, this was an acceptance of what was being said. The middle ground had fallen, the chasm opened up and there was no way the MMC, or because of its thorough assessment of possible options, the Secretary of State, could recommend the merger going ahead. 'The only remedy which would deal with the full range of adverse effects we have identified would be the prohibition of the merger.' [MMC 2.250] Music to the ears!

The fans had made a big impact:

> Fans and their representatives who gave us evidence were in no doubt that a breakdown of the traditional structure of British football as a result of increasing inequalities of wealth would be against the public interest. This raises issues which are more for the Football Task Force than for us. Nevertheless, given the wide definition of the public interest in the FTA [Fair Trading Act] we accept that major structural changes to British football are matters within our terms of reference in so far as they are affected by this merger. In our view, the increase in inequality of wealth between clubs, arising from the merger, would be likely to . . . put at risk the ability of many clubs to compete and ultimately could hasten the demise of some smaller clubs. This may be expected to have the adverse effect of damaging the quality of British football. [MMC 2.206]

Perhaps inadvertently, the panel also pointed the way for the remedy of this adverse effect on the public interest by saying that 'effective remedies would involve a high degree of intervention by the government in the administration of British football.' [MMC 2.250] What this meant was: a) that the BSkyB deal would increase inequality in British football; b) that this was against the public interest; and c) that remedies could not be sought from BSkyB but only by government intervention. Grist to the mill of those arguing for an independent regulator.

Byers also let it be known that the e-mail, letter and fax campaigns had worked wonders. The press was on the whole delighted. Andy Walsh had many calls from journalists who had been following the story, calling him to congratulate IMUSA. James Lawton put *The Express* fully behind the decision and recognised the role of fans:

> The government couldn't wave a wand and hand football back to the people. It couldn't throw out the 'suits' as the money lenders were once kicked out of the temple . . . But the decision to ban the take-over of Manchester United by BSkyB is certainly a matter for celebration. The voice of the fan has sounded louder than the usual pathetic whimper . . . He has taken so much, the ordinary fan, in recent years. He has seen his game turned into a day out for the well-heeled and the trendy, a social outlet rather than a passion of the streets. He has been moved from the tyranny of the hooligan to that of the money man. He has seen the Halls and the Edwards' and the Bates' annexe it for themselves and the shareholder. No, the government couldn't do much about this. But it could say – as it has – that enough is enough.' [*Daily Express*, 10 April 1999]

Charlie Whelan waded into New Labour in *The Observer*, and issued a warning:

> As far as I know, Rupert Murdoch has never watched a football match in his life. Peter Mandelson, his friend who was in the government, goes to see his local team Hartlepool only so that he can be photographed following the people's game. Football means nothing to these men. Yet the BSkyB bid for Manchester United indirectly cost Mandelson his political career and could lose New Labour the crucial support of the Murdoch media empire . . . The astonishing thing is how this government has got into such a mess over the future of football, given the passion for the game at all levels in New Labour . . . If the OFT gets its way, all clubs will do their own deals. Who would bet against BSkyB winning exclusive rights for all Manchester United games? [*The Observer*, 11 April 1999]

Of course, the Murdoch press were somewhat less enamoured. Rob Hughes, a one-time 'friend of the fan' ('my own roots as an individual are with those who stand often in contented squalor on the terraces'), said that the decision was an 'own goal' for supporters. Citing the media ownership of AC Milan and Paris St Germain, he asked, 'If it is acceptable business across the Continent, and in South America, where this type of liaison is vibrant, how can England stand apart? At once, the cry will go out that this writer, this newspaper, is biased.' Well, yes, especially when he claimed, 'The private television company paid an enormous price to sell its dishes, because football is the biggest turn-on . . . but in the era of football's direst need, it was BSkyB that rescued it.' [*The Times*, 10 April 1999] A quite incredible rewriting of history and dumbfounding failure to acknowledge that BSkyB had made huge amounts of money out of selling dishes and televising football (paid for by the football fans!).

The Times editorial set out what was in effect Murdoch's response, distancing the man they liked, Blair, from the party whose minister had made the decision: Byers 'had taken the decision by himself earlier this week. He had not spoken at any time to Tony Blair about the subject . . . the DTI decision . . . is unlikely to make any substantial change to *The Sun's* relationship with Labour. It is expected to remain broadly supportive of Mr Blair but implacably hostile to his line on the euro.' [*The Times*, 10 April 1999]

Indeed, Labour's long-feared reaction of Murdoch was quickly scotched:

> Rupert Murdoch denied his papers would wage a 'jihad' on the government for deciding to block BSkyB's £623m bid for Manchester United, as the Tories seized on evidence that ministers tried to influence the outcome. 'I'm disappointed but we're not going to start a jihad on the government or anything like that,' Mr Murdoch said yesterday. [*The Independent*, 12 April 1999]

The City was similarly disenchanted, as shares plummeted from a pre-decision high of 215–220p to 186p by 3.30 p.m. on decision day. The *Financial Times* was unimpressed:

> Leaving aside populist concerns for 'possible damage to British football' . . . This is a barely veiled attack on both companies' ethical standards. And had it been inclined to do so, the commission could probably have imposed conditions to circumvent this danger. [*Financial Times*, 12 April 1999]

The *FT* also derided the Commission's statement that 'it does "not believe" the media company's claim that other broadcasters without Premier League rights could create similar channels. It also says a "Chinese wall" between BSkyB and Manchester United to prevent the parent company influencing its subsidiary in broadcast rights talks "could not be effectively monitored and enforced".' It reflected much of the surprise of the City at the strength of the Commission's rejection: 'Competition lawyers said that the Commission seemed to have bent over backwards to find objections to the deal. "They have painted a very black picture of the take-over and seem to have dismissed virtually all BSkyB's arguments," said one.' [*Financial Times*, 10 April 1999]

In the week the bid was announced, Greg Dyke, the only member to speak out against the deal, had taken a bet with Mark Booth that the deal would be blocked. Presumably after collecting his bottle of whisky he expressed his delight: 'I always saw an independent Manchester United as a club with a great future. My view was that United had more to lose than gain from the deal.' [*Mail on Sunday*, 11 April 1999] Dyke obviously saw an opportunity which the share price fall represented and snapped up £110,000 worth. Others, such as SUAM and IMUSA's share guru Duncan Drasdo, urged fans to take the chance to increase the fans' ownership of the club.

Over the weekend, the e-mail lists and website – such important cogs in the campaign machine – spewed messages of congratulations. They came from Sweden, 'Congratulations to you and your friends! You did it, you defeated Murdoch, it's "big" and it's important even for us here close to the North Pole,' said Frederik; New York: 'Business surely has its place but so do those whose support transcends the boundaries of capital, Dan'; and Los Angeles: 'Heard the wonderful news, thank you for a job well done. The next step is to make sure that similar take-overs cannot happen.' They continued nearer to home: 'With Eric (I mean God) on our side, it was always possible,' said Dave Blatt from London; and Manchester-based author Stephen Kelly said: 'I never thought Labour would dare defy Citizen Murdoch.' Malcolm Clarke gave the FSA's reaction:

> Brilliant – what else is there to say? Nobody gave you a dog's chance at the beginning, but you did it! Many congratulations! I was at the Task Force today. Roland Smith was decidedly grumpy when someone raised the subject at the start and then suddenly and unexpectedly buggered off at lunchtime – I wonder why! It is particularly nice that Murdoch should get a bloody nose in the week of the tenth anniversary of Hillsborough, after what *The Sun* did to the Liverpool fans. But we should see it as a magnificent victory in a major battle in a much longer war which we wage on many fronts, and not as winning the war. Fans united will never be defeated.

IMUSA were careful to thank the massive support received from other clubs – 'We could not have done this on our own and we have had support from fans all over the country, from Slough Town to Newcastle United, and that is why this is a victory for football' [*The Independent*, 10 April 1999] – and the feeling was reciprocated:

> I would just like to say what a relief for football fans everywhere that this take-over bid has been stopped. Well done and glad greedy 'bastard' Edwards didn't get his ninety mill pay-out!! All the best for Europe and see you next season!! [Tim, Ipswich Town]

IMUSA and SUAM, as well as the host of allies they had brought together, had proved themselves on both the national and the international stage; in the media, amongst supporters, on the Internet, with government and Parliament and in the Monopolies Commission, they had been a focal point for opposition. Linda Harvey wrote, 'The tears are still coming. Remember this date – as important as any other date in the history of Manchester United. Feels good to know we did it together, doesn't it?' Paul Windridge: 'I always believed, right from the start, that we would make this, but when I first heard the news it took my breath away. For once, I couldn't actually believe it.'

Andy returned late on Saturday night, tragically missing the moment of glory but having at last had time with his family. Co-operation between some of those most closely involved had secured him a ticket for the Cup semi-final. 'Walshy is without a ticket for Sunday, and although he is not the begging sort, I am – if there is anyone who knows of a ticket going, make sure it ends up in his hands,' said Mick Meade. It was on Sunday, 11 April, and Arsenal awaited. That the referee had ruled in IMUSA's favour over the Sky deal had its payback. That day David Elleray did what David Elleray does and wrongly ruled United out of victory in a poor game. But even then United lived to fight another day. Barely had the dust settled on the grave of Murdoch's bid to buy the club when United were straight into the chase for a treble dream. For many Reds it was now like going for the quadruple.

EIGHT

JUST WHEN YOU THOUGHT
IT WAS ALL OVER

After the months of campaigning, it was hard to take in what had been achieved. The derision, scepticism, defeatism, even pity which had greeted the start of the campaign was in many ways well founded: Murdoch doesn't lose many battles; Manchester United usually get their way; fans usually get shafted. But a unique combination of determination, solidarity and strategy had brought together an alliance of forces to win. In the end the strategy that campaigners set out at the very start was followed all the way to a victory as complete as anyone could have hoped for. From getting an OFT inquiry, to an OFT delay, to an MMC referral, to putting the opposition to the MMC, to the PR and media battle, to building bridges with other fans, to the final rejection of the bid. At every single turn of events, the targets of the campaigners were achieved.

Looking back, it still seems improbable. But it was an improbable season all round. Five days after Stephen Byers' announcement, Ryan Giggs, with his team down to ten men in the FA Cup semi-final replay, and staring defeat square in the face, picked the ball up and single-handedly trounced the toughest defence in Europe in a dazzling fifty-yard run on goal, which saw United through to victory over Arsenal. That Roy Keane had been sent off, that Arsenal had a goal disallowed, that Peter Schmeichel, in his last season at the club, saved a last-minute penalty from Dennis Bergkamp, made the night one of the most memorable matches ever. Seven days later, the club flew to Turin to complete the second leg of their Champions' League semi-final against Juventus, having only drawn 1–1 at home. Within ten minutes of the start of the match, Juve were ahead 2–0. By half-time United were level, ahead on aggregate and, with a Yorke–Cole combination adding a third in the second half, reached the final. It was the first time United had won on Italian soil and the first time Juventus had been beaten in European competition at home for over thirty years. United were now back in the European Cup final for the first time since 1968.

Although there were the odd low moments – the scousers coming back from 2–0 down to equalise at Anfield (clearly the highlight of their season) – the pinnacle of winning over Murdoch merely revealed another peak, and another after that. After beating Middlesbrough, drawing with Blackburn and in so doing sending Ferguson's former number two to Division One, United clinched the title at home to Spurs, again after going behind. The FA Cup final against Newcastle United must have been one of the biggest non-events for anyone not on a treble roll, with an easy 2–0 victory seeing United to their third League and Cup double in six years. However, what seemed like a fairy tale looked well and truly over when Bayern Munich held on to a 1–0 lead until the dying moments of the European Cup final. But, with a Nou Camp two-thirds full of Reds, and with Bayern seeing their luck run dry as they hit the bar, the super-subs Sheringham and Solskjaer pinched victory in spectacular fashion from a Bayern team becoming complacent in their superiority. The final summit had been climbed. Reds were on top of the world. In a mirror of the campaign's series of improbable victories, after losing in the same week that IMUSA saw the MMC, United were not defeated again.

Few could dismiss what the team had achieved, but some did try to dismiss the victory over Murdoch. It won't change the future direction of football (*The Times*); it wouldn't stop other media take-overs (*Financial Times*); it was only because it was Murdoch (Deloitte and Touche); it wasn't down to the fans, but the objections of the football authorities (David Mellor); United fans are still stuck with Edwards (take your pick). Edwards' reaction was to declare that the manager would only have limited funds to strengthen the squad, whilst finance director David Gill denied that the take-over had ever had anything to do with extra transfer funds. Even as Edwards was throwing his toys out of his pram, the contradictions of the deal continued to be exposed.

Some of the more sensible comments probably had a point. Murdoch wouldn't give up his aim of dominating the pay-TV sports market that easily. He couldn't come and darken United's door again, but, by controlling the TV market for live football, he would continue to blight the lives of the match-going fans. Indeed, as this book goes to press, Martin Edwards decided to sell half of his shares, below market value, exclusively to institutional shareholders. Not only is this a kick in the teeth for Shareholders United and others wanting to broaden and democratise the ownership of the club, it also leaves BSkyB as the single biggest shareholder in Manchester United. Battle won, the struggle continues. The Restrictive Practices Court went well into extra time and the outcome remained unpredictable to the end. If the collective selling of TV rights was outlawed, the prospects for the majority of football clubs and football fans were not good. Those clubs with large followings would secure lucrative PPV deals, and would no longer have any obligation to share any of it with anyone else. Even with the OFT's defeat, profits look set to climb further for those who will benefit from PPV, although players' wages remain on a trajectory of which the Space Shuttle would be proud. The latter of these is likely be continually used as justification for making supporters pay yet more for their football. With price increases for the 1999–2000 season in the region of 15 to 20 per cent, what was once a game for everyone, will continue to narrow its appeal as one of the more expensive elements of an 'entertainment' industry. Money will continue to pour straight out of the game.

Already the revamped Champions' League means that the top three clubs will have a big head start when it comes to resources. One Premier League insider said that soon, because of the cost of competing at the top, the worst place to finish in the Premier League will be fourth. Further perversion of that once-great European competition cannot be ruled out. Nor can the prospect that Murdoch, Berlusconi and/or others will attempt to assert direct control – possibly through ownership – of European Leagues. The European Commission's current investigation into multi-club ownership needs to be closely watched. The European Court has already wrought havoc by conceiving of football in the same way as concrete-making, with the Bosman ruling exacerbating the wealth gap in the game everywhere. If they rule that any restriction on having two clubs owned by the same company or individual is a restraint of trade – ignoring the threat this poses to the independence of clubs and fair, *sporting* competition – they will be making similar mistakes again. This time it will be unforgivable and irretrievable.

Although the Office of Fair Trading, which ironically played such a strategically crucial role in the defeat of Murdoch, lost their RPC case, matters may continue to deteriorate. Pressure to reduce the numbers in the Premier League may lead to the creation of Premier League Division Two. The Premier League will almost certainly introduce pay-per-view at some point and this will increase the clamour of the 'yo-yo' teams to be given a trampoline instead. It may also jettison the collective sale of TV rights itself: if just six clubs think that selling their rights individually would be preferable they could block any future collective deal by forcing a stalemate. Expect a showdown, starring Martin Edwards and Sam Chisholm, at the Lancaster Gate corral anytime in the next two years. Just when you thought it was safe to go back to the match . . .

What is certain is that although current arrangements remain until 2001, trends continue, and a lot of the Football League will realise that their tanks are empty, they are freewheeling downhill and they will smack into the wall at the bottom sooner or later. Some may be repairable, for sure; some may even follow the models at Northampton and Bournemouth; but the long-term future of the competition they thought they were in – the collective pyramid of football, complete with Gordon Taylor's 'dream factor' – is surely doomed unless changes are made, and fast. Watford have shown that social mobility in football is still alive, even if, as favourites to go straight back down, ridden with disease. But it will surely not be long before thirty or so clubs will look at the situation, decide that they are more likely to meet their balance-sheet performance targets without the rest, and cut themselves off.

So was it all a wasted effort? Was it, like the Indians surrounding General Custer, a last great victory before the war was lost?

Indeed, no sooner had Murdoch been shown the door than United were embroiled in an unseemly row over their participation in the World Team Championship. This concoction is precisely the kind of TV-driven, contrived affair which many foresaw the club being lowered to if Murdoch had succeeded. Manchester United's plc willingly took up the offer to travel to Brazil in January, the middle of the season. To their eternal shame, they removed the holders and record winners from the FA Cup. The English game's guardians, the FA, did what they do best, sank to their knees and forfeited the integrity of their flagship competition, the oldest cup in football, believing that it would deliver them the 2006 World Cup. The whole affair stinks of the sickly sweetness of new bank notes, not the mud and pies of football. That the government – in particular Tony Banks, who had been so supportive in the battle against BSkyB – should be entangled in and soiled by it all is saddening.

So, was it all a last hurrah for the fans? In short, no. If Murdoch had been allowed to proceed with BSkyB's take-over of Manchester United, the game would already be up. The future direction of both the club and football would be in the hands of television. Despite the medium's influence, its commercial power and its ability to blind those charged with steering the football fleet through choppy waters, it is not in control, it is there to be *dealt* with, literally. The victory over Murdoch maintains that situation – football can still decide its future. 'Dunkirk' it might have been, a desperate scramble to avoid obliteration, but that means that at least there is another battle to be fought.

Even over the FA's recent decision, and the plc's wish for Manchester United to miss the FA Cup, alliances involving fans' groups, the PFA and managers, as well as MPs and enormous public pressure is forcing a rethink at the time of writing. Another battle, another defiant stance, another refusal to accept what seems inevitable.

So, we also say no, because in many ways the defeat of Sky was a symbolic victory. At the 'top' of the game the perception was that the tide of commercialism, the forward march of television could not be stopped. It was 'progress'. One commentator even said that the government and fans had 'acted like King Canute' in dealing with the take-over! Well, no one is drowned yet. The victory over Murdoch may yet prove to be a landmark. The decision to block the deal could be a watershed. IMUSA, SUAM and their allies proved that even where the commercial stakes are at their highest, involving the richest club in the world and the most powerful media mogul of them all, victories can be won for supporters. Not so much a throne in the sea, then, as a line in the sand.

But what of the other claims – that other media take-overs will happen, resulting in the same outcome that had been campaigned against; that it was only because it was Murdoch; that it wasn't a fans' victory?

Certainly, the fact that it was Murdoch helped. There was a well of antagonism toward him which stretched from the anger within football at *The Sun* following Hillsborough to a more general dislike of the antics of his tabloid paper. Then there were the well-publicised links between New Labour and the News Corporation, and there were the complaints about his involvement in other sports which came in from across the globe. Yes, that it was Murdoch maybe turned the PR campaign in IMUSA's favour.

But there were also very good reasons for this: it was *his* company which was the leading sports broadcaster; it was *his* companies which had wrecked sport elsewhere; it was *his* domination of the rest of the UK's media; it was *his* priorities which threatened the future of the game. However, even if it had not been Murdoch there would still have been one hell of a fight and core objections. The MMC were charged with *only* considering the effect that media ownership had on football in this instance and as such couldn't make broader objections. But the implications are very clear: any TV company would be sitting both sides of the Premier League negotiating table; any broadcaster as parent company would have priorities which would overrule those of the club, football and the fans; any media buy-out would further concentrate wealth and damage British football; and any media ownership of the building blocks of the game threatened breakaways, new competitions and a reduction in competitive balance. At the time of writing, the DTI is reportedly to produce guidelines on the circumstances in which media companies can be involved in the ownership of clubs. The same arguments may, therefore, have to be made again. But that does not belittle or lessen them just because the last time they were made, it concerned a company owned by Rupert Murdoch.

Retired MMC panel member Nicholas Finney confirmed this in July 1999, saying that the threat to competition from the merger would have stood whoever had been in charge. What does remain a threat is the possibility of other clubs being bought by media companies where the size of the business does not qualify the take-over for investigation by the Competition Commission. Government action is necessary.

As for the relative importance of the fans in blocking the take-over, it is simple: without the involvement of football supporters the deal would never have been stopped. The campaign against the take-over showed what a broad church not only Manchester United, but all football fans are. IMUSA and SUAM collected together football fans ranging from City analysts to a milk float mechanic, an IT consultant to corporate lawyers, academics to MPs, and journalists to actors. It involved football fans from Bournemouth to Bayern Munich, Slough Town to South Africa, and America to Altrincham. But most of all it involved dedicated fans of Manchester United. Without the massive and united support football fans showed, without the resources which were pulled in and the organisations lobbied, the scale and depth of contributions, the bid would have gone through, possibly without any investigation.

The amount of political pressure, the sheer volume of submissions made to the OFT, the referral to the MMC, the questions which the MMC sought to address, and even the number and quality of the arguments made to the MMC – at each stage those involved in the campaign played vital roles. Furthermore, the fact that the MMC verdict was so unequivocal, that it upheld the public interest concerns which were top of the fans' agenda, that it supported the claims that the fabric of British football was something that should be protected, and that this whole agenda was even part of their considerations was effectively down to the issues raised by campaigners.

But what now? Where to from here? How can the game and the club be safeguarded? At the time of writing the speculation about who will make offers to buy all or part of the club is intense and ranges from an Irish stud-farm owner to the Sultan of Brunei. However happy many fans will be to see the end of the Edwards era, the only safeguard for the club is for supporters to establish a sizeable stake in the club. Protecting the club and raising the interests of fans means uniting as many of those individual shareholders – around 25 per cent of the club – as possible. Shareholders United have taken up this challenge and already have over a million shares pledged to their organisation – a small percentage, maybe, but an encouraging start. The ultimate aim of forming a shareholders' trust which can act on behalf of small shareholders *en bloc* is now a priority.

Indeed, the concept of clubs as mutual organisations – where fans own the clubs – is now very much on the agenda, something argued for by Jonathan Michie in *New Mutualism: A Golden Goal?*. The issues raised in debates at the 3 February conference, in the wake of Sky's bid, were followed up at a major gathering again at Birkbeck College on 8 July. The ideas even enjoyed government support, with then Sports Minister Tony Banks arguing in a foreword to *New Mutualism*: 'Greater supporter owner-ship of clubs offers a solution to a number of perceived problems in the game and is an idea whose time has clearly come. And the example of Barcelona shows that there is no reason why these ideas should be limited to smaller clubs.' Everything, it seems, is still to play for.

The effects of the campaign have certainly gone beyond Old Trafford. Newcastle United fans, faced with the bid from NTL, collectively rubbed their hands with glee at the prospect of ridding themselves of the Mary Poppins fans and brothel twins, Douglas Hall and Freddie Shepherd. Mark

Jensen, editor of their fanzine *The Mag,* is quoted as blaming IMUSA and United fans for saving Hall and Shepherd's skin by getting the Sky deal thrown out! NTL did not hang around for a similar ruling from the DTI on their bid, withdrawing it within days.

More broadly, the issue of an arm's-length or independent regulator for football is very much a possibility, although the likelihood of the government taking up such a proposal even if the Task Force recommends it must be remote, at least before the next election. However, the debates about the governance and direction of the game will continue and those involved in the campaign against Murdoch will be at the forefront of calls for the reform of football, to take up the challenge in the MMC's report. Indeed, Finney has said that although the MMC could not make recommendations on protecting the interest of British football beyond blocking the merger, the report contained 'the heaviest possible hint' that the widening wealth gap in football requires the attention of policy makers.

At the first committee meeting since the bid was blocked, IMUSA decided that whilst it will certainly be involved in ownership issues, it now needed to reorientate and focus back on some of the coalface issues – ticketing, European travel, the stadium – around which it was formed. Its involvement in the campaign to have United reinstated in the FA Cup has been the first example of this. However, the organisation also has problems to face up to as a consequence of the success in defeating Rupert Murdoch. Substantial debts have been incurred; campaigners have barely had time to catch their breath and recuperate after the seven-month struggle; and the reputation of the organisation now means it is called upon, particularly by the media, more than ever. As with all fans' organisations, it is voluntary, lacking in resources and in urgent need of some sustainable finances to pay for administration and recruitment.

Such was IMUSA's profile towards the end of the campaign that a number of ex-players were getting in touch to offer their support, including former Busby-era keeper Harry Gregg. So many players are referred to as legends that the term has been demeaned, but Harry is a real-life hero, both on and off the pitch. The man was not just a great footballer but he went back into the flames at Munich to rescue others from the crash and he has a fearsome reputation for fighting for what he believes in. Harry telephoned to ask for IMUSA's assistance in another matter but wanted first to pass on his heartfelt congratulations to the organisation for fighting to defend his club. 'That club belongs to you and me,' he said. 'It is not for Martin Edwards and the board to sell it off.' When the same phraseology that IMUSA had been using throughout the campaign was being repeated by somebody of Harry's stature it filled everyone with pride. IMUSA had eulogised about 'the traditions of Manchester United' and the club 'being built by the great players of the past' despite the fact that most of the committee, apart from the likes of Eddie Taylor and Ray Eckersley, were under the age of forty and had no recollection of '68, let alone Duncan Edwards. But as United fans you are brought up with the tales of the great sides of the '50s and '60s. It is part of the 'family history'.

This was why when it was reported that Dennis Viollett, another Busby era player and holder of the club's scoring record, had been taken ill in the States IMUSA joined others in raising funds for his medical fees. Paul Windridge, who is mentioned elsewhere in this book, co-ordinated efforts and got quite close to Dennis and his wife Helen, visiting them at their home in Florida. Paul produced a series of prints to raise funds before Dennis's eventual sad death, and when his ashes were scattered on the pitch in front of the Stretford End, Helen invited Paul and Andy Walsh along to the ceremony. Also in attendance that evening were Martin Edwards and Peter Kenyon who, by the looks on their faces, were none too pleased at the presence of Walsh and Windridge. Helen reassured Paul and Andy that what IMUSA had done in saving the club from Murdoch was in line with Dennis's views. One of the more bizarre sights that evening was seeing United players like Albert Scanlan and Denis Law queuing up for Paul's prints and asking him to add a dedication and his autograph to the bottom of the picture!

When BSkyB talk of football being a Whole New Ball Game they are only partially right, because the game is as much about history as it is the present day. It does not exist without its past. It is about shared memories and identities constructed around eleven men on a field. It becomes a central plank of the personal make-up of thousands of fans, as well as ex-players such as Harry. That is why the idea of a TV company whose owner knows nothing of the game short of how to make money from televising it, and whose Chief Executive could not name Denis Irwin as the team's full-back, taking over an institution like United caused absolute horror. It was this, the desire to protect what is left of the integrity of the club and the game as a whole – to protect the history as well as the future – that led IMUSA, SUAM and others to go to such lengths to stop BSkyB's take-over. And, although undoubtedly the events of that warm May evening in Barcelona will live on in the history books and stories for future generations as the first time the treble had been achieved, another event will also become part of football's history and Manchester United's identity. That is the decision on 9 April to stop BSkyB taking over the club, to which so many had contributed so much.

BIBLIOGRAPHY

Boon, G. (ed.) (1999) *England's Premier Clubs: A Review of 1998 Results*, Manchester: Deloitte and Touche

Brown, A. (ed.) (1998) *Fanatics! Power, Identity and Fandom in Football*, London: Routledge

Brown, M. (1998) 'The Football Task Force' in *Chelsea Independent*, 1998

Chester, Sir Norman (1968) *Report of the Committee on Football*, London: HMSO

Conn, D. (1997) *The Football Business: Fair Game in the '90s?*, Edinburgh: Mainstream

Crick, M. and Smith, D. (1989) *Manchester United: The Betrayal of a Legend*, London: Pan

Dunphy, E. (1991) *A Strange Kind of Glory: Sir Matt Busby and Manchester United*, London: Heinemann

Football Association (1991) *Blueprint for the Future of Football*, London: FA

Football League (1990) *One Game, One Team, One Voice*, Lytham St Annes: Football League

Football Task Force (1998a) *Eliminating Racism from Football*, London: DCMS
(1998b) *Improving Disabled Facilities at Football*, London: DCMS
(1999) *Investing in the Community*, London: DCMS

Goldman Sachs International (1998) *Recommended Offer by Goldman Sachs International on Behalf of British Sky Broadcasting Group plc and Manchester United plc*, London: Goldman Sachs

Hopcraft, A. (1969) *The Football Man*, London: Sportspages

Hornby, N. (1994) *Fever Pitch*, London: Simon Schuster

Kiernan, T. (1986) *Citizen Murdoch*, London: Dodd Meade

Labour Party (1996) *Labour's Charter for Football*, London: Labour Party

Lee, S. (1999) 'The BSkyB Bid for Manchester United', in J. Michie *et al* (eds) (1999)

Michie, J. (1999) *New Mutualism: A Golden Goal?*, London: The Co-operative Party

Michie, J. *et al* (eds) (1999) *A Game of Two Halves: The Business of Football*, Edinburgh: Mainstream

Monopolies and Mergers Commission (1999) *British Sky Broadcasting Group plc and Manchester United plc: A Report on the Proposed Merger*, London: The Stationery Office Limited

Salomon Brothers (1997) *Football Values*, London: Salomon Brothers

Salomon Smith Barney (1998) *UK Football: After the Bubble*, London: Salomon Smith Barney

Taylor, Lord Justice (1990) *The Hillsborough Stadium Disaster: Final Report*, London: HMSO

Taylor, R., Ward, A. and Newburn, T. (1995) *The Day of the Hillsborough Disaster: A Narrative Account*, Liverpool: Liverpool University Press

White, J. *Are You Watching Liverpool? Manchester United and the '93–'94 Double*, London: Heinemann

Submissions to the Monopolies and Mergers Commission

All Party Football Group of MPs

Adam Brown, Manchester Institute for Popular Culture, Manchester Metropolitan University

Independent Manchester United Supporters' Association (a) Public Interest

Independent Manchester United Supporters' Association (b) Competition Issues

Jon Leigh

Jonathan Michie *et al*, Birkbeck College

Shareholders United Against Murdoch

Paul Windridge

Fanzines

Red Issue
United We Stand
Red News
Red Attitude

INDEX

NOTES TO THE INDEX

The Independent Manchester United Supporters' Association (IMUSA) and Manchester United *per se* have not been included in this index as a result of their predominance in relation to the text. Page numbers followed by 'q' (e.g. 24q) indicate that the reference includes quoted material.